AGRARIAN REFORM
UNDER ALLENDE

AGRARIAN REFORM UNDER ALLENDE

Peasant Revolt in the South

Kyle Steenland

UNIVERSITY OF NEW MEXICO PRESS

Albuquerque

Fried. 6.50|5.85|9|25|81

Library of Congress Cataloging in Publication Data

Steenland, Kyle, 1946–
  Agrarian reform under Allende.

  Bibliography: p. 235
  Includes index.
  1. Land reform—Chile. I. Title.
HD506.S73   333.7′6′0983   76-57540
ISBN 0-8263-0450-8

To Ambrosio Badilla
who fought for the peasants of Cautín and who
was murdered, after the military coup,
like tens of thousands of other Chileans.

Dime porque vas llorando, cuando recién te levantas
dime por qué vas llorando, dime por qué ya no cantas?
Yo lloro por mis hermanos, yo lloro por mis valientes,
que los tienen prisioneros, en jaulas de hierro ardiente.

Tell me why why are you crying, when you have just gotten up,
tell me why are you crying, tell me why you no longer sing.
I am crying for my brothers, I am crying for my brave ones,
who are held prisoner in cages of burning iron.

"Dime, dónde vas morena," a song from the Spanish Civil War

Contents

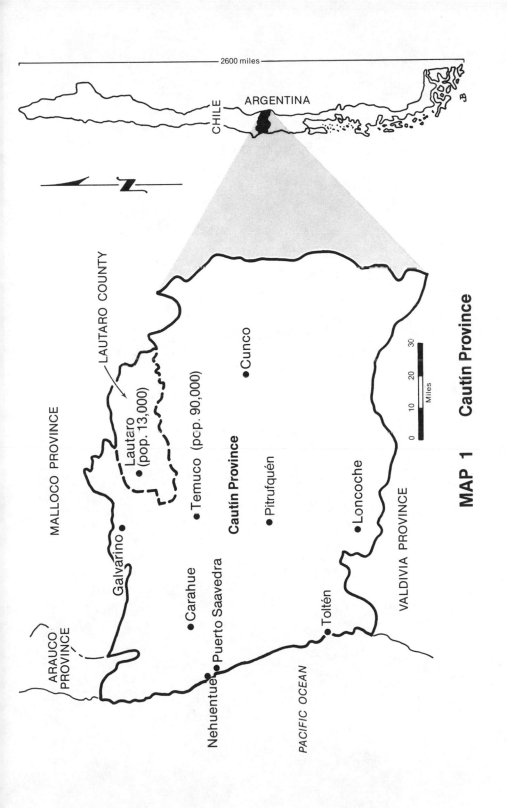

2600 miles

ARGENTINA

CHILE

B

LAUTARO COUNTY

MALLOCO PROVINCE

ARAUCO
PROVINCE

Galvarino

Lautaro
(pop. 13,000)

Temuco (pcp. 90,000)

Cunco

Cautín Province

Pitrufquén

Carahue

Puerto Saavedra

Nehuentue

Loncoche

VALDIVIA PROVINCE

Toltén

PACIFIC OCEAN

0   10   20   30
Miles

MAP 1   Cautín Province

Acknowledgments

This book would not have been possible without the generous financial assistance of the American Studies Department at the State University of New York at Buffalo. The department supported what was an unusual research project and gave me complete independence to sink or swim as best I could as a North American loose in Allende's Chile. Special thanks go to my advisor Liz Kennedy who read the text and offered detailed criticisms which helped in the editing; also to Mike Frisch who read the text and gave me valuable comments.

Special thanks are also due to Susan Steenland who spent a considerable amount of time wandering around southern Chile with me, who shared the fear and the horror of Chile after the coup, and who confronted with a great deal of courage the tragedy of that time.

Numerous Chileans helped me along the way, fundamentally by accepting me as a friend instead of an enemy. After all, there were many Americans in Chile during that time who were agents of the CIA, and Chileans were rightly suspicious of Americans who asked a lot of questions about Chilean politics. Unfortunately, I cannot name the names of all those who so unselfishly helped me because to do so could jeopardize their safety. The military junta reacts harshly against its critics and even the friends of its critics.

I also want to thank all those who have worked in the Chile solidarity movement in this country to denounce the crimes of the military junta and to demand a change in the shameful U.S. policy of supporting that junta. Their example and encouragement have helped me with the sometimes dreary task of finishing this book. Especially helpful here have been those who work with Non-Intervention in Chile (NICH), a national organization of Chile solidarity groups, and with NACLA, a research group which publishes information on Latin America.

Finally there have been a number of people who have done specific tasks along the way. Ann Schneider typed the final draft of the manuscript. Liz Ward assisted with the maps, and Bob Rothschild helped print the photographs.

Introduction

The three years of Allende's government in Chile were followed with intense interest throughout the world. Many saw the Allende experiment as a model that could be followed by others in the fight against economic underdevelopment. The programs enacted during the Allende period have been, and still are, discussed extensively. One such program was the agrarian reform.

The Chilean agrarian reform under Allende was the most thorough agrarian reform attempted in Latin America since the Cuban revolution. As all the programs of Allende, the land reform generated intense opposition on the part of the wealthy and intense hope on the part of the poor. Critics attacked the land reform as underfinanced, overambitious, and poorly planned. Stronger criticism labelled the reform immoral, a Marxist conspiracy to control the nation's food supply. Supporters claimed the reform was the first serious attempt to help the rural poor.

Part 1 of this book analyzes Allende's land reform. Chapter 1 discusses the policies of expropriation, the effects of the expropriations on production, the new social organization in the countryside, and the effects of the land reform on both peasants and landlords. In addition background information is provided about Chilean agriculture since the 1930s, and particularly about the land reform under President Eduardo Frei during the 1960s.

There are many questions about any major land reform. Did the policy of massive expropriations result in a disruption of agricultural production? Were the new cooperatives formed on the expropriated land as productive as the private farms they replaced? Did the peasants support the land reform actively, or was it the government that took most of the initiative? Did the landlords really lose a great part of their wealth, or was the monetary compensation sufficient? Did they continue producing on the land remaining to them, or was the threat of expropriation so great that they refused to make any new investments? Did they join the chorus of those who were demanding that Allende be overthrown?

These are classic questions that confront any government which seriously attempts to change the balance of power in the countryside. For Allende these questions were particularly important. Although Allende controlled the presidency, he did not control the other important institutions of the state, the Congress, the courts, and most important, the military. He had only limited tools with which to carry out his reforms. He tried to carry his programs so as to gather more support from the Chilean population, with the goal of eventually gaining more power within the government. This very lack of power made it difficult for Allende to carry out his reforms.

Furthermore, Allende's Popular Unity government had to play a tricky balancing game. In many cases major reforms to alleviate some of Chile's desperate poverty required difficult and radical changes, the positive effects of which might not be seen for years. But the Popular Unity could not afford to lose any short-term support because its hold on the executive branch itself was tenuous. Thus it frequently had to concentrate on rapid reforms that would quickly gain more mass support. At times such rapid changes could only be carried out at the cost of economic disruption.

The situation was further complicated by splits within the left. The Popular Unity was a coalition of six or seven parties; internal disagreements frequently meant that no coherent policy could be agreed upon and carried out. This was often the case with the land reform program. In addition, the MIR, a leftist party with influence among the peasants of southern Chile but outside the government coalition, at times came into conflict with the Popular Unity over land reform.

The author hopes that Chapter 1 can shed some light on the successes and failures of the Chilean land reform, and land reforms in general, so that lessons can be learned for land reforms to come. Most of the population of Latin America is still peasant, and the peasantry still bends its back under the weight of the wealthy landlords. There are many reforms due.

Future land reforms in Latin America will take place in order to resolve the same problems that Chile's land reform was designed to solve. These are inefficient and stagnant agricultural production, on the one hand, and desperate poverty by the mass of landless or nearly landless peasantry on the other. More and more, the peasantry will not resemble the classic picture of oppressed serfs tied to the all-powerful landlord. Instead the peasants will be wage earners who work a fixed number of hours per day. Often they will not live on the landlord's property. The landlord will be just another boss, and the peasant will be more like an urban worker than a small farmer. In other words, agriculture in Latin America is becoming more and more capitalistic, leaving behind its feudal past. Recent land reforms in Latin America, such as those in Cuba and Chile, have affected capitalism, not feudalism, in the countryside. The major land reform before these recent examples occurred during the Mexican Revolution and was directed against the more traditional feudal oppression of the peasants.

What is the difference between feudalism and capitalism in the countryside? If Chilean agriculture was capitalist during the Allende government, how did it get to be this way? What holdovers from feudalism, if any, affected the land reform in Chile? These are questions addressed in Chapter 2. Here the author provides a short history of Chilean agriculture from the time of Spanish conquest through the 1930s.

In addition to providing a review of Chilean history that helps to explain how Chilean agriculture came to be the way it is, this chapter also addresses a theoretical question with relevance to Latin America as a whole. Much of the debate about how to overcome underdevelopment in Latin America has centered on how to approach land reform. One view holds that Latin American underdevelopment stems largely from a backward agricultural sector controlled by a few traditional landlords. This view sees Latin American agriculture as still held back by feudalism; the dynamic forces moving to modernize Latin America are the capitalists, the industrialists, in the cities. Change must occur through the elimination of feudalism in the countryside, allowing capitalism to flourish there and ridding the government of the backward influence of the landlords. A second position is that in most of Latin America feudalism has already been replaced by capitalism in the countryside. But this has been done without a major land reform. Instead the landlords themselves have seen fit to make this change. Yet agriculture remains in a backward state, and the new capitalist landlords are scarcely more efficient than the old feudal ones. The peasantry still lives in desperate poverty and a land reform is still needed. Instead of a simple division of agricultural property among the peasants, more stress is to be laid on collective production and the formation of cooperatives. The struggle for land reform in the capitalist countryside may well be linked to a struggle against capitalists in the cities. The author believes that this second position is more correct, but in many cases vestiges of feudalism remain in the countryside and have important effects. Chapter 2 shows how this has been the case in Chile.

Part 2, the larger part of the book, focuses on southern Chile and tells the story of three years of land reform in one particular area.

The Mapuche Indians, who make up the majority of the peasantry in southern Chile, occupied hundreds of farms illegally during the Allende government. They claimed that the land was rightfully theirs, that it had been stolen from them by the conquering Chilean army in the late 1800s. The Mapuches planned to keep the land and farm it.

The action of the Mapuche peasants and their allies threatened the most powerful interests in the area. Southern Chile is predominantly agricultural. The wealthy of southern Chile saw the source of their wealth cut off in a series of swift blows. They didn't like it, and they began to organize against it. Since they controlled much of the media, we can find out what their opinions were by reading their newspapers. For example, on March 7, 1971, the *Southern Daily* of Temuco, Cautín Province, ran the following:

> At the shout of Netuain Mapu (We shall recover the land)
>
> ### THE SHADOW OF CHE IS CRUSHING CAUTIN
> *The south of Chile is the focus of a continental Castroite-Maoist conspiracy.
> *The actions of the ultraleft are supported by the weakness of the government.
> *In 10 months more than 80 farms and 52,800 acres have been illegally taken over

The landowners complained that the followers of Che Guevara were creating havoc in the south. According to them, law and order had broken down, and the government encouraged it, acquiesced in it, or was too weak to do anything about it.

In late 1970 and early 1971 the province of Cautín in southern Chile was the most explosive area in the country (see Map 1). The future struggle between the right and left throughout Chile was first outlined in the south.

Minister of Agriculture Jacques Chonchol moved to Cautín for a month and a half in 1971. He carried out a series of expropriations of the occupied farms, using the agrarian reform law. He thereby lent legality to the illegal actions taken by the peasants. Minister Chonchol believed the expropriations were just and helped right many years of cruel exploitation. He also wanted to defuse a tense situation. He hoped that massive expropriations would cause the peasants to feel that the government was supporting them. The illegal occupations would then slow down. The peasants would follow the advice of the government, which was to await the normal process of the agrarian reform in order to gain control of the land. An end to the illegal occupations would, he hoped, calm the right wingers who had launched a full-scale national propaganda effort against the violence and "anarchy" in the south.

The landowners themselves were responsible for much of the violence. The first serious incident occurred in December 1970 at Ruculán, a farm in western Cautín. A group of landowners attacked some peasants who were occupying a farm, and three peasants were wounded by rifle fire. At the same time a small leftist party which was not part of the government, the MIR, was encouraging further occupations and organizing peasant self-defense militias. The expropriations by the government were supposed to change this explosive situation.

In the long run it didn't work. In Cautín itself the illegal occupations and violence continued throughout 1971. Armed incidents in April, May, October, and November resulted in five deaths. The number of farm takeovers did not decrease until late 1972. Then, however, illegal occupations began to flare up in other provinces, such as Ñuble and Santiago. The agrarian conflict on a national level continued until the military coup in 1973.

Claiming that they were stepping in to maintain "law and order," and strongly supported by the United States, the military took over the government on September 11, 1973. It soon became clear what they meant by "law and order"; thirty thousand murdered Chileans, systematic torture of tens of thousands of political prisoners, and the abolishment of Congress, political parties, most of the press, trade unions, and so forth. It was more like lawless disorder. For the peasants, the coup meant an end to the agrarian reform, and in many cases the return of the expropriated farms to their former owners.

It is this story of three years of land reform in the south that is told in Part 2. The focus is on one particular country, Lautaro, in Cautín Province. It was one of particularly intense conflict (see Map 1). The peasants were more thoroughly organized than in other places, more farms were taken over, the land reform went deeper, and the repression was more intense when the coup came.

The narrative in Part 2 alternates between a description of one particular farm in Lautaro County, and a description of the more general events in the surrounding area. Each chapter covers one year. A special chapter is devoted to the coup in September 1973, and a final chapter summarizes the events over the three years in the county.

It should be pointed out that in the chapters that cover the history of one particular farm in Lautaro County, the farm chosen is not a specific, but a kind of "average" one. It is an amalgamation of the typical experience of many specific farms in the county.

In the same way that no specific farm is discussed in detail, many dates and names are changed. These precautions have been taken in order to protect those who are now living in Lautaro County. Although information is only partial, we do have reports that the military government has executed one member of the Peasant Council of Lautaro and one peasant leader from the farm El Luchador. One man in the land reform administration in the town of Lautaro has reportedly been tortured and has disappeared. Another member of the Peasant Council was arrested right after the coup, tortured, and then imprisoned in Temuco where he remains today. Their names respectively are Catalina Carbolao, Luis Mora, Esteban Perle, and Rafael Railaf. Another report indicates that the governor of Lautaro County, Fernando Teillier, was shot down by a right-wing gang on the outskirts of the town of Lautaro shortly after the coup. We can be sure that many more are dead or near dead, many whose names we do not as yet know.

In all those cases where the information would not damage any supporters of the Allende government, strict accuracy of dates and names has been maintained. The dates of public events and the names of all right-wing participants are accurate.

Much of the drama of Chile during the Popular Unity government of Salvador Allende was played out in miniature in Lautaro County. It is this drama that we try to capture in the second part of this book. A detailed story of one area should help in understanding the whole. It is especially crucial to record any part of what happened under Allende since the military dictatorship has systematically attempted to distort or ignore this history.

This author also hopes that through the very details of life in one particular area, the reader will be able to capture a sense of what was going on in Chile under Allende. An over-all account of the Allende years of necessity must concentrate on important national political events, frequently sacrificing a description of the life of the average Chilean.

This author had the opportunity to live in Chile for almost two years during the Allende government. A year of that time was spent in Cautín

Province, mostly in Lautaro County. In Lautaro the heavy winter rains turn many of the roads into mud. The temperature is cold and the peasants have little heating. They wait patiently through the miserable rains until spring once again brings a dry earth, until once again the smoke from the volcano Llaima is visible every day, coming from the Andes to the east. In much the same way they are waiting through the present military dictatorship. They will not forget the benefits gained under the Allende government or the brutality they have suffered from the military. They are waiting for the day when they will once again work for themselves on the land where they now work for the landlord. They will do what they can to hasten the arrival of that day.

PART ONE

PART ONE

Rural Strategy Under Allende

Introduction

Chile, unlike most Latin American countries, has a predominantly industrial economy. Only 25 percent of the population lives in the countryside. Only 8 percent of the gross national product is generated in rural areas. Such statistics would lead one to think that the agrarian reform carried out under the Allende government would have played an important but decidedly secondary role in the struggle for power in Chile. However, two factors gave the agrarian reform an unexpected importance. First, food shortages and their role in the political struggle made the question of agricultural production crucial. Second, as the battle between the Popular Unity* and the opposition sharpened, both groups desperately attempted to win the support of uncommitted sectors of the population. One of these uncommited sectors was the peasantry, largely unorganized until the late 1960s.

Beginning in the second half of 1972 and continuing in 1973, food shortages played a crucial role in politics. Basic products such as cooking oil, bread, sugar, meat, rice, and milk became difficult to get, and some of the most important political battles between the working class and the opposition occurred over the issues of production and distribution of food. The shortages were used as a major, if not the major, propaganda tool of the right wing. Under such conditions the internal production of food took on an unusual importance.

Since the 1930s Chilean agriculture has been practically stagnant; the

---

*Allende's government was called the Popular Unity; this was a coalition of political parties, principally the Communist and Socialist parties (in Spanish, Unidad Popular, or UP).

growth of agricultural production has been slightly below the growth in population.[1] Increases in food consumption have come about through importations. Importations of agricultural products have risen slowly since the 1940s; they reached an average of $184 million a year during the government of Eduardo Frei (1964–70). Such importations in an under-developed country greatly damage the economy, wasting large amounts of scarce foreign exchange. Total exportations averaged $1.065 billion a year under Frei. Approximately 20 percent of this hard-earned foreign currency had to be spent to import agricultural products. About three-fifths of these importations could have been produced in Chile.[2]

This situation continued under Allende and got much worse. The important redistribution of income carried out by the Popular Unity in 1971 led to a sharp rise in the demand for food. Internal agricultural production increased slightly during 1971 and 1972 (4 percent and 2 percent, respectively) and went down as much as 15 percent in 1973. To satisfy increased demand, importations were greatly increased. They jumped to $265 million in 1971 and $535 million in 1972, at a time when the credit blockade carried out by the United States had made dollars extremely scarce. Part of this increase was due to the increased prices of agricultural products on the world market. Such prices went up an average of 50 percent in 1971 and 1972. The devaluation of the dollar accounted for some of the increase. Nevertheless, the jump in importations was much greater than the increase in prices, signifying an increased quantity of food available for the population. Importations of food accounted for an average of one fifth of the food available for consumption in Chile during the Frei government. Under Allende they accounted for about a third. The quantity of food available for consumption rose about 3 percent a year under Frei. In 1971 and 1972, under Allende, it rose 12 percent a year.[3]

Nevertheless, the tremendously increased demand and the right-wing control of distribution (the government controlled only approximately 30 percent of the distribution of basic consumer items) meant serious shortages. In such a situation it was imperative that internal production increase and that, at the same time, the government control a much greater proportion of the distribution. It is obvious that Chile could not continue to import over $500 million of agricultural products per year, the majority of which could have been produced internally. Agricultural importations in 1973 represented about 50 percent of the total quantity of dollars earned by Chile a year in exportations. The food crisis made the question of the relationship between the agrarian reform and agricultural production a crucial one.

The other crucial question in relation to the agrarian reform was its effect on the political sentiments of the peasantry. Given the intensity of the battle for state power in Chile, both the Popular Unity and the opposition sought to win the support of the peasantry. It can be said that generally the Popular Unity had the support of the majority of the landless peasantry and that the opposition had that of the small landholders. The medium and large landholders, as is logical, supported the right wing. The majority of support given by small landholders to the opposition represented a failure on the part of the Popular Unity.[4]

The two main questions for the Popular Unity, then, were how to carry out the land reform so as to maintain or increase the production of food, and at the same time organize and gain the active support of the majority of the peasantry. In its attempt to fulfill these goals, the Popular Unity encountered several major obstacles.

The first came from the lack of control of state power. The Popular Unity's lack of control of Congress meant that it had to use the Agrarian Reform Law passed in 1967 under Frei. The Popular Unity in many senses pushed that law to its limit. The limitations of the law, at first hidden, became painfully apparent as the Popular Unity radically increased the rate of expropriations and the organization of the peasantry. The three most obvious deficiencies of the Agrarian Reform Law were that it: (1) enabled the government to expropriate property of the large rural bourgeoisie only in order to strengthen the medium rural bourgeoisie; (2) created a reformed sector which favored only a small percentage of the peasantry and did not encourage collective exploitation of the expropriated land, but rather led directly to its division; and (3) permitted the expropriation of only land for which the owner was paid, while allowing the owner to remove livestock and machinery.

In addition to the limitations of a bad agrarian reform law and the inheritance of an unwieldy and reactionary bureaucracy to carry out that law, the Popular Unity was hindered by fundamental differences within its own ranks over agricultural policy. These differences were never publicly discussed; in fact, they were rarely even explicitly discussed within the Popular Unity itself. This and the continued disagreements led to an inability to apply unified criteria to the application of the agrarian reform. Instead each current struggled to implement its view, resulting in inefficiency and at times, something close to anarchy.

One view, generally represented by the Communist Party, claimed that production could be maintained only by providing guarantees against government interference to the small latifundistas (landlords) and by not fundamentally altering the class structure in the countryside. This view held that it was necessary to organize the peasantry in order to lend an effective support to the government but not to exercise a decisive control over the production process, which was to remain in the hands of the state apparatus and the small latifundistas. The process of expropriations was to be carried out in such a way as to favor a small percentage of the peasantry in the reformed sector. This reformed sector was not to be organized to exploit the land collectively, this being a stage postponed until a later date. The Peasant Councils, which were the organizations set up under Allende to unify all sectors of the peasantry (minifundistas, wage earners, reformed sector), were conceived of as mediators between the state bureaucracy and the peasant masses. The Peasant Councils were to assure that the production plans outlined by the state were carried out.

The other main view, represented generally by the Socialist Party and more consistently by the MIR, maintained that the state should stretch the Agrarian Reform Law to the limit in order to expropriate as much rural bourgeoisie property as possible. The peasantry was to be organized to exercise effective power in the countryside, controlling the production of the latifundistas who escaped expropriation. The Peasant Councils were to be given effective power. They were eventually to take on the role of a dual power, representing the beginnings in the countryside of a new state which would replace the actual bourgeois state. In case the intensified class struggle led to an institutional crisis, the Peasant Councils would fulfill a function similar to that of the Peasant Soviets in Russia in 1917.

The reformed sector was to integrate not only the workers on the expropriated farms but also as many landless peasants and minifundistas from the nearby areas as possible. Production in the reformed sector was to be organized as much as possible in a collective manner, so that when the working class obtained state power the transition to socialism in the countryside would not be so difficult.[5]

In general, the first of these two strategies was the one carried out, although the second had effect in certain areas. It often depended on which political parties controlled crucial posts in the bureaucracy at the local level. Such posts were allotted by quota, and each party struggled to control its own area or its own bureaucratic organizations. (An exception must be made here for the MIR, which was not in the government and, therefore, controlled no bureaucratic positions.)

In some senses the differences between these two strategies corresponded to the classic differences Marxist parties have had with respect to agrarian reforms in underdeveloped countries. The same kind of differences arose in Russia between 1925 and 1927 as seen in the debates between Preobrazhenski, whose position would correspond to that of the

Socialist Party in Chile, and Bukharin, corresponding to the Communist Party in Chile. Similar arguments were voiced during the course of the agrarian reform in China. In Russia and China the questions about the treatment of the smaller bourgeoisie, the necessity of maintaining production, and the organization of the state sector were of much more importance due to the overwhelmingly rural nature of those countries. Despite historical differences, the questions confronting the Popular Unity in relation to the countryside were similar. The Popular Unity, however, did not control the state apparatus; thus, the possibilities of action were more limited than they were in Russia and China.[6]

Agrarian Reform, Christian Democratic Style

Ever since the 1930s Chilean agriculture has been stagnating. The principal cause of this stagnation has been low profits, a result of low prices for agricultural products. When the depression hit Chile, the agricultural bourgeoisie lost their dominant position. The urban bourgeoisie gained control of the state and kept food prices down by using the state to subsidize the importation of agricultural products.

Between 1930 and 1965 the land under cultivation increased only 10 percent. The rural population increased 50 percent over the same period of time, while the urban population increased 220 percent. Unemployment in the countryside was chronic and reached levels of 25 percent. The value of agricultural production had doubled between 1910 and 1930, but between 1930 and 1950 it increased only 27 percent.[7]

According to the CIDA study of 1966, the class structure in the countryside was the following:[8]

Class	Number	% of Population
Latifundistas	12,737	2
Rich Peasants (who permanently hire outside labor)	42,980	7
Middle Peasants (occasionally hire outside labor)	141,474	21
Minifundistas (own their land but hire no outside labor)	132,021	20
Foremen and Custodians	45,971	7
Inquilinos (wage workers living on farm)	82,367	12
Medieros (sharecroppers)	26,861	4
Afuerinos and Voluntarios (wage workers from outside farm)	179,778	27
Total	664,189	100

As can be imagined, the distribution of income among these groups was extremely uneven. From the same study by CIDA we have the following distribution:

Class	% of Income
Latifundistas	36.7
Rich Peasants	15.4
Middle Peasants	12.7
Foremen and Custodians	
Medieros	35.2
Afuerinos and Voluntarios	

This was the situation the Frei government confronted when elected in 1964. Frei, elected on a populist program, promised that he would carry out a thorough agrarian reform. This was the time when the United States was most sensitive to the possibility of another Cuban revolution in Latin America, and both the Alliance for Progress and the Organization of American States had encouraged land reforms in order to lessen rural discontent that might prove a breeding ground for guerillas.

Frei's Agrarian Reform Law of 1967 had as its purpose the elimination of the largest and most unproductive landholdings and the incorporation of a small section of the peasantry into the expropriated land. The expropriated land would be organized into cooperatives (called "asentamientos") for three to five years, after which time the land was to be divided among the associates of the cooperative except in exceptional circumstances. Expropriations is really a misleading word since the expropriated land was to be paid for: a certain percentage was paid for immediately (between 1 and 10 percent) and the rest paid in quotas over the space of twenty-five to thirty years. The majority of the quotas were to be adjusted for inflation. The exact terms of the payment were to be determined in correlation with the efficiency with which the expropriated land was being exploited at the time of the expropriation. The owner maintained the right to withdraw his livestock and machinery. All land over a set limit was expropriable. That limit was about eighty hectares (1 hectare = 2.4 acres) of good *irrigated* land in the central valley. One such hectare was called a Basic Irrigated Hectare (BIH). As a very general rule, it can be said that eighty BIH correspond to about five hundred hectares in central Chile. The owner who had had expropriated a farm greater than eighty BIH was entitled to maintain in his possession a reserve of no more than eighty BIH. This meant that, in practice, many owners kept the machinery, the livestock, and the best part of the farm while the peasants who received the expropriated land were left with very little. Land could also be expropriated if it were inefficiently exploited. Inefficiency was measured not only in terms of productive efficiency, but also in terms of the owner's treatment of workers. The determination of inefficient exploitation was done by the Corporation of the Agrarian Reform (CORA). If the owner disagreed with their evaluation, he had the right to appeal to the Agrarian Tribunals, special courts set up to consider owner complaints in relation to the agrarian reform.

Such was the general nature of the 1967 Agrarian Reform Law. It was passed with much fanfare but without much opposition on the part of the big landowners. Those whose lands were expropriated would use the indemnity to invest in more productive activities. Those who remained with reserves would be paid for the land expropriated and would maintain the best land, all the machinery, and their livestock. Depending on the political situation, after the three-to-five-year transition period the expropriated land could once again be bought from individual peasant owners. All in all, the law was an attempt to modernize capitalism in the countryside, an attempt which most sectors of the bourgeoisie heartily favored.[9] The continued scarcity of agricultural products, despite the large importations, was one of the main factors in the chronic inflation that created working class unrest.

The Frei government expropriated some 15 percent of Chile's agricultural land; that is, 15 percent of the BIH of the country. The expropriations benefited twenty thousand peasants, substantially less than the goal of one hundred thousand set by the Frei government. The great majority of the twenty thousand were inquilinos. Approximately half of the expropriated land was voluntarily offered to CORA by public institutions with land holdings. The other half was largely composed of land that exceeded eighty BIH, and reserves were generally left to the owners. The average cost to the state for each peasant incorporated into the reformed sector was $10,000, counting the costs of paying for the land, and providing credits for salaries, machinery, and livestock. The cooperatives formed on the expropriated land that were to continue during this three-to-five-year transitional period were called asentamientos.[10]

Expropriations Under Allende

The period after Allende's election was a period of great weakness for the momentarily disorganized and confused bourgeoisie. The Allende government was able to take advantage of this in relation to the agrarian reform by rapidly expropriating a great number of farms. These included not just those exceeding the limit of eighty BIH but also many that were inefficiently exploited.

The Allende government was also aided in its policy of increased expropriations by the large number of illegal occupations of farms by rural workers. These occupations were verbally condemned by the government but were not repressed, following the government's policy of not using the police to repress popular actions. In fact, the illegal occupations were a great benefit to the Popular Unity since they cut off the farm owner's profits immediately and made him more willing to sell out to CORA rather than follow a two- or three-year bureaucratic appeal process in the Agrarian Tribunals. The figures on illegal occupations are as follows, according to the ICIRA diagnosis:

Year	Number of Occupations
1960–66	36
1967	9
1968	27
1969	148
Sept–Dec 1970	192
1971	1,278

In over 50 percent of the illegal occupations under the Allende government, workers from outside the farm participated. This was an entirely new phenomenon.

One point of clarification. Despite the right-wing hysteria about violence in the countryside, most of these illegal occupations were carried out without physical violence. What violence there was came from well-armed groups of landowners who killed about fifteen peasants during the Allende years. Only one owner was killed.

The rapid increase in expropriations can be seen from the following figures, which cover the period through June 1972:[11]

Number of farms expropriated		Hectares Expropriated	%
1965–70	1,408	3,563,554	40
1971–72 (30/6)	3,282	5,296,756	60
Total	4,690	8,860,310	100

The increased expropriations practically eliminated the farms of over eighty BIH. In 1973 there were only some two hundred left. However, the bourgeoisie maintained control of an enlarged sector of farms between twenty and eighty BIH. Most of these farms should be labelled latifundias. They were the bastion of the rural bourgeoisie. These farms employed numerous permanent laborers (averaging between five and ten) and even more numerous temporary workers. Their owners did not work their farms and, in most cases, did not live on them. The Popular Unity announced the end of the latifundia once all the farms over eighty BIH were expropriated. This was an illusion. It was to accept the definition of latifundia set up by Frei's Agrarian Reform Law, a definition rejected at the time by the same leftists who later worked in the Popular Unity government. What happened was that the rural bourgeoisie was forced to accept the expropriation of the largest farms which in many cases were very poorly exploited and had great amounts of land not in production. The big landowners retreated into the strata of farms between twenty and eighty BIH. These farms were overcapitalized, receiving the machinery and livestock that were withdrawn from the expropriated land. Meanwhile the reformed sector suffered from undercapitalization and was barely able to produce more efficiently than the former owners, despite an increase in the land under cultivation. The retreat of the bourgeoisie to the strata of farms between twenty and eighty BIH can be seen in the following chart, which covers the period from 1965 up to June 1972:[12]

Farms according to BIH	% of farms in each strata		% of total hectareage in BIH	
	1965	1972	1965	1972
less than 5 (Minifundistas)	81.4	79.3	9.7	9.7
5/20 (middle peasants)	11.5	11.3	12.7	13.0
20/40	3.0	3.3	9.5	11.6
40/60	1.3	2.5	7.1	14.5
60/80	.8	1.6	5.7	12.8
more than 80	2.0	.1	55.3	2.9
reformed sector	0	1.9	0	35.5

This chart shows the effect of the division of fifteen hundred farms greater than eighty BIH between 1965 and 1967, which created forty-five hundred new farms. Such divisions were carried out to escape expropriation. It also takes into account the reserves left to the owners after the expropriation of farms greater than eighty BIH. Although exact figures are not available, it is estimated that reserves were granted in 35 percent of the expropriations, forming approximately sixteen hundred new farms.

A more graphic way to represent the power of the bourgeoisie in the countryside under Allende is to list the different strata with statistics on labor force and production as of June 1972:[13]

Strata	Amount of land in BIH	Permanent and Temp. Workers	Value of Production	Value of Prod. Commercialized	% of Production Commercialized
Reformed Sector	35%	18%	29%	29%	80
Minifundia and Small holdings up to 20 BIH	22%	60%	28%	15%	45
Greater than 20 BIH	42%	22%	43%	56%	95
Totals	100%	100%	100%	100%	75

The chart shows that the reformed sector covered less land, had fewer workers, and produced less than the sector of private agriculture, latifundias of more than twenty BIH. As pointed out in the ICIRA diagnosis, the situation is similar to that of Mexico in 1940 after the land reform begun during the Revolution had come to a halt, and to that of Cuba in 1963 after the first land reform but before the second. In Mexico the private sector gradually swallowed up the reformed sector while in Cuba it was the other way around. What would have happened in Chile largely depended on the struggle for state power carried out by the urban workers. It is unlikely that the situation would have been changed by further expropriations given the balance of political power in 1973. The bourgeoisie was much better organized in 1973 than in 1971 and was effectively resisting expropriations for inefficient exploitation. In fact, the owners were contesting the expropriations already carried out. There were about three thousand cases before the Agrarian Tribunals in 1973 in which the expropriated owners were contesting the expropriation itself, or the amount of compensation paid, or the size of the reserve granted. A very broad guess would indicate that approximately a fifth to a quarter of the expropriated farms were involved in judicial action with the Agrarian Tribunals.

Taking From the Rich to Give to the Poor

There are no statistics about the actual structure of classes in the countryside in 1973; but, making extremely broad generalizations based on the 1965 agricultural census and the ICIRA diagnosis, the following distribution can be estimated:

Class	Number of People
Latifundistas	6,000
Rich Peasants	40,000
Foremen and Custodians	35,000
Middle Peasants and Minifundistas	350,000
Afuerinos	160,000
Medieros	50,000
Voluntarios	40,000
Asentados (reformed sector)	75,000
Inquilinos	30,000

It can be seen that the reformed sector, although greatly enlarged, was still small compared to the number of salaried workers in the countryside. According to the ICIRA estimation cited earlier, the remaining latifundistas employed 22 percent of the workers (temporary and permanent) in the countryside; the reformed sector employed only 18 percent. In many cases the reformed sector had begun to take on the same role in relation to the minifundia around it as had the latifundia before. Many asentamientos, as the new cooperatives were called, hired outside labor and paid them lower wages than the asentados themselves received. The asentados, or the workers on the asentamientos, received a daily wage from the state, generally the minimum daily wage for workers in Chile. In addition, they maintained their small plot of land within the asentamiento. Unfortunately, within the reformed sector many asentados devoted most of their time to their small plot and little to the collective farming of the asentamiento.

The average inquilino in the Central Valley during the Frei government got 54 percent of his income from his work on his small plot of land and the rest from salary.[14]

The asentado under Allende probably got even a higher percentage of his income from his small plot. ICIRA estimated that, while only 13 percent of the land of the reformed sector was officially reported as pertaining to the small individual plots of the asentados, one-third of the production of the reformed sector came from these individual plots. Given that the asentado received more income from working on the individual plot than on the collective part of the farm, he had little incentive to work collectively. It was a fact that generally the asentado was paid his daily wage for the entire month whether or not he had actually worked the entire month for the asentamiento. There was no external control of the asentamiento which made sure that the wages were being paid for effective work.[15]

In general, the asentado had little sense that after three to five years he was to become responsible for the debts of the asentamiento. For this reason it was not uncommon for the debts to go on increasing. Many asentamientos were hopelessly indebted to the state bank. The Allende government continued to give new credits nonetheless, and many debts were written off by not adjusting them for inflation.

It is difficult to establish exactly which peasants have made up the reformed sector, but from the available figures it would seem that about 50 percent of the asentados were former inquilinos. The rest were landless workers from outside the farm, mainly afuerinos.

The Popular Unity made an effort to organize the reformed sector in order to incorporate more afuerinos as well as to make the participation of the outside labor within the reformed sector democratic by giving the outside workers the right to vote in the assemblies of the asentados which determined the policy of the asentamientos. For this reason the Popular Unity created the CERA, or Centro de Reforma Agraria. CERAs were to be the Popular Unity alternative to the asentamiento set up under Frei. They were also supposed to collectivize profits and ensure the continual existence of the cooperative after the transition period.

The CERAs that were formed were generally the product of bureaucratic manipulation by the CORA. In many cases the peasants did not fully understand what was meant by the CERA, what its differences were from the asentamiento. In addition the membership in an asentamiento was valued as a privileged position, and many peasants resisted the incorporation of more afuerinos in the CERA.

The Popular Unity on the whole was not able to combat these ideas effectively. In fact, the existing CERAs were in most cases exactly like the asentamientos, with the exception that they were not to be divided after the period of three to five years. The decision to organize the CERAs was reached late, toward the end of 1971, and the agreement was reached only after resistance from some sectors of the Popular Unity. Once the agreement was reached, it was not able to be implemented efficiently because those parties who were not really convinced of the advantages of the CERA did not campaign for them.

Another alternative that the Popular Unity had proposed for the reformed sector was the Centro de Producción, or CEPRO. The CEPRO was a state farm where the workers received a straight salary and where the state had an administrator. The CEPRO workers also had their individual plots, but it was not permitted that collective work be slighted in favor of individual exploitation. The CEPROs were financed by the state, and the peasants working on them had no debts to pay off to CORA or the state bank. To some degree the CEPROs corresponded to the Russian *sovjos*, while the CERAs and the asentamientos corresponded to the *koljos*.

The CEPROs were created where the Socialists had predominant influence in the CORA bureaucracy; the Communists opposed the CEPROs, although not publicly. In 1973 there were 116 CEPROs which covered 14.2 percent of the expropriated land and gave employment to 6.3 percent of the work force employed in the reformed sector. There were about two-hundred CERAs and fifteen-hundred asentamientos.[16]

In general the definition of the CEPRO was as unclear and varied as that of the CERA. The CEPROs which were created were the result of local initiative without coherent national direction. The CEPROs were so new that it is difficult to evaluate them, but in any case they appear to have been a step forward as far as the organization of the reformed sector. At least one party, the MIR, had proposed CEPROs for all new expropriated land whenever possible.[17]

In general, then, it can be said that, with the elimination of a small group of latifundistas and the creation of a somewhat privileged strata of asentados, there was significant but still limited change in the class structure in the countryside.[18] Little help was offered to the minifundistas. They received increased credit but suffered the difficulty of obtaining scarce consumer goods in the towns.

Production and Commercialization

Agricultural production increased 6 percent in 1972–73 but decreased 15 percent in 1973 because of a 15 percent decrease in the area cultivated. This decrease was largely due to the lockout, carried out by the bourgeoisie in October 1972, which prevented seed and fertilizer from arriving during planting season. On the whole the production increase in 1971 and 1972 was due to increased productivity per acre and increased area under cultivation in the reformed sector, both of which compensated for the widespread sabotage of production by the latifundistas.

However, as pointed out in the introduction, distribution was the main problem in the availability of agricultural products. The state in 1971 bought only 10 percent of total agricultural production. This was because the state paid very low prices. In 1973 these prices were two or three times below the black-market prices for products such as potatoes, wheat, and corn. What is more surprising, in 1971 the state bought only 14 percent of the production of the reformed sector. In 1971 the problem of inflation and parallel black markets was not yet very serious: in 1972 and 1973 it was. The state decreed buying monopolies for various products, mainly wheat, potatoes, and corn. It was likely that these monopolies increased the quantities of these products that the state bought from the reformed sector, but the tremendous difference between black-market prices and state prices had the opposite effect. It is possible that the reformed sector sold as much as half of its collective production on the black market. It is certain that the peasants of the reformed sector sold almost all of the production of their individual plots. The fact that the state was paying the salaries and giving credits to the reformed sector and yet could not control the marketing was due to the paternalism with which the reformed sector was constituted in the beginning. No correlations were set up between credit received and fulfillment, or production plans, or delivery of crops to state buying agencies. When the problem had gotten to be much more serious in 1972 and 1973, it was very difficult to turn the clock back.[19]

In any case, logically it would have been better to clamp down on the latifundistas whose production was sold almost entirely on the black market. But the Popular Unity, despite having the legal tools to prosecute, had no enforcement mechanism to do so. The police and the court system were generally on the side of the latifundistas. In addition the policy of the Communist Party to give guarantees to the rural bourgeoisie in order not to interrupt production came into play. The Popular Unity did not push the buying monopolies for all they were worth, fearing that the right wing in the countryside would once again sabotage production. But here the Popular Unity was caught in a contradiction. The rural bourgeoisie was producing, but all of its production was going to the black market. From there it was sold to the customer who could afford it. Most of the profits went to the middleman. The urban wealthy could afford to buy the products, and the urban working class could not. The redistribution of income carried out by the Popular Unity in 1971 lost much if not all of its force due to the inflation and the black market which destroyed the system of official prices.

Peasant Power and the Bureaucrats

Up to this point the discussion of the agrarian reform has been somewhat technical, but a description of the development of peasant organization under Allende necessarily enters the terrain of politics and controversy. The main cause of this controversy was the Peasant Councils. The Peasant Councils were planned by the Popular Unity as organizations which would bring together the different sectors of poor and middle peasants. Recognizing that the peasantry was divided into different strata, which at times had very different interests, it was felt that the Peasant Councils would unify the various strata to struggle against the big landowners and to support the government. The Popular Unity conceived of the organizations as being formed from representatives of already existing organizations, such as the asentamientos, the peasant unions, the committees of small farmers, and so forth. The first Peasant Councils were the spontaneous product of the peasant militancy in the first months of 1971 and they soon surpassed the goals set out for them by the government, especially the Communist Party. The CP felt that the Peasant Councils should aid in the production process by acting as a mediator between the state bureaucracy and the peasant masses. The Socialist Party, and to even a greater extent the MIR, felt that the Peasant Councils should co-direct the production process and form the basis for a dual power (which would act as the representative of a new socialist government once the working class was victorious in its struggle for state power). The MIR, which for years had sustained a bitter polemic with the CP, was perhaps the most active party in the formation of the first Peasant Councils. This led to the nonparticipation of the Communist Party (which controlled many of the peasant unions). This, in turn, signified that the Peasant Councils and the peasant unions went their different ways. Within the left a theoretical debate developed about the role of the peasant unions or the Peasant Councils as vanguards in the countryside. This debate was mixed with a great deal of political sectarianism that often lent an air of unreality to the discussion.[20] The MIR was not in the Popular Unity. The Communist Party wanted nothing to do with the ultraleftists. If the ultraleftists controlled a Peasant Council and asked for a peasant union to send a representative, and if that peasant union was controlled by the Communists, then that peasant union received instructions not to participate in the Peasant Council. This situation did not take place in all of the country, but it did take place in one of the most conflictive areas, southern Chile, where the first Peasant Councils were formed. It should be remembered, however, that the influence of the MIR in the countryside was limited. While strong in the south, it had less influence in the other areas of the country where the Socialist and Communist parties were strong.

During 1971, 186 Peasant Councils were formed in as many counties. By 1973 probably every province in Chile had some counties with Peasant Councils, but their performance varied. On the whole it can be said that the Peasant Councils did not exercise a decisive influence upon the decisions made by the state about the countryside. Few Peasant Councils were able to resist the hostility or noncooperation of the local bureaucracy of CORA in those areas where CORA was opposed or indifferent. The councils had no financing of their own, and the peasants in Chile were very poor. It was difficult for them to pay bus fares and meet often. If a Peasant Council either was not given or did not take real power, it gradually died. In those areas where the Peasant Councils were most vigorous, they formed Provincial Peasant Councils. This took place only in Magallanes, Valdivia, Cautín, and Malleco, or in four of Chile's twenty-five provinces. In counties where the Peasant Councils were strongest, they effectively united the different strata of poor peasants to the exent that this was possible. They also exercised a good deal of real power, though still in a very limited way. In Cautín one Peasant Council organized the direct delivery of industrial goods from expropriated factories to the countryside, avoiding the black market and middlemen. When the crops came in, this Peasant Council made sure that the produce was sent to the factories from which the Council bought industrial products. In June 1973 in Santiago Province a Peasant Council joined with industrial workers to organize the occupation of forty farms between forty and eighty BIH. This Council also organized an open market to sell rural products, again to avoid the black market. Where Peasant Councils were strong, they exercised a control over the local bureaucracy of CORA and to some extent they oversaw the policy of expropriations in their area. It was very common that the Peasant Councils organized the distribution of food to the countryside. Such popular distribution, although it controlled only a very limited quantity of merchandise, was institutionalized by the Popular Unity to go through the Peasant Councils. The state controlled only 30 percent of the distribution of basic consumer products, and of that 30 percent very little was dedicated to the Peasant Councils for distribution in the countryside. But what there was helped greatly. The peasantry had neither the time nor money to come into the town, stand in line, make the necessary contacts in order to buy basic goods such as cooking oil, soap, rice, or tea on the black market. The best organized Peasant Councils were elected directly by Sectorial Assemblies in the countryside. These assemblies brought together all the peasants in a given local area. Another important factor was the participation of peasant unions. In those counties where the peasant unions were strong, the Peasant Council did not succeed unless the peasant unions participated.[21]

Under Allende the peasant unions continued their rapid growth. (Peasant unions began to exist in 1967. They were first organized on a large scale by the Christian Democrats, under the Agrarian Reform law.) From 131,307 members in 1970, they had grown to 207,910 at the end of 1971. The influence of the Popular Unity parties in the unions grew greatly. Sixty-three percent of the membership of the unions belonged to unions controlled by parties in the Popular Unity by 1972.[22] The problem with the unions was that many existed only on paper and that they integrated many asentados and minifundistas into organizations which were theoretically made up of salaried workers on private farms. They often did not include many afuerinos, the most numerous and the most class-conscious strata of the peasantry, but also the most difficult to organize. Just about the only organization that the afuerinos had was given to them by those very few Peasant Councils that organized lists of unemployed peasants (who were to have been given priority for membership in the reformed sector in case of new expropriations). It is hard to judge the peasant unions as the Peasant Councils because their composition and performance was so varied. In some areas they were the most dynamic force among the peasantry, in others they scarcely existed or were made up of minifundistas.

The intensification of the class struggle caused the rise of independent popular power organizations in the cities. These latter cooperated with the organizations of the peasantry. The appearance of Industrial Belts and County Comandos offered the possibility of constituting a center of workers' power similar to those of the Russian soviets between February and October 1917. The comandos brought together urban workers and peasants in order to exercise real economic and political power in a county. These County Comandos flourished only in moments of political crisis, notably during the October 1972 employer's strike and the frustrated coup of June 29, 1973. At such times the bureaucratic control of the executive branch of the state was insufficient for the Popular Unity (which momentarily depended directly on the working class in order to maintain control of the situation). At such times the working class and the peasantry formed an effective alliance and one that threatened the bourgeoisie to the point where it was hesitant to push the class struggle to its ultimate consequences. The Popular Unity made use of this threat to force the bourgeoisie to back down; but, when the crisis was over, official government support of the County Comandos weakened. The bourgeoisie maintained a continuous campaign against the County Comandos, the Industrial Belts, and the Peasant Councils, denouncing them as constituting alternative powers not authorized by the constitution.

It was through an effective worker-peasant alliance that the peasantry made its weight felt on a national scale. When the crisis was acute and the opposition was threatening to overthrow the government, it was then that each side tried desperately to mobilize the peasantry. The left had more success than the right. The support that the right had among the peasantry was passive: it showed itself at election times in the form of passive resistance to expropriations or government agricultural plans. It was composed of the support of some minifundistas and many middle peasants.

The most class-conscious and the most active elements of the peasantry supported the left, and showed it. During the attempted coup of June 29, 1973, they cut off roads and occupied hundreds of private farms, awaiting a possible call to move to the cities. The failure of the right to secure such *active* support was evident during the employer's strikes of October 1972 and August 1973. At those times the right called for a peasant strike; but only a very, very small sector of the peasantry responded. Right-wing peasant unions were unable to get their members to adhere to the strike despite strenuous efforts.

The Strategy of the Latifundistas

The traditional organization of the big rural landowners is the National Agricultural Society (NAS), set up over a hundred years ago. It held decisive power over the government until the 1920s. Already in the government of Frei the NAS had abandoned its traditional argument that "private property is sacred" in order to argue that private ownership of land was more efficient than inept state control. However, even the NAS did not oppose the Agrarian Reform Law head on, recognizing that they could scarcely claim that private ownership of the big latifundias had proved efficient. Their tactic was to cleanse their organization of political figures and elect "technical" experts to defend the "professional" interests of the big landowners. They then pressured the Frei government to make sure that the Agrarian Reform Law contained a clause prohibiting the expropriation of "well exploited" farms under eighty BIH. Furthermore, they pressured to make sure that the Agrarian Tribunals set up by the law would favor the owners in subsequent disputes with CORA.

It is interesting that the image of "professionalism" pushed by the NAS was torn to shreds by the confession of the president of the organization, Benjamin Matte, that he was a member of the fascist sect, Patria y Libertad. Matte resigned from the presidency of the NAS in early 1973 in order to pursue his fascist activities, and after the frustrated coup of June 29, 1973, he sought refuge and political exile in Ecuador. It is clear that the rural bourgeoisie is one of the main components of the extreme right. Most of the latifundistas were members of the National Party, many with close links to Patria y Libertad. Their farms served as airports and training grounds for the fascist movement. The most reactionary elements of the upper class formed a strange alliance with thugs and hoodlums in the pursuit of fascism in Chile.

The NAS was largely successful in crippling the expropriation process during Frei's government. The election of Allende, however, was a serious blow. At first on the defensive, the latifundistas then developed a series of tactics which threatened completely to halt the process of expropriations.

In order to do this they used the Agrarian Tribunals, composed of judges and right-wing agronomists. The NAS maintained several offices permanently staffed with lawyers in Santiago. Whenever a member of the NAS (NAS membership was now about five thousand) was threatened with expropriations, he called a phone number and got immediate legal help.

For example, in Santiago in June 1973, the CORA announced the expropriation of some forty farms. Immediately the Agrarian Tribunals issued staying orders preventing CORA from taking possession of them. Thus, the owners gradually perfected their legal tools until they could paralyze expropriations.[23]

In the political realm, the right introduced a Constitutional Reform in the beginning of June 1973. This Constitutional Reform, presented by the former head of CORA under Frei, Rafael Moreno, required that (1) CORA divide up the asentamientos into individual plots in a period of two years after expropriation; (2) CORA give a reserve to every expropriated owner of at least forty BIH; and (3) that, in those cases where farms greater than forty BIH had been expropriated and the owner had not been given a reserve of at least forty BIH, CORA now gave the owner that reserve. Congress approved the law. If enacted, it would have practically destroyed the agrarian reform. Allende vetoed it, but Congress rejected his veto by a majority. The bill was simply one more factor in the institutional crisis provoked by the Congress in order to force the capitulation or the outright overthrow of Allende.

In the military realm the right used their shield of the corrupt and class-based court system to attack and kill peasants with impunity. Of the some fifteen murders of peasants during the Allende government, not one resulted in the conviction of a landowner, despite the fact that in almost all the cases the landowners were clearly identified by many witnesses. On the other hand, peasants who were attacked by landholders were often jailed for a year without bail with only the flimsiest charges against them.

Many armed groups of landowners, especially in southern Chile, operated permanently in close connection with Patria y Libertad. Beginning around the end of 1971, and increasingly thereafter, the landowners succeeded in reoccupying farms occupied by peasants, using arms and protected, if not openly aided, by corrupt police officials.[24]

Conclusion

Allende furthered a land reform that did not basically differ from the traditional pattern of reformist parties in Latin America (APRA in Peru, Acción Democrática in Venezuela, and the Christian Democrats in Chile). The radical nature of the Chilean land reform stemmed from the greatly increased rate of expropriation. The Popular Unity pushed a traditional, progressive land reform to its ultimate consequences within the context of capitalism.

There were inevitable limitations given that the Popular Unity government did not control state power. Nevertheless, there were more radical options which the Popular Unity did not choose to exercise. Among these were greater reliance on the Peasant Councils, an emphasizing of collective work relations on the expropriated farms from the beginning, and a greater control of agricultural markets and the private latifundia. That these options and others were not chosen was due partly to conscious political decisions and partly to an inability to foresee the depth of the agricultural crisis which took place in 1972 and 1973.

Despite all the criticisms of Allende's agrarian reform, we must remember that because of it tens of thousands of Chilean peasants took control of their own lives for the first time. Even if only for a brief moment, the agrarian reform righted many wrongs that had oppressed the peasants for centuries.

The military intervention in September 1973 put an abrupt end to all that.

Since the Coup

The agricultural policies of the military regime began with the brutal repression of the peasantry wherever signs of resistance were encountered or even merely imagined. For example, in the provide of Valdivia, in the county of Panguipulli, the military decided there was a guerrilla group, led by the MIR, operating. The area was surrounded by three or four thousand troops and about ten helicopters were brought in. Air Force jets bombed two small towns in the area. The troops closed the circle, killing many and arresting others, later subjecting them to systematic torture. In October 1973 there were five hundred political prisoners in the capital of Valdivia Province. The peasantry has been terrorized in the same way as the rest of the population.

Since the coup there have been no leftist guerrilla attacks in the countryside. The countryside in Chile offers no cover for guerrilla activity. There is a developed system of roads, and there is little forested area. The best area for rural guerrilla activity would be southern Chile, but over the years the military has created a series of bases that strategically blanket the area. On the other hand, the soldiers in these bases are peasants themselves and undoubtedly are uncomfortable in their role as persecutors of the peasantry. Unsuccessful rebellions within the military took place right after the coup in Temuco and Valdivia.

The military, of course, immediately announced the dissolution of the Peasant Councils and the Marxist peasant unions. Prices for agricultural products were decontrolled. Labor policies in the reformed sector were tightened up considerably. As in the city, a free market for products has been created; at the same time the free play of the market in labor has been restricted by taking away all rights of the peasantry to organize while conferring those rights on the landlords.

The military has adopted a mixture of right-wing policies concerning land ownership, some from the Christian Democrats and some from the National Party. From the Constitutional Reform Bill proposed by the Christian Democrats comes the policy of dividing up the farms in the reformed sector among the asentados. All members of the cooperatives (asentamientos) are, supposedly, to be given title to the land in a few years. This, of course, will create many small landholdings which can be bought up by the large landholders, re-creating the latifundia, as happened in Mexico. Restrictions on the sale of divided land from the cooperatives, which are written into the Agrarian Reform Law, have been removed.

From the National Party, which has much more influence with the government than the Christian Democrats, comes the idea of returning the expropriated farms outright. The government has decreed that all farms being legally contested during the Allende period in the Agrarian Tribunals may be returned following a case-by-case review. This involves from one-fifth to one-fourth of all the expropriated farms. In some areas, such as the provinces of Linares and Cautín, the old landlords have simply taken back their farms by force, with the approval of the local military authorities.[25] There is no way to judge how widespread this has been nationally, but it surely has been relatively common.

According to the government's own statistics, by the end of 1975, 23 percent of the land in the reformed sector had been returned to its previous owners.[26] In some cases this was done "legally"; in others force alone was used. The results are the same. In addition, the government has been busily dividing up former cooperatives into individual plots. It is difficult to tell how far this has proceeded. We can assume that it has affected less land than the 23 percent that has been directly turned over to the old owners. Eventually, however, it should affect more. It appears as if the government is not planning on conserving any of the cooperatives over the long run.

The military has also disbanded the ten-year-old agricultural institutions, CORA, INDAP, and SAG. More than 40 percent of the technicians working for these agencies have been fired. CORA is now nothing more than an accounting office that oversees the division of the cooperatives. Peasants in the reformed areas now receive little or none of the technical assistance these agencies provided under Allende.

Production for export has increased due to the junta's campaign to increase exports in order to improve the balance of payments. Easy credits have been available to agricultural exporters, but the bulk of Chilean agricultural production has been hurt. One of the main problems has been the wheat crop. Over the three years of the Allende government wheat production averaged 1,300,000 tons, despite disruptions like the 1972 truck owners' lockout. The junta has averaged only about 700,000 tons in its first three years of producing wheat. The first year's crop, 700,000 metric tons, was undoubtedly hurt badly by the economic sabotage carried out by the right just prior to the coup. The second year's crop was officially predicted to be 1,100,000 tons at the beginning of 1975. But in May 1975 the *Mercurio*, Chile's major newspaper, said that official estimates were only 600,000 tons.[27] By the end of 1975 (the crop was harvested in June) the government marketing agency claimed a total of

800,000 tons.[28] The 1975–76 crop appears to have been about 600,000 tons.

It is difficult to trust official statistics. The best figures available since the coup are from the March-April 1976 issue of *Mensaje*, one of the few publications in Chile which is critical of the junta (*Mensaje* is allied with the Roman Catholic Church). The *Mensaje* article uses a variety of sources to try to get an accurate picture of agricultural production. Using statistics from the Agricultural Engineering School, the article concludes that the overall agricultural production dropped 8 percent in 1974–75, compared to the 4 percent increase claimed officially by the government. This 8-percent drop is in comparison to the 1973–74 production. Given the right-wing sabotage of late 1973, we can assume that the 1973–74 production must have been as bad or worse than the last year of production under Allende.

Furthermore, the *Mensaje* article predicted that the 1975–76 agricultural production would show a decline with respect to the previous years. There are several reasons for the decreased production. There has been a decrease in the area sown with crops. Credit for agricultural production has been drastically reduced as has technical assistance to farmers. Division of the reformed sector has been followed by sharply decreased production.

The Central Bank has estimated that there was a 5 percent reduction in the area sown with wheat between the 1973–74 crop and the 1974–75 crop. A study by ODEPA, the state agricultural planning office, estimated in 1975 that the use of nitrate fertilizers in Chile had dropped by *half* since the coup; and phosphates, which must be imported, by at least that much as well. The same study reported that loans from the state agricultural bank had dropped by half since the coup.[29] All these trends continued in 1976.

Prices for agricultural products have gone way up, but prices for agricultural supplies have gone up even more. For example, in early 1973, 100 kilograms of wheat could buy 320 kilograms of nitrate fertilizer or 220 kilograms of phosphate fertilizer. In early 1975, however, 100 kilograms of wheat could buy only 100 kilograms of nitrate fertilizer or 50 kilograms of phosphate fertilizer.

Despite the decreased agricultural production and the higher percentage of production going to export, the junta has not increased its imports of food. On the contrary it has sharply reduced imports in order to improve its badly deteriorated balance of payments. Agricultural imports soared under Allende, and in 1973 they totalled $700 million. In 1974 they were down to $555 million, and in 1975 they were only $330 million. Wheat imports dropped from a million tons in 1974 to only 400,000 tons in 1975. This means that in 1975, adding together imports and internal production, only 1,200,000 tons of wheat were available for consumption. The junta itself was claiming in February 1975 that minimal internal requirements were 1,600,000 tons.[30]

The drastic decreases in food imports have been translated into high food prices that are beyond the reach of the average Chilean. This has meant that malnutrition, severe enough to cause mental damage, is more widespread than it has ever been among working-class children in Chile.[31]

That wheat still imported into Chile has been financed by United States loans. The Ford administration used the food export program to get around congressional restrictions on aid to Chile. United States government food exports to Chile (Public Law 480) since the coup have been greater than to any other Latin American country (they were cut off during the Allende government). While the following list may not be complete, it does cover many of the credits made under Public Law 480 to Chile:

Date	Amount
October 1973	US $49 million
October 1974	$17 million
April 1975	$52 million
May 1975	$58 million

These credits have been made available not in money but in grain, mostly wheat and corn. With copper prices going through a very low period and with oil prices jumping, the United States has financed the junta's food imports, thereby easing the crisis in the balance of payments.[32]

To give an idea of how difficult it has become for the average Chilean to eat, it is worthwhile to look at some statistics comparing income and food prices. In late 1976 a typical salary for a worker was about fifteen pesos per day. Prices for many food items are listed below.[33] A kilogram is 2.2 pounds.

Food	Price
Bread (kilogram)	4.8 pesos
Milk (quart)	2.2 pesos
Cooking oil (quart)	15.0 pesos
Beans (kilogram)	15.0 pesos
Rice (kilogram)	6.0 pesos
Potatoes (kilogram)	2.5 pesos
Eggs (dozen)	15.6 pesos

Given these kinds of wages and these kinds of prices, it is no wonder that many Chileans are literally starving under the military junta.

None of these statistics can adequately describe the repression and poverty to which the masses of Chilean peasants have been subjected by the present military regime in Chile. The initial brutal repression, with its tortures and murder, was followed by the return of much of the expropriated land to the old owners. Since then the landlords have had free rein to exploit the peasantry as they choose. Occasionally some news of this filters through, even though all the newspapers are heavily censored. In April 1976, for example, an item appeared about an interview between the military and a leader of the Christian Democrat right-wing federation of agricultural workers in Cautín. (The junta has allowed the right-wing peasant unions that supported the coup to continue to exist, at least formally.) The Christian Democrat denounced "arbitrary firings" of peasants and claimed that "more than 40 percent of the landlords in Cautín are way behind in the payments they owe their workers."[34] This report indicates that even those who supported the coup have now been forced into protest.

Postscript to Chapter 1

There is a danger that in this chapter about rural strategy under Allende the reader will have been lost in a mountain of statistics and will have lost track of the human significance of the agrarian reform. Despite its shortcomings, the agrarian reform in Chile was a tremendous step forward for the Chilean peasantry. In order to get a sense of the problems of the peasants prior to the agrarian reform, it might be worthwhile to read some of the correspondence which follows.

During Allende's government a diligent researcher went to the archives and discovered hundreds of letters which had been sent over the years by peasants to the president of Chile.[35] A certain faith in the president led these peasants to believe that somehow he might be able to cut through the red tape of the Chilean bureaucracy and solve some of their desperate problems. The president merely forwarded the letters to the Ministry of Labor, which forwarded them to the local bureaucrats in the area. Nevertheless, the letters provide us with an invaluable description of the problems of the peasants. The letters from the peasants are invariably handwritten, often difficult to read, with mistakes in spelling. The answers from the Ministry of Labor, of course, are typed and in correct Spanish.

Two examples are provided here. The first dates from 1947 and illustrates the problems of union organizing in the countryside. Because of repressive legislation, it was very difficult to organize rural unions in Chile until the mid 1960s. The second example dates from 1966, and the problem of the peasant is solved not by the slow creaking of the bureaucracy but by the agrarian reform which leads to the expropriation of the farm in question. Both cases come from Cautín Province. The landowner involved in the second example owned farms throughout southern Chile, including Lautaro County.

Case 1: Letter from the peasants near Puerto Saavedra.

To: His excellency Gabriel González Videla
     Presidential Palace, Santiago
From: El Plumo farm, near Puerto Saavedra, Western Cautín Province
Date: January 10, 1947

Your Excellency:

We make this complaint about the Governor of the Imperial district and the Inspector of Work for the same district who came to solve our conflict at the farm.

These servants of the public administration called a meeting of the workers at the farm. But, when they arrived at the meeting, they were both drunk.

They came with an officer from the Tucapel Regiment in Temuco, named Luis Esmeralda. This officer started right off by attacking harshly the leaders of the C.T.Ch. (the labor union), calling them loafers and refusing to allow them to speak in defense of the peasants.

The Inspector of Work refused to recognize the union, saying that he was not willing to give legal status because everything that was asked for in our list of grievances was unjust and because of that he rejected completely our list of grievances.

But your Excellency,

Is it unjust that we want a school to teach our children, who now grow up in ignorance?

Is it illegal that we ask that our houses are repaired and improved since right now we live in straw huts with one room where we fix our food, eat it, and go to sleep?

Is it unjust that we ask for a raise when we have to sell our own belongings because of the low salaries and the high prices?

It is illegal that we ask the boss for the temporary use of the land on the hills for growing wheat and oats, when there is so much good land in the valley which he is not even using and which is gradually being covered by weeds?

We ask your Excellency that this land be divided up so that we can have access to part of it. Anything to stop this war without truce that our boss has been carrying out against us for trying to form a union, something that is not a crime. The boss, Mr. Antonio Kind, is working hard to get us thrown off the farm by the police, using all kinds of lies and slanders.

Respectfully,

José Diaz, Gerardo Sepúlveda, Sotero Nera, Armando Ariáz, Rafael Donoso, Juan Aguilera, Feliciano Cruces, José Mellao, Eugenio Sepúlveda, Luis Soto, Claudio Mejía, Juan de Dios Flores, Luciano Mella, Eusebio Pardos, Juan Rivera

Case 1: Letter from the Inspector of Work which concludes the investigation of the complaint. The president had forwarded the complaint to the National Work Inspection Office.

To: The Ministry of Labor
From: The Inspector of Work for the Imperial District
Date: January 24, 1947

Dear Minister of Labor:

In answer to Documents Nos. 12 and 13 of the Provincial Office of the Ministry of Labor, corresponding to Documents 60, 180, and 192 of the Ministry of Labor, and Nos. 414 and 757 of the National Work Inspection Office, I must point out the following:

The complaints made by the C.T.Ch. are completely false and are only one of the many lies about the Work Inspectors which are spread by the Communist Party. With the documents I am sending and the account I will give of the events both the Minister of Labor and the National Work Inspection Office will be able to fully understand what happened at the El Plumo farm near Puerto Saavedra.

On January 4, 1947, I went with the Governor of the District, the

Secretary to the Governor, and other officials to El Plumo farm in order to investigate a complaint by the owner of the property. The owner complained that eight peasants working on the farm refused to leave despite having been legally fired. When we got to the farm we called a meeting of all the peasants there. When they showed up they were accompanied by a member of the C.T.Ch. from the town of Imperial, who did not have any business being there. This was pointed out to him by me, by the Governor, and by the owner of the property, but he said that he was going to stay and defend his class brothers. The authorities and the owner of the property were kind enough to allow him to stay with the condition that he could not speak.

After long deliberations and having confirmed that the peasants had been legally fired and notified, it was discovered that the peasants had refused to receive their final pay from the owner. An agreement was reached that I would return to the farm on the 11th, Saturday, in order to arrange the final pay of the peasants.

On Saturday the 11th I went back as had been agreed. The peasants involved did not show up in spite of having been fully informed. Given the situation I wrote up a citation asking that the peasants and the owner show up at my office on the 17th at 3 P.M. This citation is enclosed.

The peasants and the owner, Juan Antonio Kind, appeared at my office on the 17th, and the conflict was solved. The peasants received their final pay as indicated by the receipt which I enclose.

As for the aggression and insolence contained in the letter from the C.T.Ch. to which I am responding, I am enclosing a note from the Governor of the District which verifies that all the charges made in the C.T.Ch. letter are false. The Governor also states that the number of peasants involved in the conflict was only eight, not fifteen as it seems from the C.T.Ch. letter.

After reading these documents the Minister of Labor and the National Work Inspection Office will be able to see to what point we have gotten with the lies and slanders from individuals who have no business getting involved. Such individuals for no reason sling mud at officials who are only fulfilling the thankless job that has been assigned to them, that of being worthy officials of the Work Inspection Office, a job that is difficult and is little understood by people of slight intelligence.

In closing I must point out that I did not answer you on time because the Governor was out of town and the note from him was very important to add to these documents.

Respectfully,

Hector Manriquez Solís de Ovando
Inspector of Work, Imperial District

(Author's note: The C.T.Ch. was a labor union federation. The Communist Party was a leading force in the federation, which tried to organize rural laborers, especially in the years 1946 and 1947. This organizing drive was broken when the Chilean government, at the instigation of the U.S. government, outlawed the Communist Party in 1947 and severely restricted the legal rights of the peasantry to organize.)

Case 2: Letter from José Marinao, a peasant living near Carahue, in Cautín Province.

To: His Excellency President of the Republic, Eduardo Frei
    Presidential Palace, Santiago
From: José Marinao Machacán, La Sirena farm, near Carahue, Western Cautín
Date: December 28, 1966

Your Excellency:

I, José Marinao Machacán, Identity Card No. 1673, from Carahue, living in La Sirena farm, am writing Your Excellency in order to obtain your help in guaranteeing me my right to continue living on the small parcel of land which I presently occupy on the La Sirena farm. La Sirena farm, property of Ana Schleyer widow of Kaham, is my home. I live there with my eight small children and my wife. I have made a complaint to the Minister of Land and Colonization, which I am enclosing, along with the response. That complaint was made on April 10, 1966. My complaint is that the foreman of the farm will not let me live in peace and prohibits me from working the small parcel of land which belongs to me. I have been living on this parcel for the last fourteen years as an inquilino. Domingo Ormeno Cerda, the foreman, is preventing me from working the parcel, which I must do to feed my family.

I also ask that Your Excellency help me obtain the family allowance and the social security contributions which are owed me by the boss, Mrs. Ana Schleyer. She owes me them for the last fourteen years, ever since she took me on as an inquilino here.

I hope that Your Excellency can help me. I have been complaining about these problems for years.

May God watch over Your Excellency,

José Marinao Machacán

Case 2: Letter from Inspector of Work in Cautín Province to Ministry of Labor in Santiago. The president had sent Juan Marinao's letter to the Ministry of Labor, which sent a note in January 1967 to the Inspector of Work in Cautín Province, asking him to investigate the complaint of José Marinao as soon as possible. The Inspector of Work in Cautín Province did not reply to the note for more than two and a half years.

To: Ministry of Labor, National Work Inspection Office, Santiago
From: Rafael Correa Luco, Provincial Work Inspector for Cautín
Date: August 30, 1969

Dear Sir:

In reference to the complaint of José Marinao Machacán, contained in Documents Nos. 4242 and 5799 of the Ministry of Labor. I can inform you as follows:

On August 26, 1969, an official of this Work Inspection Office went to visit La Sirena farm belonging to Ana Schleyer widow of Kaham. The farm now actually belongs to Clara Schleyer. The official was unable to reach the farm due to the road being impassable.

The official left a citation asking that Mr. Marinao come into the Work Inspection Office.

Mr. Marianao subsequently did come into the Work Inspection Office where he stated officially that at present he drops any complaint because he is now able to work his parcel in peace and because a committee has been formed of peasants at the farm to ask for the farm's expropriation according to the Agrarian Reform Law.

The long delay in processing this complaint has led to a penalty being imposed on the Inspector who was initially in charge of the investigation.

Respectfully,

Rafael Correa Luco
Provincial Work Inspector, Cautín

These two cases are typical of thousands of others where peasants tried to obtain justice from the authorities. The absolute lack of rights of the Chilean peasant was maintained until the Agrarian Reform Law of 1967. That law began the slow process of redressing centuries of grievances.

Chapter 2

Class Relations in
Chilean Agriculture, 1540-1930

Our review of Chilean history has shown that it was capitalism, with its internal contradictions itself, which generated the underdevelopment of Chile and determined its forms; that this remains as true today as it was in the past; that Chile's underdevelopment cannot be attributed to the supposed partial survival of a feudal structure which never existed there in whole or in part.
Andre Gunder Frank, *Capitalism and Underdevelopment in Latin America*

The landowning class has not been transformed into a capitalist middle class, ally of the national economy. Mining, commerce, and transport are in the hands of foreign capital. The latifundistas have been satisfied to serve as the latter's intermediaries in the production of sugar and cotton. This economic system has kept agriculture in a semi-feudal organization that constitutes the heaviest burden on the country's development.

The agrarian problem is first and foremost the problem of eliminating feudalism in Peru, which should have been done by the democratic-bourgeois regime that followed the War of Independence. But in its one hundred years as a republic, Peru has not had a genuine bourgeois class, a true capitalist class. The old feudal class, camouflaged or disguised as a republican bourgeoisie, has kept its position.
José Carlos Mariátegui, *Seven Interpretative Essays on Peruvian Reality*

Any discussion of agriculture under Allende would be incomplete without a historical perspective. The behavior of the inquilinos (see Chapter 1), for example, cannot be understood without a historical understanding of the differences between them and wage laborers. In Chile the reliance on the inquilino as the backbone of the agrarian reform meant that the resulting agricultural cooperatives embodied relations of production which were less socialized than would have been possible if the agrarian reform had relied on wage laborers from outside the farms. The inquilinos have traditionally possessed their own means of production and have been only partially paid in wages. They therefore reacted to the agrarian reform with the desire to expand their own individual production and become small capitalist farmers themselves; the cooperatives showed little tendency to collectivize production and income. As explained in Chapter 1, the response of the Popular Unity government was to try to form Agrarian Reform Centers (CERAs) as an alternative, an attempt that largely failed. The CERAs were to incorporate wage laborers from outside the farm into the new cooperatives.

The history of class relations in the countryside in Chile is not and was not an academic question, but one that has provided a theoretical foundation for the various rural strategies of the Chilean left.

Any attempt to trace the history of Chilean agriculture of necessity involves a discussion of feudalism and capitalism. In the last few years a spirited debate has taken place about whether Chile has ever been a feudal country. Gunder Frank has taken the position that Chile has been a capitalist country since the time of conquest, basing his assumption on the fact that Chilean agriculture always produced for export during the colony and that at no time was Chilean agriculture a closed natural economy with production for subsistence alone.[1] This contention has been tied to the theory of dependency, which Frank calls the "development of underdevelopment." The dependency theory holds that Chile has always been integrated into the world market system, and it is as a result of this integration that Chile is a poor country. The metropolis has always stolen a surplus from the Chilean economy and prevented the accumulation of capital which might have been used for national development. The dependency theory is opposed to the "dualist" theory of Latin America, which states that a stagnant, feudal sector coexists with a modern, capitalist sector. The solution for underdevelopment for dualists has been the elimination of the feudal sector, the taking of political power from the landowning oligarchy, and the development of national capital by the modern, urban, and national bourgeoisie. The solution for underdevelopment for those who believe in the dependency theory is, on the other hand, a socialist revolution conducted against both the landowning capitalists and the industrial ones. The left in Latin America has been divided on these questions. One sector of the left has called for a bloc between the urban working class, the peasantry, and the national bourgeoisie to create a full democracy and a national capitalist development free from imperialism. Only at a later stage would the struggle be for socialism. This has often been the position of Latin American Communist parties. On the other hand, since the Cuban revolution, many sectors of the Latin American left have held that the revolution to be carried out must be both antiimperialist and socialist at the same time, that there is no dualism in Latin American society, and that the national bourgeoisie cannot fulfill its historical role of freeing the economy from imperialism.

This is obviously an old debate in colonized or neocolonized countries, dating at least from Lenin's discussion of the development of capitalism in Russia in 1899.[2] Its renewal in the sixties in Latin America was due to the impact of the Cuban revolution, the inability of the traditional Communist parties to carry out a revolution, the new weakness of the United States due to its loss in Vietnam, and so forth.

This author believes that the dualist conception has been quite correctly rejected by the majority of the left in Latin America. The national bourgeoisie has proved itself incapable of leading an antiimperialist and antioligarchic revolution. To the failure of such traditional reform parties as APRA in Peru, AD in Venezuela, and the MNR in Bolivia, must now be added the failure of Juan Domingo Perón's most recent presidency. The penetration of imperialist economic interests into manufacturing production in Latin America has meant a qualitatively different situation than that of countries in Africa or Asia where a comprador bourgeoisie can be isolated from a national bourgeoisie. In Latin America the industries created during the import-substitution period (1930s–1940s) helped develop an internal market. After World War II, U.S. capital took advantage of this internal market by investing directly in manufacturing, thereby either destroying or subjugating the national bourgeoisie.

There can be no stage of "national" capitalist development in Latin America because there is little "national" capital. Native capital is predominantly the willing servant of foreign capital. The most striking demonstration that a consistent antiimperialist policy in Latin America can only coincide with socialist measures has been offered by Cuba.

However, even though it opposes the dualist thesis, the interpretation of Chilean history by Gunder Frank must be rejected. Chile has not been capitalist since the mid 1500s. It is quite possible, and indeed necessary, to reject both the dualist interpretation and Frank's. As has been pointed out by numerous authors, most clearly by Ernesto Laclau, Frank's view is based on the identification of capitalism with production for the market and ignores the relations of production internal to the economy. A study of those relations of production reveals that they certainly were not capitalist throughout most of Chile's history. Indeed they have been marked by extraeconomic coercion on the part of landowners, the owner- ship of some means of production by the peasant labor force, and a restric- tion of the internal market which has impeded the development of capitalism.[3]

To jump ahead, the conclusions reached by this author are that Chile had a slave economy oriented towards exports from the time of conquest until the late 1600s. From then until the latter part of the nineteenth century Chile was a semifeudal country, after which the economy as a whole can properly be defined as capitalist as a result of the dominance of mining over agriculture. Within the agricultural sector itself feudal rela- tions of production remained dominant until the 1930s when the number of inquilinos began to descend both absolutely and relatively, and wage labor became predominant.

A few words are necessary about the definition of feudalism and capitalism, before turning to their description in Chile.

As Marx defined feudalism, and this is the definition we will use, it means: (1) an economy where wealth is predominantly based on privately owned land; (2) where the owners of the land extract the surplus produc- tion from the peasantry (production exceeding subsistence) by extraeco- nomic coercion of one form or another; (3) production is primarily for use, not for the market, and the economy is a closed natural economy; and (4) the peasantry owns its own means of production, including usually a small plot of land. Marx stressed two aspects of feudalism, the relations of production and the nonexistence of markets. The relations of production were characterized by the fact that labor was not free and did possess some means of production. In order for capitalism to develop, the peasan- try had to be free to establish a contract with the landowner or farmer and also had to be dispossessed of its means of production. The nonexistence of markets forms the other side of feudalism. Production must be predom- inantly for consumption, not for commodity exchange.[4]

Marx emphasized neither the one nor the other of these two sides of feudalism. Both are crucial. One cannot define as capitalist an economy which produces predominantly for the market but in which labor is not free. This is the main problem with Frank's analysis. On the other hand, it is clear that an economy which produces for the market, in which the main goal of the landowners or farmer is commodity exchange, cannot be called feudal. Chile from the late seventeenth century until the late nineteenth century produced predominantly agricultural exports for an external market. Yet the mass of labor force was subject to extraeconomic coercion, was not free, and continued to possess certain means of production. Therefore we cannot call Chile during this period either feudal or capitalist, strictly speaking, but we will choose the term semifeudal.

The definition of feudalism used here has a specificity which precludes economies based on slave labor. The peasant is not free, but he does possess some means of production and some traditional rights. He himself is not a commodity. Thus he is not a slave. The Indian in Chile was enslaved, first in the mines, and then throughout most of the seventeenth century. Only after that could the agricultural laborer no longer be bought and sold, and thus begin to control important means of production.

Furthermore, this definition of feudalism is not tied to serfdom. Serfdom disappeared from most of Europe in the fourteenth century, in the sense of the serf being the vassal of the lord. In that century the Black Plague reduced the labor force considerably; so did the Hundred Years War. The population boom between the eleventh and thirteenth centuries seems to have already died down before these disasters of the fourteenth. At the same time, major peasant rebellions took place, their goal the abolition of personal vassalage.[5] Depopulation due to war and plague meant that the labor force was more in demand and in a better bargaining position, and also that there was an additional amount of uncultivated land to which serfs could flee. The landlords, in the face of this difficult situation, accelerated a trend which had begun earlier. They divided their land (desmesnes) among their serfs, who then became hereditary tenants with fixed rents in money or kind.[6] Many of the onerous burdens of serfdom, including the lord's absolute right to dispose of the person of his vassal, as well as chevage, leywite, and so forth, disappeared or were sharply reduced, often in return for payment.[7] But the lord continued to exercise jurisdiction in manorial courts and to receive payments for all kinds of pasture and mill services. He continued to collect a rent in kind or money, a hereditary burden required of the peasant, who had no right to bargain. Labor remained unfree, and rent did not allow any profit for the tenant. No average rate of profit affected the amount of rent as is the case under capitalism. The replacement of labor services by money, rent, or rent in kind is not an indication that feudalism no longer exists, and much of the formal structure of serfdom as it existed from the ninth to the fourteenth centuries could largely disappear without the disappearance of feudalism.[8]

This much said about feudalism, a few words are in order about merchant capital. In Chile the landlord produced for export at first gold, then hides and tallow, and finally wheat. Sale of these exports meant an accumulation of commercial capital which at first benefitted the landlord, who was also the merchant, and then was divided between them, inasmuch as they became separate persons.[9] The accumulation of this capital did not provide a point of introduction for capitalism. Instead, the capital accumulated from exports was wasted on the consumption of the landlords and was not invested in production. The slave and then feudal relations of production remained the same or grew more intense. The accumulation of merchant capital is ordinarily associated with the destruction of feudalism in Western Europe, and rightly so. However, Marx's discussion of merchant capital makes it clear that it does not necessarily contribute to the development of capitalism; that is, to wage, labor, and the investment of capital in industry. Ironically, production for export and commodity exchange may in fact hinder the development of commodity exchange in the home market, and this is what happened in Chile. According to Marx:[10]

> The independent and predominant development of capital as merchant's capital is tantamount to the non-subjection of production to capital, and hence to capital developing on the basis of an alien social mode of production which is also independent of it. The independent development of merchant's capital, therefore, stands in inverse proportion to the general economic development of society.

Marx holds that the development of commercial capital may or may not help capitalism develop, depending on the relations of production of that society where the merchant capital develops. He writes as follows:[11]

> However, in its first period—the manufacturing period—the modern mode of production developed only where the conditions for it had taken shape within the Middle Ages. Compare, for instance, Holland and Portugal. And when in the 16th, and partially still in the 17th century, the sudden expansion of commerce and the emergence of a new world-market overwhelmingly contributed to the fall of the old mode of production and the rise of capitalist production, this was accomplished conversely on the basis of the already existing capitalist mode of production.

Historical examples of an increase of feudal labor relations at the same time as increased production for the market are well known. Perhaps the most outstanding is Eastern Germany at the end of the fifteenth century where grain for export to Western Europe was produced in great quantity at the same time as the landlords increased the feudal oppression of their peasants. Similar situations occurred in parts of England in the fourteenth century. In general it seems that market production of raw materials for export to areas of more advanced manufacturing production often produces a prolongation of feudal labor relations within the home economy. [12]

In the case of Chile, we will try to show that in fact this is what happened. Frank's assertion that Chile was a capitalist country since the sixteenth century because it depended on the production of commodities for an external capitalist market is incorrect in terms of Marx's definition of capitalism. [13] Whereas such production in Chile increased the accumulation of commercial capital, it went hand in hand with the slave or feudal exploitation of the peasantry.

Finally the terms feudalism and capitalism were first defined and employed in a thorough fashion by Marx, and we are trying to use the definitions that he developed. Most historical discussions of feudalism and capitalism must at least reflect, consciously or unconsciously, Marx's work. But Marx wrote mostly about capitalism and did not extensively discuss precapitalist economic formations. His definition of feudalism, including an equal emphasis on relations of production on the one hand and the closed natural economy on the other, has made it difficult to label economies either feudal or capitalist in those cases where one of these elements is present and not the other. Furthermore, Marx's discussion of other precapitalist economic formations, i.e., slavery, Asiatic and Ancient, as sketched out in the *Grundisse*, is only tentative. In trying to describe Chile, we are using the term semifeudal to characterize the period from about 1680 until 1860. This term is perhaps unsatisfactory because it lacks precision. But if we are to follow a Marxist approach in describing an economy, we cannot but use a compromise term like semifeudal. [14]

The transition from feudalism to capitalism, or in the case of Chile, from semifeudalism to capitalism, is by its nature different from the transition of production existing side by side and confronting one another, whereas the latter transition is abrupt, taking place rapidly. Capitalism and socialism cannot coexist for long within a given economy. In the case of the transition from feudalism to capitalism, the description of the economy as a whole depends upon which element is dominant. Clearly as soon as an average rate of profit is formed that governs investment of the majority of capital in the country, then a country as a whole may be described as capitalist. That is what happened in Chile in the late nineteenth century. Nevertheless, in the agricultural sector of the economy rents were not correlated with the average rate of profit until wage labor dominated agricultural production, and this took place in the 1930s. So we can say that even when Chile as a whole can be described as capitalist, the agricultural sector continued to be dominated by feudal relations of production for many years.

To discuss Chilean agriculture, we must start with a discussion of the Spanish economy at the time of the Conquest of the New World. It was the Spanish economy, of course, that gave direction to the society that the conquistador set up in Latin America. Spain at the time of the Conquest was divided into the Kingdom of Castile and the Kingdom of Aragon. It was the Castilian economy that served as the model for Latin America since Castile had the monopoly of trade with the New World throughout most of the sixteenth and seventeenth centuries and most Spanish immigrants to the Indies were Castilian rather than Aragonese. This Castilian dominance was to prove an important factor. In this section we will try to determine which characteristics of the Castilian economy inhibited the "normal" or classic (i.e., English) development of capitalism in Spain. Many factors that hindered the development of manufacturing capital in Castile were likewise, in changed circumstances, to hinder its development in Chile.

The tremendous accumulation of merchant capital due to the discovery of the Indies, the monopoly of its trade, and the large amounts of precious metals available there could not find outlets in the Castilian economy. Much of the development of Castile in the sixteenth century can only be explained by its peculiar past.[15] Castile did not have the traditional development throughout most of the Middle Ages which Aragon shared with the rest of Western Europe. For Castile the seven centuries of the Reconquest of the Moors (who had occupied Spain) prevented political and economic stability. Castile continued to fight the Moors until the fall of Granada in 1492. The society of Castile was a society of war.

The neighboring Crown of Aragon, in contrast, developed and matured in stability from the early twelfth century onward, isolated from the battles of the Castilians and Moors. Aragon joined the Italian city-states to become the major traders in the Mediterranean in the thirteenth and fourteenth centuries. Strong craft guilds developed in Aragonese towns. In general the development of the feudal economy in Aragon (northeast Spain) was typical of the rest of Western Europe with an exceptional emphasis on maritime trade.

Castile, which was to form the other half of the Spanish state in the late fifteenth century under Ferdinand and Isabella, was completely different. In Castile the craft guilds were opposed by the state and did not truly exist during the thirteen, fourteenth, and most of the fifteenth centuries when they dominated craft production in the rest of Europe. It was not until Ferdinand of Aragon became king of Castile that craft guilds were finally chartered, and by then they were becoming an anachronism throughout Europe, an obvious fetter on trade and development.[16]

The towns of Castile were not dominated by merchant capitalists and guilds, forces that might have at times opposed the noble landlords, as occurred in the Crown of Aragon. (An exception were some of the towns of Cantabria in northwest Spain.) On the contrary, the nobles lived in the towns and were threatened by no merchant or manufacturing capitalists. The Castilian towns resembled the Roman towns of antiquity rather than the towns of medieval Europe. The wealth of the nobility was based on the land, but the nobles frequently lived in town. This was partially due to the pattern of continual war in Castile during the Reconquest of the Moors. The same pattern was to repeat itself in the colonies of the New World.

The predominance of the nobility and the weakness of the bourgeoisie in Castile were confirmed by Ferdinand and Isabella in the Act of Resumption in 1480 which, while exacting a monetary tribute from the nobility, also confirmed its landholdings, its usurpations of Crown land and land of the military orders during the previous centuries. Ferdinand and Isabella did indeed consolidate the position of the monarchy in Spain for the first time, but it was not a monarchy independent of the nobility or linked with the urban bourgeoisie against the nobility. Subsequent Spanish monarchs in the sixteenth century were never independent of the nobility.[17]

The economic base of the nobility was land, large tracts of it in Old Castile or newly founded estates taken during the Reconquest. At the time of Ferdinand and Isabella the nobility represented about 2 percent of the population and owned about 97 percent of the land. It was also exempt from taxes. Eighty percent of the Spanish population were peasants.[18] With such a landholding pattern the 1481 decree of Ferdinand giving the serf the freedom to abandon his master remained largely a dead letter. Castilian agriculture suffered from social and technical backwardness. After 1570, Castile became heavily dependent on grain imports from northern and eastern Europe.[19]

A peculiar feature of the Spanish economy was the Mesta, the organization of sheep owners. The Mesta was controlled by the great aristocracy who used Spain as one large sheep path. In England it was the capitalist farmers who enclosed the fields and developed sheep farming at the expense of the traditional tenants and grain crops, causing "sheep to eat men." But in Spain this classic example of capitalist development was distorted. It was the nobility who developed the great sheep herds, and who ruined a large part of the country's grain-producing areas in favor of the sheep. The nobility blocked the development of a Spanish textile industry, preferring to export their wool for higher prices to foreign countries. The English textile industry provided the basis for English manufacturing and capitalism. It flourished only after the export of wool to Flanders was halted in favor of textile manufacturing at home. In Spain, on the other hand, the exportation of wool was continued; and the development of a Spanish textile industry, a crucial industry in the development of manufacturing production, was thereby hindered.[20]

This economic background explains to a large degree the course of events following the discovery of the New World. That discovery led to a tremendous flow of precious metals into Spain. The inability of Spain to use this capital to promote its own manufacturing production is the crucial cause of Spain's future backwardness.

Some of the wealth of the New World was absorbed by the expenses of maintaining the empire. Under Charles V in the early sixteenth century, Spain became an empire, joined with the Hapsburg Austrian empire and the Burgundian kingdoms. The Spanish Crown became involved in continual wars in Germany, Flanders, and Italy which cost more money than the treasury had. The silver fleets from the Indies were pledged in advance to Genoese and German bankers who had made loans to the Spanish empire (called asientos). But the costs of maintaining the empire were only one side of the problem. The other side resides in the nature of the Castilian economy as sketched out above.

The discovery of the Indies opened up tremendous possibilities to the Spanish Crown, though possibilities fraught with dangers. Spain tried to impose a customary mercantilist monopoly on trade with its colonies; this failed miserably. As early as the beginning of the seventeenth century, contemporaries were claiming that nine-tenths of the colonial trade (both legal and illegal) was being carried on by foreigners.[21] Heavily in debt, the Spanish Crown made little profit from a colonial trade it could not control. The Crown was forced to declare bankruptcy, beginning in 1557 and 1575, and culminating in the total collapse of 1680.

The Castilian economy was also hampered by the rise in prices in the sixteenth century. Prices rose faster in Spain than in the rest of Europe, at least partially due to the influx of precious metals from the mines of the Indies.[22] Higher prices in Spain meant that manufactured goods from other countries were cheaper, and despite formal restrictions, these foreign goods were increasingly sent to Latin America. Spanish merchant capital was not invested in Spanish manufacturing. Instead it was frequently invested in loans in the form of buying bonds (called juros) to the Crown. By 1565, 65 percent of the Crown's revenues were paid—in fact, were precommitted—to juro holders.[23]

All in all, the internal weaknesses of the Castilian economy, dominated by the nobility, meant Spain was not only unable to profit from its colonies, but also, in the long run, was probably the worse off for having had them. The illusions of Spain's Golden Age and its obsession with precious metals helped inhibit its own capitalist development for a long period of time. The weaknesses of Spain were to be reflected in the societies set up by the Spaniards in Chile and in all Latin America in the sixteenth century. Some one thousand conquistadores managed to conquer a continent in fifty years. They came largely from Castile, usually from the southern provinces of Estremadura and Andalucia. They were often soldiers, sons of impoverished noble families. We will try to show how the kind of society they set up in Chile reflected their origins.

The discussion of Chilean history will be divided into three parts: (1) the period of slavery; (2) the period of semifeudalism from about 1680 to 1860; and (3) the transition to capitalism after 1860. In this first part we will look at the relations of production in the early period, characterized by Indian slavery.

The legal forms under which the conquistadores founded their kingdoms in the New World were feudal. All the new world had been granted in fief to the Spanish Crown by the Pope, and the Crown in turn was the lord of all its vassals—Spaniards or Indians—in the New World. The institutions which were the basis for the division of the spoils in the new world, the merced and the encomienda, were institutions which derived first from the Reconquest of Spain itself, then from the experience of conquering the Canary Islands. The merced was a grant of land and the encomienda was a grant of Indian labor. The mercedes in Chile were issued by the Cabildo, or municipal government of Santiago, until 1575 when the Governor of Chile began to issue them. They continued to be granted until 1703 when the state began to sell its land. But by about 1650, most of the land was distributed and there were few new grants.[24]

Land grants were useless in any case without the accompanying encomienda of labor. The encomienda delivered a certain amount of Indian
labor to the encomendero, the recipient of the encomienda. The encomendero was supposed to protect the spiritual and material well-being
of the group of Indians. In return for this protection, the encomendero
was allowed to collect for his own benefit the tribute which the Indian
vassals owed to the Crown. In Chile, this tribute was paid in labor (even
though personal service tribute was decreed illegal in 1542 and 1549 by
the Spanish Crown). In Chile this arrangement between lord and vassal,
encomendero and Indian, was very different from what it was in Europe.
The vassals were of a different race and were far from the protection of the
Crown. They had no history of traditional rights as did the serfs of
Europe. The encomendero, as a result, abused the encomienda system
and often turned it into a system of slavery. No spiritual or military
protection was offered in return for the tribute. Military protection in fact
was a contradiction in terms. The Indians of the encomienda were looked
upon as potential enemies. They were of the same race as the southern
Araucanians who fought the Spaniards from the time of Conquest until
1884 and at times jeopardized the very existence of the colony. The
encomendero of central or northern Chile worried that these vassals
might join the southern Araucanians (Mapuches) in a general uprising.

What usually occurred in Chile was that both mercedes and encomiendas were granted in the same area to a given person. The merced of land
was located near an Indian community which was given as an encomienda
to the Spaniard who had received the merced. Encomiendas were
granted by the Governor of Chile from 1541 until 1791 when encomiendas were finally in practice abolished.

The encomendero had another fundamental obligation to fulfill in return for the encomienda, that of serving his lord the king militarily. In
Chile, a country continually at war with its own Indian population, this
obligation was basic. There was no organized army paid from royal funds
until the first decade of the 1600s, after the defeat of 1599 inflicted by the
Mapuches had made the inadequacy of the Chilean military system apparent to the Crown. Even after this, the encomendero had to fullfill
military service although more and more frequently he was able to avoid
it. Domingo Amunátegui, in his basic work on the encomiendas in Chile,
discusses the military obligation of the encomendero as follows:[25]

The grant of the encomiendas in Chile rested, then, from the beginning upon an essentially feudal base. The beneficiaries received a

more or less large number of servants who were placed under their command with the condition that those encomenderos would continue fighting in the conquest of the territory.

In Spanish Chile, which was continually threatened by extinction by the Araucanian Indians, the old military ties of fealty took on the importance they had had during the Reconquest of Spain or during the ninth century in France. As Amunátegui points out in the same passage, the encomenderos were called the "citizens with fiefs" (vecinos feudatorios).

To discover the substance behind these feudal legal forms, however, it is necessary to investigate the relations of production within the encomienda. We can point out three basic characteristics of the early period (1541 to 1599). First, the economy was based on gold and silver extraction. Second, Indian labor was basically slave labor. Third, the encomenderos were physically eliminating the labor force by killing the Indians despite the Crown's attempts to make the encomienda system protect the Indian.

The Spaniards wanted land not to farm it, but to extract gold. Inasmuch as the land did not have gold or silver on it, it was viewed as a prestigious possession but of little immediate value. But the precious metals declined rapidly, and by 1600 they had practically disappeared. In 1568 the royal fifths from the mines amounted to between thirty-five and forty thousand pesos, in 1583 they had decreased to twenty-two thousand pesos, and in 1600 they were an insignificant two thousand five hundred pesos.[26]

The encomiendas were designed so that an Indian community would continue to live together and farm its own land. Mercedes to Spaniards could not be located, in theory, on Indian land. The tribute paid to the encomendero was not to be burdensome and was to allow the Indian community plenty of time to work its own land. But the Spaniards' desire for gold and their need for Indian labor to get it led to the transformation of this system into a living hell. To the first one hundred and fifty conquistadores in Chile it appeared as if the labor supply was inexhaustible. Indeed, estimates are that some one to one and a half million Indians lived in Chile at the time of conquest, with about seventy or eighty thousand around Santiago, the first settlement. With abundant labor and seemingly abundant precious metals, the Spaniards sent the Indians of their encomiendas to work all year round in the mines, breaking up communities, and often sending them to a totally different part of the country. These practices were illegal, but Spain was far away. Its representatives in Chile needed the support of the first Spaniards for military defense and were not about to refuse them rewards for their efforts.[27] The work in the mines consumed the Indians as undoubtedly did the diseases brought by the Spaniards. Pedro de Valdivia had originally granted sixty encomiendas in 1544, but in 1546 he cut them back to thirty-two because of the shortage of labor and his desire that new encomiendas be granted after further conquest in the south.[28]

The president of the Royal Tribunal (Audiencia) in Chile in 1559 issued regulations for the encomienda after an investigation. In his description of the encomienda we can find the essence of the early relations of production:[29]

> I found, by talking with priests, that the [Indian] mothers did not even want to give milk to their own children, and that in this way they killed their own children, saying that it was better that way. Otherwise, when their children reached the age of 7 or 8, the encomenderos would take them to the mines, and they would never be seen again, and they would never be a source of joy to their parents.

Any system where the owners of wealth have complete control over the laborers, and the laborers are more or less easily replaced, can degenerate into slavery. The Spaniards, as shortsighted as perhaps any group of colonizers has ever been, looked only to the short-run gains and ignored the progressive disappearance of the Indian population. Only the Crown tried to preserve the labor force. The history of colonial Chile is to a large extent the history of the failure of the Crown to exert any control over the encomenderos. According to Amunátegui, "the Chilean colony was one of the colonies in America least willing to obey the orders of the sovereign."[30] The Crown wanted above all to suppress the use of Indian *labor* to pay the tribute, instead calling for the payment of tribute *in kind* from the Indians' own production on their own land. Until the 1700s when the encomienda lost its economic significance, the Crown tried unsuccessfully to eliminate forced labor on the encomendero's land, in his mines, or in his house. Again, according to Amunátegui, the Spaniards in Chile[31]

> never accepted the suppression of personal obligatory service in order to benefit the Indians of their encomiendas, no matter how much these Indians proved themselves submissive, and no matter how much all the Kings from the glorious Emperor to his Majesty Carlos III, emphatically ordered such suppression in hundreds of royal decrees signed by their nearly divine hands.

The encomenderos did what they pleased, and what they pleased soon put the whole colony in jeopardy. By the first decade of the 1600s there were only about 5,000 encomienda Indians left in Spanish-occupied Chile, which meant a total Indian population of about twenty thousand.[32] The overwork in the mines, the loss of the south in the Mapuche uprising of 1599, the continual slaughter of the Indians who fought in wars with the Spaniards, the deaths from disease—all these causes served to reduce abruptly the numbers of the native population available to the Spaniards as a labor force.

The reliance on slave labor largely eliminated the possibility of an internal market. Each Spaniard assured himself of his own food supply for his own consumption, and as many manufactured items as could be extracted from the labor of his own Indians. In the early 1600s a contemporary source commented on the lack of an internal market:[33]

> Each Spaniard has his own vineyard, some bigger, some smaller, and land from which to get bread, by harvesting wheat, and land for corn, peas, beans, melons, and other vegetables: so that there is no place where anything is sold, nor stores.

What manufactured goods could not be made by the Indians were imported from Peru in exchange for gold. No artisan class of Spaniards developed in the early days of the remote colony. A few encomenderos organized local industries for cloth and for rigging for ships. These were operated by Indians; and, when the Indian population dwindled to almost nothing, these local industries closed. They were not reopened until the mid 1700s, by the Jesuits.[34] In the 1600s the only real internal market was the permanent army, and production for it was subsidized from Peru.

The Crown tried to prevent this situation by fighting the abuses of the encomenderos. Shortly after the Conquest, the Crown tried to abolish the encomiendas altogether throughout Latin America in the comprehensive New Laws of the Indies of 1542. These laws were met by armed rebellions by the encomenderos in Colombia, Mexico, Peru, and Paraguay. As a result the Crown retreated.[35] For Chile, the Council of the Indies frequently suggested another solution, the importation of black slaves. But contemporaries just as frequently replied that it was too expensive. Indians were simply much cheaper even though they were disappearing.[36]

The disappearance of the precious metals and the labor to work them meant that Chile faced a disaster in the late 1500s. The uprising of 1599, which took the whole south of Chile away from the Spaniards until the 1800s, accentuated the already approaching crisis. The solution for Chile was threefold. First, the military question was taken care of by payments from the budget of Peru, and a professional army was established. Second, an export was found. Tallow and hides from cattle and sheep replaced gold and silver as the export items, so that the Spaniards in Chile were able to import the manufactured items they needed. Still, such exports never created enough wealth to pay for the army, which remained dependent on Peru until the early 1700s. Third, the solution to the labor problem was found in the legal enslavement of Indians caught in war. This was made possible by a Royal Decree of 1608 although in fact it had been going on for some time. The raids on the south, malocas, meant that slavery, which before 1608 had been illegal but de facto, then legally became the main source of labor for the colony.[37] In addition, the grazing economy needed far fewer workers than the mines.

The seventeenth century was a dismal one for Chile just as it was for Spain. The population barely rose at all. The colony would have been abandoned except for the Royal determination to keep it Spanish in order to avoid the invasion of European navies by way of the Straits of Magellan. The brief Dutch occupation of the Island of Chiloé in the early 1600s scared the Crown.

The destruction of the Indian communities of northern and central Chile meant that even before the Royal decree of 1608 the majority of the Indians of encomienda came from those captured in war. A contemporary source estimated that over half of the Indians in encomiendas in the district of Santiago in the first decade of the seventeenth century were captured in war. Such Indians lived on the land of the Spaniard, not in any separate community.[38] They joined the displaced Indians of the pacified areas (Yanaconas) on the landlord's ranch unlike the Indians who remained living in their original communities (indios de pueblo). As the century went on the indios de pueblo almost completely disappeared, and most encomiendas were made up of yanaconas and other Indians who were captured in war. Together these groups were known as indios de estancia, or ranch Indians, because they lived on the landlord's ranch. There they farmed their own plots of land. They thereby formed a model for the future labor system of inquilinos which came to be the dominant form of labor in the countryside from the early 1700s until the 1930s (see Chapter 1). The ranch Indians were not the direct predecessors of the inquilino, due simply to the progressive extinction of all the Indians of north and central Chile, but the relations of production exemplified by the ranch Indians were similar to those later found between inquilino and landlord.[39]

It was not until the 1670s that the Crown prohibited the enslavement of Indians captured in war.[40] The Crown at that time also proposed the freeing of all slaves in Chile, but Governor Henríquez protested, saying that the Indian slaves were more numerous than the Spaniards and that their freedom might lead to a rebellion. But the late 1600s did see the end of Indian slavery as the basis for the work force. It continued to be difficult to capture sufficient Indians by raiding the south. Meanwhile, the Indians working on Spanish land were gradually destroyed by disease and brutality. The resulting shortage of manpower was accentuated by the change from livestock ranching to wheat farming, the latter needing more workers. The solution to the labor problem was the use of the mestizo (part Spanish, part Indian) or poor Spanish workers. Such workers were not slaves. Their incorporation into the wheat farms meant that slave relations of production were replaced by feudal ones.

In the late 1600s wheat became the main export crop to Peru. By 1680 also, the basic land tenure system in Chile was established. The big landowners had consolidated their holdings, and their farms remained intact until the 1870s and 1880s.[41] The farming of wheat completely transformed the relations of production. The farm replaced the ranch (hacienda replaced estancia) and the inquilino became Chile's serf. The smaller landholdings owned by some Spaniards in 1604, when Jines de Lillo (a Crown engineer) measured the land, disappeared by the 1680s. Whereas in England the introduction of sheep to replace grain meant the transition from feudalism to capitalism, in Chile grain replaced livestock and feudal relations of production replaced slavery.

In the 1600s wheat frequently had to be imported from Peru, so slight was Chile's production. In 1624–26 and 1637–40, for example, wheat was imported. Wheat exports from Chile were prohibited several times as in 1611–12.[42] All this changed in the 1700s.

The trend toward wheat production for the Peruvian market had begun even before the 1687 earthquake which disrupted Peru's own wheat production. The commerce had been stimulated by the natural superiority of Chilean soil to Peruvian for wheat. By the early 1700s wheat exports to Peru were already above one hundred thousand quintales (100 kilograms = 1 quintal) a year. Over the course of the century they rose gradually. In the period 1787 to 1795 they averaged one hundred and sixty-eight thousand quintales a year with the price, which was controlled by the merchants of Lima, having remained steady or fallen slightly since the beginning of the century. In 1787 wheat exports to Peru, the principal market for Chile until the mid 1800s, were valued at three times more than exports of tallow.[43]

At the same time wheat began to dominate the Chilean economy, the encomienda began to disappear. By 1788, three years before the abolition of the encomiendas, there were only 49 left in all Chile. In 1655 there had been 107 encomiendas of more than 10 Indians each in the district of Santiago alone. When they were abolished in 1791, there was little or no protest. The encomienda had become irrelevant.[44] The inquilino (mestizo or poor Spaniard) became the standard worker on the wheat hacienda. He was different from the Indian of the encomienda in that he owed no tribute to an encomendero and was not a slave that could be bought and sold. The inquilino possessed more instruments of production. In most cases he probably had his own tools, plow, and oxen. He received a small plot to work on his own and certain pasture rights. The inquilino began to work practically full time on the landlord's land and worked on his own only when the landlord did not need him. He received a ration of food while working for the landlord, but at first he received no salary. The fact that the inquilino used his own animals and tools differentiated him from the Indian and made him more similar to the peasant in Europe who paid his rents with labor services. Frequently it was the children of the in quilino who worked the family plot while the inquilino himself worked on the landlord's land. The inquilino's possession of his own tools and animals stemmed from his background, which was that of a poor but independent farmer who rented a part of the landlord's property in exchange for a token payment in goods (perhaps a small number of sheep) and the labor of watching the livestock and fences. This arrangement was known as préstamo.[45] The rent and labor exacted were slight. Land was cheap and abundant, and the independent farmer performed basically the functions of a caretaker on the landlord's property. When wheat replaced livestock, land became more expensive. This poor independent renter-farmer, often a mestizo, saw his rent become much larger. He no longer paid part of it in goods, but with much more labor. He became an in-quilino. The inquilino was not a rural proletarian or wage laborer. He entered into no contract voluntarily with the landowner. He was a peasant who paid his rent with labor services and who provided his own means of subsistence by working his small plot of land. His landlord was not a capitalist who invested in agriculture because he was assured of a return on his investment equal to the average rate of profit in a society where industrial production was well developed. On the contrary, there was no average rate of profit and no industrial production. The landlord exported the agricultural product. Internal demand was slight.

This system, which dominated Chile's economy until the mid 1800s, was similar to that described by Karl Kautsky when he was discussing the revival of feudalism in Eastern Europe in the sixteenth century after the nobles had crushed the Germans peasant revolts:[46]

> The victorious nobility began itself to produce commodities for a system which was a singular mixture of capitalism and feudalism. It began to produce on large tracts of land, using almost always not wage labor, but forced labor of a feudal character.

What for Kautsky was a singular mixture of capitalism and feudalism in Europe, was a characteristic mixture in Latin America. Chile became a semifeudal country when wheat production was developed and the inquilino replaced the slave as the main type of labor.

The boom in Chile's economy in the eighteenth century was reflected in figures for shipping. Towards the end of the sixteenth century about two thousand metric tons were shipped from Chile per year, while, at the end of the eighteenth century, the figure was about forty thousand metric tons per year not counting contraband (equal to about 25 percent of the legal trade).[47] Population also increased rapidly in the 1700s. It jumped twenty to thirty times in the first half of the century alone. All this growth, however, failed to develop an internal market. In a report to Governor O'Higgins in 1795, a contemporary described the economy as follows:[48]

> There is nowhere to export. There is no one to sell to. This can be seen by the complaints about the lack of consumers amongst the population itself.

The scarcity of export markets was to be solved by independence from Spain and colonial trade restrictions. But the lack of an internal market was not to be solved, given the poverty of the inquilino and the feudal relations of production. A modern Chilean historian comments:[49]

> At the end of the eighteenth century . . . Chile was presented with the real possibility of giving an enormous impulse to its agricultural and mineral production and even of perfecting certain branches of manufacturing or establishing new ones. In other words, national production could have increased in quantity and at the same time acquired more variety.

However, two factors conspired very actively against those expectations, the narrowness of the internal market and also the limitation of the external market. The former was composed of a population which was less than 500,000, the majority of whom, due to the prevalent social situation, lived by satisfying their basic needs with only a few simple items. It was a limited market that was not an effective stimulant of greater production.

The lack of money in circulation was another indication of the weak market. It was not until the late 1700s that enough money circulated so that it was even theoretically possible to pay monetary salaries to agricultural workers. It was not until then that Chile got its own mint.[50] The payments from Peru for the Chilean army continued to be in kind until the early 1700s, and after that were only sporadically in money. The lack of money in circulation continued to plague the Chilean economy until the mid 1800s. We find Governor O'Higgins complaining about it in the late 1700s, even after mining production had again picked up:[51]

There is no doubt that the interior commerce in Chile is weakened by the lack of circulation of money and the scarceness of money. That which is produced goes straight from the Royal Treasury to the ship's treasury to be exported to foreign countries.

On the other hand, the limitations of the external market (limited to Peru) were swept away with the independence of Chile in the early 1800s. The entire period between 1810 and 1830 was one of war. First the Chileans defeated the Spaniards, then the royalists defeated the patriots, and finally the forces of independence achieved a definitive victory in 1819. The following decade was marked by continued royalist resistance in the south of Chile and by feuds between various sectors of the ruling class who favored independence. During this period of conflict some revolutionary reforms were proposed, passed, and then eventually ignored or repealed. The reactionary triumph of Diego Portales and the subsequent stability of "law and order," which lasted until the 1850s, put an end to the political experiments of the 1820s. (The present Chilean military regime has named its headquarters after Diego Portales, appropriately evoking their reactionary predecessor who represented the most conservative aspects of Chile's ruling class.)

The forces that brought about independence certainly were not interested in changing the social structure in Chile. They wanted freedom from the restrictions placed on Chile by Spain in both economic and administrative matters.[52] But the predominance of the army in the years 1810–30 meant that the landlords were not in a position of control at all times. The army reflected advanced ideas insomuch as it, to a very limited extent, represented the mass of the population. Some of these ideas led to ephemeral reforms which provide us with an opportunity to discover something about Chilean society in the early 1800s.

The congresses of the 1820s first brought up the question of land reform and generally advocated the superiority of small property holdings. In 1825, for example, José Miguel Infante presented a law to Congress which suggested that the property, expropriated from the convents during the war against the royalists in the previous decade, should be subdivided in small lots and sold at public auction. This proposal did not succeed. In 1823 Representative Montt suggested that the large landlords be forced to rent out their property to small farmers to avoid the waste of large tracts of land lying fallow. In 1825, in yet another measure which attacked the landlords, José Miguel Infante proposed a direct tax on land as opposed to the indirect tax (diezmo) which was easily avoided by the landowners. Here we see for the first time a proposal which criticized the low taxation of the large landholdings: such low taxation has continued right up until the present day.[53] All reforms listed above were either repealed by Portales or were stalemated in one or another of the congresses of the 1820s.

The only reform which was carried out was the abolition of slavery, which affected about ten thousand blacks, most of whom were house slaves. This reform was allowed to remain on the books by Portales probably because the slaves were so few in number and did not represent an important work force for the agricultural economy. Nevertheless, the landlords fought the proposal tooth and nail in the 1820s in the halls of the Congress where arguments about the sacred rights of property were used, the same arguments used by the conservatives to attack Frei's Agrarian Reform Law in 1967 and Allende's agricultural policies during the Popular Unity government.[54]

The civil war of 1829–30 put an end to all these radical experiments. The group centered around Portales organized a part of the army which proved victorious, and Chile was not to see another military conflict among its ruling class until the 1850s when the powerful mining sector demanded government control and finally succeeded in taking it away from the landowners.

The dominance of the landowners in the period from 1830 to 1860 was a reflection of the dominance of agriculture in the economy. The mining, which grew to be more important later on, was still weak. At the political level, certain measures taken by the government in this period show a marked favoritism for the landowners and their exports. The building of the railroads, for example, which the state undertook under the government of Montt between 1850 and 1860, discriminated against the miners. The government railroad went from Santiago to Valparaíso and from Santiago to Talca and therefore favored the exports of wheat for the landowners of the Central Valley. The mine owners of the north, however, had to build their own railroads from their mines to the ocean with their own (and a good deal of British) capital, without state aid.[55]

The state also freed wheat exports from taxes and at the same time imposed taxes on mineral exports. These measures were not without economic importance. They so irritated the mine owners that they were among the major causes of the civil wars of 1851 and 1859.[56]

In the 1850s the mining interests gained control of the state. The civil wars of 1851 and 1859 resulted in military defeats for the mining interests and victory for the landowners, but the relative drop in world prices for Chilean agricultural exports and the sudden loss of the wheat markets of California and Australia led to a momentary economic crisis in Chile from which the mining interests emerged triumphant.[57]

> The revolution of 1859 was a face to face confrontation between the government, supported by the feudal landholding class, and the liberal mining bourgeoisie, which was vigorously expanding. This is the merit of that revolution, which in spite of the defeat of the mining interests, signalled the end of the conservative feudal governments and opened the way to the liberal era.

Vast economic changes, which provided the basis for this change in power, occurred in Chile between 1830 and 1860. The relations of production in the agricultural sector also changed although their fundamental characteristic, the feudal oppression of the inquilino through extraeconomic mechanisms, remained the same.

The replacement of the landlords by the mine owners did not mean that a national bourgeoisie defeated a feudal class, as in Europe. On the contrary, the mine owners were exporters too, tied to the world market. Soon enough they became junior partners to the British nitrate interests. They developed no manufacturing base. Instead they continued to import manufactured goods from Europe, principally England. When they invested their earnings in something other than mines, it was often in agriculture itself. After they gained control of the state, they rapidly learned to use it to their advantage. Once the British had gained control of the nitrate mines, the Chilean ruling class began to rely on the state as a source of wealth. The state began to receive large revenues from taxing British exports, and these revenues were appropriated one way or another by those who were already wealthy. Mining capital, which might have been a source of manufacturing capital, instead turned to usury and speculation. The unhealthy financial dependence of private capital on state revenues began to develop, an alliance which was to lead in the twentieth century to a kind of state capitalism.[58]

The first serious attempt to create a national manufacturing sector was made by José Manuel Balmaceda in the late 1880s. (There were some industries which had sprung up during the 1879 War of the Pacific to supply the army, but they disappeared after the war.) Balmaceda attempted to use the enormous state revenues accrued from taxing British nitrate exports to generate Chilean industry. However, he represented no organized faction of the ruling class, and he did not organize either the petty bourgeoisie or the working class to support his program. He was therefore defeated in 1891 in yet another of Chile's civil wars. (It was not until the 1930s, with the economy in crisis due to the depression, that a national manufacturing sector developed, on the basis of import substitution.)

Although mining dominated the economy after the 1850s, agriculture did not do badly in the later 1800s. The discovery of gold in 1848 in California and Australia led to a tremendous though short-lived jump in demand for Chilean wheat. The California market disappeared by 1854 and the Australian by 1859. After 1860, however, the European market, principally English, took up the slack. Between 1844 and 1860 agricultural exports increased five times.[59] The Peruvian market remained regular and even increased. The increased production was largely attained by an increase in the area cultivated, by 200 percent between 1842 and 1875. Increased production also resulted from increased mechanization and from better irrigation. It is likely that this improvement of techniques of production did not come from the traditional landholding class but from the mining sectors which began to invest in agriculture.[60] As for the increased incomes of the traditional landowners, a contemporary commented on their use in the 1850s:[61]

What have we done during 8 years of agricultural prosperity and national prosperity for the good of agriculture? Nothing or almost nothing. The earth has provided us with animal fats and meat; but we have given ourselves brocades, golden Parisian carriages, well-dressed footmen. . . . Each hacienda has provided the wealth to build a palace in the capital.

At the same time agricultural income was increasing, the mine owners expanded production. Their exports surpassed those of agriculture. Silver, gold, and copper mines produced the wealth. Estimates differ, but between 1844 and 1880 agricultural exports were somewhere between only 30 and 45 percent of the value of total exports.[62]

The mine owners were capitalists. They employed wage labor. The attraction of the mines for the rural laborer was strong. The construction of railroads offered another possible escape for the inquilino. Under pressure the landlords had to offer more advantages to their inquilinos. At the same time the demands put upon the inquilino for labor increased tremendously. At times the inquilino was obliged to provide not one but two workers every day, so that one of his family had to work for the landlord as well. The landlord began to pay a small salary to the inquilino in addition to the benefits of land, daily ration, and pasture rights. With the increased possibility of alternative employment in other areas, the landlord saw fit to increase this salary during the 1850s.[63] The population increased from 1,080,000 in 1843 to 1,820,000 in 1965, but agricultural laborers were still in short supply. A modern Chilean historian comments:

> The incorporation of peasants in new public works, especially railroads, obliged the landlords to raise salaries to avoid the migration of their labor force.

The fact that the inquilino began to receive a small part of his income in salary should not be mistaken for his having become a member of a rural proletariat. The same Chilean historian points out:[64]

> [Benjamin] Vicuña Mackenna confirms this point in his study of Chilean agriculture at the middle of the 19th century, where he observes that the inquilino often did not receive his salary in money, but in cloth or food which was paid to him at a price which was higher than the price anywhere else.

This kind of salary did little to increase internal demand. One author of a recent study, discussing the difficulty of calculating the internal demand in the mid nineteenth century, comments:[65]

> An important sector of the population cultivated its own food or received rations of food in exchange for work on the farms. Only cities like Santiago, or Valparaíso, or the northern mining districts

and the railroads constituted a real market for commercial agriculture.

In the mid 1800s, before the conquest of the Mapuche south, some two thousand landowners held 70 percent of rural property. The newspaper *El Mercurio* (now the bastion of the military junta and the recipient of large doses of money from the CIA) at that time represented the mine owners instead of the landowners. In May 1861 it commented:[66]

It seems necessary to us to divide agrarian property, both because this would work in favor of both debtors and creditors and because it would permit small capitalists to become owners; and the production would increase due to the improved care that can be given to a small farm.

But no agrarian reform would occur until the 1960s.

The period between 1860 and 1930 can be characterized as capitalist because of the dominance of mining capital in the economy. Nevertheless, feudal relations of production continued to prevail in agriculture until the 1930s when rural wage laborers became more important than inquilinos.

Wheat exports continued to be significant all the way up until the 1930s, even though they were less than mineral exports. But after 1900 the value of wheat exports dropped even further. An extreme example is provided by the year 1908, for example, when nitrate exports were valued at 234 million pesos while wheat exports for that year were only 12 million pesos. In 1929 agricultural exports made up 13 percent of the total, and mineral exports the other 87 percent. It should be remembered that these mineral exports were not Chilean. After the War of the Pacific in 1879 they became largely European. In 1910, for example, they were 65 percent European. The state began to be directly supported by taxes on the nitrate exports. In 1880 two-thirds of state revenues came from the taxes on exports and imports, and by 1910 the figure was seven-eighths with all direct taxes having been lifted on property in Chile.[67]

The predominance of mining over wheat was increased by two factors external to Chile. One was the falling price on the world market. Between 1873 and 1896 wheat prices dropped 50 percent. At the same time, partially as a cause and partially as a result of the price drop, production in other countries increased enormously, dwarfing Chile's. The United States, India, Australia, Russia, and Argentina all increased their wheat production for export; and Chile became only a small factor in the world market.[68]

Within Chile itself the large landholdings which were consolidated in the late 1600s began to break up in the 1870s and the 1880s, another indication of the loss of power by the landlords. This breakup, however, was relative. Only in comparison to the colony was land less concentrated. In 1925, five hundred properties still accounted for 62 percent of the land.[69]

In 1900 the proportion of wheat produced for the internal market to wheat produced for export was about 3 to 1, but after 1900 the proportion became 7 or 8 to 1. In addition to new competitors abroad and falling world prices, the War of the Pacific had brought new markets within Chile in the northern mining districts.[70]

The internal market took on increased importance for the landowners. In 1874 the National Society of Agriculture commented:[71]

In Chile we can have very high prices [for wheat] that are not caused by bad harvests within the country but by the prices in foreign markets.

The landowners would sell their wheat only at world prices within Chile itself. After the 1930s this situation was dramatically reversed. Chilean prices for wheat were then lower than the world market. Internal production was insufficient, and the state imported wheat to make up the deficit. This imported wheat was subsidized by the state, and it was sold in Chile at less than world prices as part of the drive by the state to keep urban prices down, and therefore urban wages down. This of course favored the industrial bourgeoisie which became prominent in the 1930s.

This period up until the 1930s was also a period when the wage laborer was gradually beginning to replace the inquilino. This was a slow process which only succeeded hesitantly. It was encouraged by the fact that the population increased sufficiently to provide a surplus of laborers in the late 1800s. Furthermore, the population was increasingly urban; and in the cities, as in the mines, wage labor was the norm. In 1865 the population was 72 percent rural, in 1907 the figure was 57 percent, and in 1930 it was 50 percent.[72]

Nevertheless, the situation of the inquilino remained one of extraeconomic oppression by the landlords. In 1907 the inquilino made between .2 and 1 peso a day in salary. In addition he made even more nonmonetary income from his own subsistence plot and his pasture rights. (In fact, it was not until the mid 1960s that the salary of the inquilino would make up more than 50 percent of his income.)[73] In 1907 the migrant agricultural worker (afuerino) made .8 to 1.6 pesos a day. Factory women and children made about 1.8 pesos, and factory men made about 3.8. Miners made anywhere from 2 to 5 pesos with the higher wages paid in the distant north.[74] As for the percentage of agricultural workers employed on a capitalist basis, different figures exist. Alexander Schejtman, a contemporary source, says that in 1930 there were 104,000 inquilinos and that they represented only 20 percent of the active agricultural population which included small owners. In 1935 an agricultural census was taken which may be considered relatively accurate, and the total number of inquilinos was listed as 107,000. It seems likely that Schejtman is correct when he says that the early 1930s represented the beginning of the decline of the inquilinos, both relatively and absolutely.[75]

Extraeconomic coercion on the part of the landowners toward the inquilinos was, of course, more difficult to bring to bear in a situation where agriculture was declining in importance and wage labor was becoming predominant. Yet abundant testimony exists about such coercion. In the mid 1800s a contemporary pointed out:[76]

> Of course the landlord has the advantage of having an inquilino who has no contract, and the advantage of frequently being the creditor of an inquilino in debt, and the equally important advantage of being the military chief and magistrate for the inquilino. The landlord is thereby both judge and plaintiff in some legal suits, having all possible influence, both that of wealth and that of authority.

Writing some seventy years later, George McBride provides us with similar information. In discussing the early 1930s, he says:

> Until recent decades it has been customary for the hacienda to exercise a certain amount of civil jurisdiction within its bounds. Crime was formerly punished by the hacendado [landowner] himself, who was looked upon, if not legally commissioned, as magistrate. Some of the farms had cells or dungeons, and some are said to have maintained stocks in which to punish their more recalcitrant inquilinos. Much of his authority has now passed out of the hands of the farm owner, but in minor matters an appeal is seldom made to public officials.

McBride provides us with other information about the inquilino:

If an inquilino decides to leave the hacienda on which he has been employed, it is almost impossible for him to find placement on another. A hacendado [landowner] in the same neighborhood is generally unwilling to receive a tenant who has left an adjoining property. Courtesy to his neighboring landowner forbids his receiving a workman who has abandoned a former "patron." Even if the inquilino is able to move into some other province or to a great distance from his former location, he finds that the fraternity of landowners is so strong that it is difficult for him to obtain employment on another hacienda. . . . Thus, though legally free to move from a hacienda, he finds himself virtually fixed on it.

In such conditions, labor was not a commodity, the price of which varied with supply and demand. Although wage labor was taking over, many peasants still worked under feudal conditions. Even the inquilino's ability to sell his produce on the market was restricted. Again, according to McBride, referring to the 1930s:[77]

The inquilino has no opportunity to gain further income than that supplied by the farm as he is not allowed to utilize even his free time working on neighboring farms or at any employment outside his own hacienda, nor is his family free to seek employment elsewhere. He may not even engage in money-making enterprises, not being permitted to buy or sell upon the farm or beyond its bounds.

However, one important basis for the feudal relations of production in agriculture was disappearing in the period between 1860 and 1930. Increased mechanization meant that the wooden plow was replaced by the iron plow, and the inquilino was not able to afford it. The inquilino was no longer able to bring his own tools to work on the landlord's land. He continued to use more crude tools on his own subsistence plot. The trend toward mechanization was even more pronounced in those areas where landowners bought threshing machines which revolutionized wheat production. In 1875, according to a modern Chilean historian, there were only three thousand agricultural machines whereas in 1920 there were 158,000. The inquilino could not, of course, afford these machines.[78]

In summary then, despite continued importance of the inquilinos, after the 1930s wage labor and capitalist relations of production predominated in the countryside.[79] Yet the inquilino was to have an importance in the 1960s and 1970s which far outweighed his numbers. There were two reasons for this exaggerated importance. First, the Christian Democratic land reform of 1967 was planned to benefit the inquilino rather than the wage laborer from outside the farm (afuerino). It was the inquilino who became a member of the cooperative (asentamiento) set up on the expropriated land and who was destined after a three-to-five-year period to riated land and who was destined after a three-to-five-year period to become a private small owner. This trend was not counteracted effectively by the Allende government. In fact, the tendency of the inquilino to favor small ownership as opposed to cooperative production was even increased under Allende. The historic trend towards increased monetary salaries for the inquilino was reversed on the cooperative farms. The peasants on the cooperatives, perhaps half of whom were former inquilinos, increasingly derived most of their income from their production on their own small plots rather than from their salaries during 1970–73.

The second factor which gave the inquilinos more importance in recent years was that they were a year-round work force whereas the wage laborers from outside the farm frequently worked only seasonally. This made these wage laborers harder to organize. It was easier, besides being ideologically more suitable, for the Christian Democratic government to base its agrarian reform on the inquilinos who lived and worked on the farm all year.

Besides the predominance of wage labor, another important change took place in Chilean agriculture between the late 1800s and the 1930s. Agriculture moved south. The basis for the increased production of the mid 1800s was an extension of the cultivated area, but by the 1800s most of the land in the Central Valley was being used. The conquest of the Mapuches in the south in 1884 meant that vast new lands suitable for wheat became available at the same time that the land of the Central Valley was becoming less productive. Wheat produced in the Central Valley decreased absolutely, as did the amount of cultivated area, between 1880 and 1910. The Frontier Region, as the south is called, took up the slack and gradually became the most productive wheat area in Chile. In the Central Valley much land was dedicated to cattle for the internal market. In 1874 there were 250,000 head in Chile, and in 1919 there were 2,160,000.[80]

The incorporation of the Frontier into the rest of Chile meant that the Mapuche Indian became the basis of agricultural labor in the south. But frequently, the inquilinos in the south were Chileans of Spanish descent; the Indians worked only seasonally on the farm, living the rest of the year on their reservations. The reservations became gradually smaller, as their lands were stolen by the landowners, while the Mapuche population increased. This combination meant that the Mapuche was forced out of the reservation to seek employment and that he became a seasonal worker. Nevertheless, his strong ties to the reservation meant that, unlike the afuerino of the Central Valley, his main desire was for land and not for better working conditions. He continued to want to own his land again, that which was stolen from him by the big landowners. Under Allende, the Mapuches who worked on the cooperatives, like the inquilinos, frequently preferred to give priority to individual rather than collective production.

It is to the Mapuches and agrarian reform in the south that we now turn our attention, having concluded this rather broad history of Chilean agriculture.

PART TWO

PART TWO

Chapter 3

The Farm: 1970

Peypiken anay
kuyfi pu riku kay
tufachi pu riku
muntu nïnmapaeyu
taiñ mapu peñi
pifin tañi pu peñi
tañi pu peñi kay
fepifilu inche
nïtramkafiñ inche
nïtramkafilu kay
kiñe huinca tïfa
anïmiwkïlepay
keñi ni ruka meo
epe akuley kay
tañi linia pu peni
pifin anya pifin
uniwliiñ kay nga
fachi pun amuaiñ
yenieaiñ yenieaiñ
pikota pikota
pala yenieliñ
yenieaniñ tralka kay
akulu fachi pun
fachi pun amuaiñ
kareta yeaiñ
nïtuaiñ mapu kay
peñi anay peñi anay
julio pingey kiyen
rangï mawin anay
tralkantukumekey
fachi pun akuiñ
rangï pun puwuiiñ

tïfa tañi mapu
pepatun tañi mapu
peñi anay peñi anay
kïpalnge pikota
kipalnge alampre
entupe ehtaka
yetufiiñ ïyeu
fantepakefuy kay
taiñ mapu anay
kom mapu inchiñ
kom lelfin tati
pifiñ tañi peñi
kuyfi pu antigu
engañangepayngin
kimnolukimnolu
tïfa welu femlay
femlayayngïn kay nga
inchiñ meo inchiñ meo
wïni fachiantïkay
fachiantï akuay
pu kayñe kay nga
feypiafiiñ kay
inchiñ taiñ mapu
tïfa feula kay nga
akuy nga akuy kay
a la nueve pingey
antï kay
akuy pu soltau
feypipayeyu kay
fepipay
iñey anta elueymeo permiso
tami nïtuael tami mapu

kuyfi kïla pataka tripantu   tïfachi pu riku
kuyfingekefuy iñ   tïfa femeuelaymi
inchiñ taiñ mapu   tïfa ta mïtronkïwe
tïfa nïtufiiñ   kupafentufiiñ
lakonaiñ kay   amutuynigïn kay nga
lakonaiñ kay   wetha put alwe kay
inchiñ taiñ mapu meo   wetha pu alwe
feypiiñ kay nga   tïfa tïfa tïfa
nïtuaiñ mapu   kime feletuiñ
feypifiiñ kay nga   feymeo feymeo feymeo
tati huinca nga   feypikefiñ kay
ulelkafilu kay   tañi pu peñi kay
ulelkamekefuy   engañangewelayyaiñ
kuyfi tañi pu peñi   kuyfi reke kuyfi reke
langïmka kulliñ eyiñ meu   piken any peñi.
langïmka sanchueymeo

—Pedro's song about the fence-running at Rinconada farm. Translation from Mapuche is as follows:

I say that long ago the rich people took our land away from us.
I said that to my brothers. I spoke to my brothers about this.
When I spoke to them, I said: "The huinca [white man] settled here,
built his house here, and now he even wants what little land is left to me."
I spoke to my brothers and said: "Let's get together tonight,
let's take shovels and picks. Let's take weapons. When it gets dark
we will go to take back our land, carrying the equipment in our cart."
I spoke to my brothers in this fashion in the month of July.
It was raining, and we left about midnight, carrying our weapons.
"This is my land, brothers. I have finally returned to my land.
Bring the pick, bring the wire, pull up the fence posts.
Let's take them over there, to where the fence line used to be.
All this land is ours."
I spoke to my brothers, "This is where in the past our ancestors were
    deceived.
They were ignorant, but now that can no longer happen.
They can no longer deceive us."
The day broke. "Today the enemies will arrive. We will tell them
that this land is ours."
Just then the police arrived. They asked, "Who gave you permission
to occupy this land?"
We said to them: "Three hundred years ago all this land was ours.
Now we are taking it back, and we are prepared to die for our cause.
In the past the wealthy beat us with sticks, and killed our animals.
But you will no longer do this to us."
We drove them out with sticks. Now we are fine.
That is why I always say to my brothers: "We will no longer be deceived like
    before."

Southern Chile, Cautín Province, Lautaro County

It was July 1970, mid winter. It was raining hard that particular night, and it was cold. Some eighty Mapuche Indians left a house on the Juan Catrileo Reservation about 11 P.M. and walked the half mile to the fence line which separated the reservation from the Rinconada farm. They had a few old shot guns and a pistol or two, but mostly they carried sticks and some tools. The tools were shovels, picks, and post-hole diggers. They also brought some wire. When they got to the fence, they dug up the fenceposts and carried whole sections of the fence about a hundred yards into the Rinconada farm. Then they dug new postholes and put the fence back up. This same operation was repeated along the entire fence line, for a distance of about a quarter mile. It took them until dawn. When they finished, the rain had slowed down and the sun was coming up over their backs. They gathered along the new fence line and awaited the events of the day.

By 9 A.M. Fernando Schultz arrived in his truck, carrying six policemen with him. The Mapuches knew Fernando well. He had owned Rinconada for over ten years and had harassed them continually, whether they were working for him or whether they were just minding their own business on the reservation. A frequent trick of his was to shoot the pigs and sheep from the reservation which wandered onto "his" land. Then he would sell or eat the animals. This was the penalty he exacted for animal trespassing.

The Mapuches figured that Fernando would be angry, and so he was. But it was the police officer who spoke first. He exhibited a map, showing the land in question to belong to the Rinconada farm. Carlos Melipeu in turn exhibited the original title to the reservation, dated 1914. The original title in fact showed that the land in question belonged to the reservation. Carlos Melipeu had gotten the map only a week or so before from the Bureau of Indian Affairs. Originally the reservation had one copy and the Bureau of Indian Affairs had another, but the reservation had lost theirs over the years. Carlos had managed to get a photocopy of the original from the files of the Bureau of Indian Affairs. It was this map that he showed to the police officer.

Given the circumstances, the police officer made no further comment and withdrew. If it came to attacking the Mapuches and throwing them off the land, he was going to wait until he had both orders from his superiors and a lot more force. Fernando Schultz, on the other hand, couldn't control his temper. He and one of his farmhands drove the truck into one of the fields which was not then occupied by the Mapuches, but which

was claimed by them. They had put their animals in it to graze, during the
night, thereby staking their claim. All in all they were claiming a total of
one hundred hectares; their reservation was 125 hectares, but it had been
225 in 1914. The total size of Rinconada, on the day before the fence-
running, was 560 hectares (one hectare = 2.4 acres).

Fernando drove his truck into the field and began to chase out the pigs
and sheep belonging to the Mapuches. Seeing this, a group of Mapuches
ran over to the field and surrounded the truck at the gate, just as
Fernando was about to chase the animals out. The police ran over too, and
after a lot of shouting, Fernando had to retreat. The animals remained in
the field. Fernando and the police left. So far the Mapuches were victorious. After Fernando and the police left, 150 more Mapuches joined the 80
at the fence. They had been sitting on top of the nearby hills watching the
confrontation, too afraid to take part in the fence-running itself. But when
the fence-runners won the first round, those sitting and watching at a
distance came down to join them.

Fernando went back into town and initiated a court suit to get the
group thrown off his land. He had suspected that something was up. He
had seen, in the past few months, strange vehicles coming down the road,
and occasionally he had seen some young people he did not know. Think-
ing that the reservation was planning to run the fence, he had instructed
his six farmhands to rotate in a patrol of the fence-line at night, carrying a
shotgun. But after two months, when nothing happened, he withdrew
them. As soon as he did, the Mapuches ran the fence.

The court suit wasn't going to do him much good either. The judge
ordered several Mapuches in to testify, and Fernando testified too. The
suit dragged on and on. Basically the issue was a political one. If the judge
had ordered that the police clear the land, a confrontation would have
occurred.

During the Frei government (1964–70), many illegal occupations had
occurred, mostly in the cities. Homeless families would occupy vacant
lots and began to construct shacks. The usual response of the Frei government and its court system was to throw them off, using the police. This
had led to violence. The most famous case occurred in Puerto Montt
where the police murdered nine people, including women and children,
in an eviction in 1969. The last few years of the Frei regime were noted
for extensive repression of popular demonstrations.

But in Lautaro County the Mapuches were claiming that the land
belonged to them legally. They showed a deed which dated from the time
the reservation was founded. In normal times, this would not have

counted for much. But the fence-running at Rinconada did not occur in normal times. First of all, it was only one incident among many. In the winter and spring months of 1970 about fifteen fence-running incidents occurred in Lautaro County. Chasing several hundred Mapuches off the Rinconada farm was hard enough, but the act would have had to be repeated in many other places.

More important, everyone was awaiting the September elections. The administration of the county belonged to the Christian Democratic party, and they did not want a whole series of violent incidents to occur just before the elections. Three candidates were disputing the presidency; Radomiro Tomic for the center (Christian Democrats), Jorge Alessandri for the right (basically the National Party), and Salvador Allende for the left (the Popular Unity coalition, made up principally of the Socialist and Communist parties). The wheels of justice in Lautaro County were creaking slowly because of the political uncertainty in the country as a whole. If the Marxist Allende were elected, the cause of the Mapuches would be distinctly favored. On the other hand, if Alessandri were elected, repression was the likely outcome. A Tomic victory would mean an unclear mandate. In the ensuing months, Fernando was to tell the Mapuches many times: "Just wait till Alessandri wins the elections, and then you'll get yours."

Alessandri never won the election. Allende did. And Fernando was to have much bigger problems to worry about than the one hundred hectares. (In December 1970 the Mapuches were to take over the rest of the Rinconada farm, 460 hectares of it.) The judicial actions concerning the fence-running died quietly in late 1972 when the statute of limitations ran out.

The fence-running itself did not just occur spontaneously. It was organized beforehand, and the issue had been fermenting for many years. It was difficult to find out the full story about the more distant past, but at least one man at the fence-running had worked for three different owners at Rinconada, and he remembered back to the 1920s. His name was Claudio. He said that the first owners of Rinconada were the Mapuches, which was clear enough.

The town of Lautaro had been founded in 1881, and before that there were only Mapuches in the area. The Spaniards had fought the Mapuches unsuccessfully for three centuries. In fact, the Mapuches were the only native people in Latin America who were able to defeat the Spaniards militarily for such a long period of time. They used a kind of guerrilla warfare and took advantage of the hilly dense terrain and the bitter winters. It was not until the 1880s that the Spaniards finally occupied the region in southern Chile which is still called the Frontier. Even then it remained sparsely populated.

After the conquest, the state sold the land to speculators, and small areas were set aside for the Mapuches. The Mapuches had been accustomed to roam, fish, and hunt as well as grow their vegetables. No land had been owned; land had only been temporarily occupied. But the white man, or "huinca" as the Mapuche called him, insisted on dividing up the Frontier into plots so that it could be bought and sold. The Mapuches were left with the plots where they were actually living at the time of the first surveys. These plots became known as reservations. Of course the Mapuche were used to living in a much wider area, but the conquerors arbitrarily restricted them. The Juan Catrileo Reservation had been set up in the 1880s at the time of the first land survey. At that time the land next to the reservation had been bought by a speculator. The speculator sold his land around the time of World War I to a certain Medina. Medina then founded the Rinconada farm and began to cultivate the land. In 1914 a second official survey was carried out. It showed that the Juan Catrileo Reservation consisted of 225 hectares of land and 41 people, an average of 5.5 hectares per person.

According to Claudio, who had a good memory, Medina never lived at the Rinconada farm. He left it in charge of an administrator. The years passed, and in the 1930s Medina sold the farm to a man named Guillermo Henriquez. Henriquez was a lawyer, and he had built up a reputation for swindling the Mapuche out of their land.

All this time the Mapuches continued to live on the Juan Catrileo Reservation. They were surrounded by numerous other reservations (about 160 of them), interspersed with farms owned by Chileans (see Map 7). The total population of the country was (and is) about 25,000, mostly rural dwellers and mostly Mapuche. The huincas (Chileans) owned the best land, to be sure. They usually employed a few permanent laborers (inquilinos) who were often huincas as well. In addition they hired the Mapuches from the surrounding Indian reservations as seasonal laborers.

Henriquez hadn't built up his reputation and his landholdings for no reason. When he began to operate on the Juan Catrileo Reservation, he moved quickly and effectively. His goal was to get hold of some of the land of the reservation in order to enlarge his Rinconada farm. His first move was to get the reservation legally divided in order that individual Mapuches on the reservation could sell him their land. To do this he took advantage of the legislation of the 1920s and early 1930s which had been passed by avaricious white landowners. This legislation allowed a reservation to be divided if only a minority of the Mapuches living there agreed to the division. The 1927 law declared that the reservation would be divided if only one of its members asked for the division. In 1931 this was improved slightly when the law was amended so that one-third of the Mapuches on the reservation had to ask for its division.

The lawyer Guillermo Henriquez knew how to get that one-third to agree. Whether it was through threats, bribery, or legal mumbo-jumbo, Henriquez managed to get a third of the members of the Juan Cartileo Reservation to agree to its division in 1938. Or at least so he claimed. What actually happened is a secret between him and his friends, the judges in the Indian courts. In any case the courts decreed the division of the reservation, and in the next two years Henriquez moved swiftly to buy or steal one hundred hectares of the reservation from the then individual owners. One of his methods was to rent a piece of land at a high rent and then fix the papers so that they read that it was a sale. The Mapuche, who were illiterate and often scarcely spoke Spanish, had no way to fight back.

The reservation, then legally divided, quickly understood what Henriquez was doing and stopped any dealings with him. The Mapuches on the reservation continued to act as a community and continued to resent what Henriquez had done to them.

In 1960 Henriquez finally died and left Rinconada to his daughter and son-in-law. The son-in-law was Fernando Schultz.

In early 1965 the reservation decided to take some kind of action to try to recover the lost land. The situation had grown desperate. By the late 1960s there were 140 people on the 125 hectares of land still held by the reservation. The ratio which had been 5.5 hectares per person was now down to .9 hectares per person. The members of the Juan Catrileo Reservation wrote a letter to the minister of land who forwarded it to the Bureau of Indian Affairs. The letter read as follows:

> Very respectable Minister of Land, we write you about stolen land on the reservation Juan Catrileo. The land is about 100 hectares. The community asks that this land is returned to it. This land has been taken by the Rinconada farm. It was bought by a lawyer named Henriquez, who was a swindler. This happened in 1938.

The Bureau of Indian Affairs decided to send someone out to the area to check it out, but they never did. This was the usual result. But in the meantime other forces had entered the scene. In the summer of 1968 students from the University of Concepción arrived in the area of the Juan Catrileo Reservation. Supposedly, they were there to do volunteer work, such as teaching the Mapuche how to read. In fact, they were there more as political agitators. They made some contacts in the area, and they learned the story of Henriquez and the swindled land. When they went back to Concepción, they told the story to members of the MIR (Movimiento de Izquierda Revolucionaria, or Movement of the Revolutionary Left), a new left-wing political group. The MIR was founded largely by students at the University of Concepción in 1965, but only really organized itself in 1967. Inspired by the Cuban revolution, the MIR described itself as the "revolutionary" left in contrast to the older well-established Socialist and Communist parties (described as the "traditional" left). The MIR from the beginning chose a semiclandestine type of organization.

In late 1969 members of the MIR visited the Juan Catrileo Reservation, and by March 1970 they moved there to live. Their goals were to help the Mapuches get back their land. Originally the MIR had tried to organize coal miners in the mines at Lota, but they had been chased out by the traditional strong political organizations of the Communist and Socialist parties there. The MIR decided to look among the most disorganized and poor sectors of the population to try to organize, and one group they chose was the Mapuche. The Mapuche represented only 5 percent of the Chilean population, but in the south they were the majority of the peasantry. They certainly had grievances and they were willing to accept the help of the MIR in order to redress those grievances.

The peasants strongly desired to right some old injustices by reclaiming land stolen from them earlier, but they were afraid. They lacked confidence in themselves, and they laced familiarity with the larger political system. The organizers from the MIR offered them both. The members of the MIR encouraged the peasants, finally convincing them that the land could be successfully retaken. The MIR offered as well the necessary organization to back up a takeover; the skills to publicize the situation, to write the letters to the government, to obtain the original maps of the reservation, and so forth. At first the peasants were suspicious of the organizers from the MIR. They seemed to be young people from the city who had for some reason, as yet unknown, come to live with the Mapuches. The peasants assumed that the organizers must have had some ulterior motive. But after several months of living on the reservation, sharing the same food and work, the members of the MIR gained the trust of the peasants. The MIR activists were the only leftists who had ever actually *lived* in the countryside. They received only an insignificant sum of money from their party. They clearly were not on some kind of vacation. They usually had had some college education, but had dropped out to do full-time organizing. Their parents were not wealthy. The "Miristas" in Lautuaro came from lower-middle-class families. They had a lot to learn from the peasants. It was not easy to adjust to the spartan life of the countryside. But the MIR organizers were dedicated. They were there to do a job. They had a sense of humor and struck up close friendships with the peasants; they were steadfast in their work. The peasants came to realize that the MIR activists were following orders from a political party and that that political party demanded discipline. The peasants understood that the MIR was generally interested in replacing the rule of the rich with the rule of the poor and that organizing the recovery of stolen Mapuche land was part of that larger project.

The next letter from the reservation was dated May 1970. It was sent directly to the Bureau of Indian Affairs, and its style was more polished, its content more determined and political. The letter stated the situation of the usurped land and referred to the documents involved, including the original title. Then it went on:

> As for the owner Fernando Schultz, he is an arrogant man who in various occasions has threatened us with arms, and has frequently killed animals belonging to members of the reservation.
>
> We have been given the runaround for 5 years by bureaucrats in offices that are supposed to solve the problems of the Mapuches. We solicit the immediate action of the competent authorities in the solution of our problems, fundamentally the problem of the land.

This letter really was just for the record. Certainly neither the MIR organizers nor the Mapuche themselves thought that the Bureau of Indian Affairs was going to do anything about it. Instead the Mapuches did something about it themselves. They proceeded to run the fence line. In the fence-running the organizers from the MIR offered advice and technical assistance, but they stayed in the background. In 1969 the MIR had gone completely underground, and the party remained in clandestinity until after Allende was elected. Even then they had very few public spokesmen. Members of the MIR were present during the fence-runnings in Lautaro County in the winter and spring of 1970. They dressed like Mapuches, and they stayed out of the spotlight.

When Allende was elected in September 1970, organizers from the MIR suggested to the Mapuches that they occupy the whole of Rinconada farm. After all, Allende had promised to extend massively the land reform begun by the previous president, Eduardo Frei. The occupation of the Rinconada would only speed up this process. In addition, with Allende in the presidency, it was unlikey that the police would be used against the peasants.

The Mapuches agreed. But it was decided (again at the MIR's suggestion) to wait until Allende actually took office. The MIR wanted to avoid any incidents which could be used to the political advantage of the right wing. The period between the September election and the taking of office in November was an extremely tense one during which the right wing attempted to prevent Allende's assumption of office by provoking violent incidents which they blamed on the left. This backfired in the attempted kidnapping of the Commander in Chief of the Army, René Schneider. In late October a group organized by retired Gen. Roberto Viaux tried to kidnap Schneider, but he resisted and was killed. The plot was exposed, to the benefit of the left.

In October in Lautaro County a meeting was held with the MIR organizers in the area and those Mapuche who had shown themselves to be the most daring and determined in the various fence-runnings. This meeting planned several occupations of farms which were subsequently carried out. There were only two members of the MIR and only seven or eight Mapuches at this meeting, but this handful was to organize and lead a massive and explosive movement in the following months. Indeed, this group of people, joined by four or five new recruits, would be behind almost all the land occupations in Lautaro County during the three years of Allende government. Allende was confirmed in office in early November. Conditions were ripe for activity to begin.

In considering the takeover of Rinconada, it was necessary to take into account the work force there. It was decided to try to win the farmhands over. As for Fernando Schultz, he lived in the city. With the farmhands on the side of the occupiers, there would be no immediate opposition to the takeover from the farm itself. There were six farmhands; two of them were huincas. Although there was some feeling that the farmhands were not to be trusted (they had not been told of the fence-running beforehand) plans were made to convert them to the side of the occupiers.

The farmhands themselves were not very contented with Fernando Schultz. Several of them had been fired in the past and then rehired only after agreeing to ask for no higher salaries. Fernando had not paid the salaries of two of the workers for months, and they were considering going on strike to force him to do so. The workers were organized into a union, called El Escudo. This union had been founded throughout the county by the Christian Democrats in 1967, after the agrarian reform law that enabled such unions to come into existence was passed. Previous legislation had in practice prohibited the formation of rural unions. The Christian Democrats organized unions which were not designed to be very effective. At Rinconada the union had not defended the workers on various occasions in the past, despite the fact that the farmhands paid their dues, 2 percent of their salaries. It was not surprising, given that one of the main organizers of the union was the mayor of Lautaro, named Herrera, and he was a good friend of most of the landowners in the area.

The workers at Rinconada, through their union, had solicited the expropriation of the farm in accordance with the agrarian reform law. This they had done in 1968, asking the Christian Democrat Rafael Moreno, who had promised an answer in thirty days. The answer never came. In fact, the Christian Democrats expropriated only six farms in Lautaro County in the period from 1967 to 1970. In any case the confiscated farms were not really expropriated in the strict sense of the term. The government had paid the owners a handsome compensation. Under Allende, the government was to expropriate some thirty-five farms in the county, sixteen as a result of previous peasant takeovers.

So the farmhands did not have much faith in their boss, their union, or the government. They complained that when the union *did* take some work complaints to the ministry of labor, that ministry would never do anything about it. In fact the work inspectors in the town of Lautaro were all friends of Fernando Schultz.

When the peasant organizers of the takeover came to talk to the farmhands, they all agreed to the plan, and they kept their mouths shut. Unfortunately, an old night watchman at a neighboring farm got wind of the planned takeover and told Fernando. From that time on Fernando quit making investments in the farm and began to sell off threshing machines and tractors. He wasn't sure that the takeover would actually take place, but he wasn't taking any chances that a bunch of wild Mapuches might capture his machinery. Under the agrarian reform law, he would have the right to harvest his crops and keep his machinery even if the farm were expropriated; but Fernando did not have a lot of faith in the Allende government. Most of his friends believed that law and order, and respect for property, had little chance for survival under Allende.

There were three peasants who took charge of organizing the takeover. All three had been at the October meeting with the two members of the MIR. The three proceeded to form a Committee to Fight for the Land.

They invited some forty-five people to join, but only twenty-two accepted. The others were afraid that the plan would not work. The twenty-two who accepted were to take all the risks, and in case the takeover was successful, they were to reap the benefits because they would stay and work the land. The six farmhands were included in the twenty-two.

The three peasant organizers, who would themselves work on the farm after it was occupied, had been aiming for a group of about twenty-five (including themselves), which they estimated as the maximum number of workers the land could handle. One of the organizers objected to the inclusion of any huinca in the group of twenty-five, but the other two opposed this idea, as did the organizers from the MIR. In the end the group included four huincas and several people of mixed blood. Almost everyone in the group knew everyone else. In most cases they were related. Two-thirds had worked at one time or another at Rinconada. Most had only a few years of school, and therefore most were illiterate. The Mapuches spoke Spanish and Mapuche interchangeably. None of the group were in a labor union except the six on the farm. All except the two most privileged and permanent farmhands were basically small owners who had so little land that they were forced to seek work elsewhere. The average amount of land owned was only about 1.5 hectares. All twenty-five were men. Their average age was thirty. Half were from the Juan Catrileo Reservation, and two-thirds had participated in the fence-running.

Over a hundred people actually participated in the takeover of the farm, called a *toma* in Spanish. Many came from nearby farms which had previously been taken over. As the fence-runnings, those who participated in one takeover then frequently helped out other neighboring groups. The hundred left late on the night of December 11 after having gathered, once again, on the reservation. About midnight they left the reservation and occupied the farm. This time they had more weapons. In other parts of the province landowners had violently attacked peasants who were illegally occupying a farm. Most of the peasants were carrying heavy sticks. The group also had about ten pistols and ten shotguns, mostly local weapons. Some were supplied by the MIR whose representatives were present. The presence of the weapons was an indication of the higher stakes. Recuperating stolen land for the reservation was one thing, but taking over a whole farm was another. The most powerful families in the county would be affected and were sure to react to an abrupt cutoff of their source of livelihood. Already several other farms had been taken

over in the past few weeks, and the whole county was in an uproar. The
representatives from the MIR said that the whole of Chile was watching
what was going on in Lautaro County. There were few newspapers in the
countryside, and few people could read them. Many, however, had transistor radios, and all the news from them was about the illegal takeovers.

That night the occupiers were all men. The women and children were
to come the next day, assuming all went well, and a camp was to be set
up. All the men wore armbands which read MCR, meaning Movimiento
Campesino Revolucionario (Revolutionary Peasant Movement). The Revolutionary Peasant Movement was the peasant front of the MIR. Most
peasants who were affiliated with the MCR were not actually members of
the MIR, but sympathized with its policies. The policies of the MIR were
understood not so much on a theoretical plane as on a practical one. The
peasants could see what results the MIR had achieved in its organization
of the fence-runnings.

The armbands meant that, unlike the fence-runnings, this time the
MIR was publicly announcing that it was organizing the takeovers. Nevertheless, its members still remained in the background, unidentified.

The Mapuches marched in formation down the road from the reservation to the farm. Arriving at the main entrance to the farm, they joined
with the six farmworkers to barricade the main gate. Then they set up
banners, posted guards, and placed the weapons out of sight (but not too
far away). Two men went further up the road and climbed up a nearby
hill. From there in the morning they would flash mirrors to signal that
vehicles were coming down the road. Any car in Lautaro County would
belong either to a landowner, the police, or the government. Buses also
ran down the road once a day, a service which had started in the early
1960s.

The reasons why the Mapuches felt justified in taking over Rinconada
were explained in a public declaration made on the morning of the
takeover. This declaration was printed on mimeograph by the organizers
from the MIR and distributed to the press. The declaration was similar to
those made public after the takeover of the fifteen other farms which were
occupied in Lautaro County during 1970–72. The declaration read as
follows:

> To public opinion. We are 25 families of small owners, both Chi-
> leans and Mapuches. We have taken over Rinconada because we are
> tired of receiving only bureaucracy as an answer to our petitions.
>   This farm was in the hands of Fernando Schultz, who is a man

who has almost no way to live, since besides owning Rinconada, he owns two other farms and a store in the town of Lautaro. It appears as if only the reactionaries have the right to live like human beings.

The rich people claim that the Mapuche is lazy and that the peasant never works hard, in order to justify the tremendous reality of misery in which we live and of which they are guilty because they have maintained the capitalist system in our country.

There are comrade Mapuches who have to maintain a family with what "their land" produces—a tiny piece of ½ or 1 hectare. This is because "our land," the land of our fathers and grandfathers, is now in the hands of the rich, who deceived our ancestors with fancy words and promises.

But this is finished. We have decided to work together at Rinconada. This means that 460 acres now return to our hands, hands which are tired of producing for others.

We know that in the Popular Unity government we will find understanding. We are ready to continue forward, convinced that we are fighting for justice, until the workers take control of Chile.

Land or Death
Revolutionary Peasant Movement

This declaration clearly betrayed the influence of the organizers from the MIR. Most Mapuches and peasants in Lautaro County had little theoretical understanding of capitalism and socialism. The members of the MIR discussed the declaration only briefly with the peasants. And yet it cannot be said that the leaflet misrepresented the peasants. They well understood that they worked to keep the rich wealthy and that they benefitted very little from their own labor. They lived in shacks, they had little to eat, and certainly they had no running water or electricity. The men who occupied Rinconada had watched one out of every three of their children die before the age of one. They saw that only six people worked at Rinconada and that the farm produced little. They planned to have twenty-five workers earning a living from the same amount of land.

About 11 A.M. the morning of the takeover, four vehicles arrived. Two carried police and detectives. One belonged to the government Land Reform Corporation (CORA). The other was Fernando's truck with Fernando and some of his family. A police sergeant began by asking why the peasants all had sticks. The reply was that they often carried sticks in the countryside. Then the police sergeant asked who the leaders were, and the response was that all were leaders. The sergeant grew angry and began to threaten some of the peasants. A police lieutenant stepped in and took over the questioning. The lieutenant was calmer and explained that he was just there to take down information. He talked quietly for a few minutes with a few of the peasants, and then the police withdrew. Fernando approached. He said that he wanted to talk to his "boys," meaning the farmhands. They refused. He asked one of them, one of the huincas, why he had gone along with the takeover. He hoped to split this man off from the others. This was the farmhand who was oldest and who had the most privileges. But the peasant replied that Fernando was six months late with his salary and that was that. Then Fernando said that the farmhands were going to have trouble with those who had come from outside the farm, again trying to split the group. At this point the peasants began to shout slogans (Land or Death, We will win), and Fernando withdrew. Then the government representative from CORA drove closer to the group of peasants. He rolled down his window and said that he was from CORA and wanted to talk to them about expropriating the farm. But his truck had no identifying insignia, and the peasants did not know him personally, so they began to push his truck and pound on it with their sticks. The government representative hastily apologized and withdrew. All four vehicles then left. When Fernando got back to town, he began another court suit which was to prove just as useless as his previous one.

The next vehicle to arrive brought the governor of the country, Fernando Teillier, and some of his friends. Teillier, recently appointed by Allende, was from the Communist Party. The peasants knew him and allowed him to approach. He explained that the farm might well be too small to expropriate and that the illegal occupations did not help the government. (The agrarian reform stipulated that only farms above a certain size could be expropriated.) The governor also complained of the influence of the MIR and the armbands which read MCR. The peasants again responded with slogans, and the governor then left. He was later to be impeached by a right-wing Congress for having done nothing to stop the illegal takeovers in Lautaro County.

The only other cars to come that day belonged to landowners. They came late in the afternoon and drove past. Then they turned around and came back. There were ten landowners in three cars. They stopped and began to get out, shouting reprimands and threats at the peasants. Once the peasants had been able to see that the *momios* (reactionaries) carried no guns, they surrounded the vehicles and forced them to beat a hasty retreat. Clearly the tables had turned, at least for the moment, in Lautaro County.

After these incidents occurred, the families of some of the men arrived. A hasty camp was set up, made of poles and burlap sacks. Fortunately it was summer and the weather was mild. Only the families of the nineteen new men who were to remain on the farm came to the camp. The six farmhands slept in their usual houses, and the other men who had come to help did not bring their families. Those who came to help would leave in a few days once the situation seemed somewhat stable.

The peasants killed a young steer and butchered it. A feast was held to celebrate the so far victorious occupation. It was a subdued feast, with no wine or dancing, because the danger of an attack was always present.

The next day the chief of the Land Reform Corporation arrived. Some of the peasants knew him, as did the MIR organizer. His car was also well identified. The peasants invited him to talk. He suggested that the farm might indeed be too small to expropriate, but that he would look into it.

The peasants were slightly suspicious of CORA and its representatives. They knew that CORA was in charge of expropriating land and then overseeing the formation of cooperatives. But the peasants themselves, with the help of the MIR, had taken over the farm. They intended to keep it and farm it with or without CORA. If CORA wanted to expropriate the farm and make the occupation legal, well and good. But if not, the peasants certainly weren't going to leave. As for forming a cooperative and relying on CORA for technical assistance and financing, the peasants weren't sure that this would be either necessary or good. If they had taken over the farm by themselves, then surely, they felt, they could organize and farm it themselves.

This attitude was not criticized by the members of the MIR who were also suspicious of the government. Although the Popular Unity government was viewed favorably, it was considered only a limited advance. The future would tell if the Popular Unity coalition would or would not move towards socialism. In the meantime the MIR encouraged workers and peasants to rely on themselves. This general strategy was applied in Lautaro County. The illegal occupations of land were a first test case of the agrarian reform under Allende. The MIR hoped to push the existing agrarian reform law to its limits, or better yet, replace it with another one. The existing law had been set up by Christian Democrat Frei in 1967, and the MIR believed it had serious defects. Rather than wait for the state *perhaps* to expropriate the land legally, the MIR encouraged the peasants to take over the land themselves. Rather than pile up debts for the state and ultimately for the peasants by paying compensation to the old owner of the farm, the MIR called for no compensation and a new agrarian reform law.

Events were later to show that so much suspicion was somewhat unwarranted. On the one hand, the peasants would soon realize that they needed all the financial and technical assistance they could get from the state. On the other, the Allende government *did* eventually carry out large-scale expropriations of land. (Of course, they were pressured to do so by illegal occupations.) The MIR's suspicions of the CORA, although partly justified, were at this early stage partly the result of excessive political sectarianism.

In any case, at the time, the CORA chief and the peasants had little to talk about. He left, and no one else came that day except journalists. Journalists continued to arrive for months. At times the peasants would talk to them, at times not, depending on whether they could prove their trustworthiness. A journalist from the United States arrived at Rinconada a few days after the takeover and got no information. At other farms, incidents occurred where journalists from right-wing magazines took pictures without permission, and the peasants took the film out of their cameras and destroyed it.

The official status of the occupied farm remained in limbo for about a month. In the meantime the peasants repaired fences, cut down shrubbery, and kept up their patrols. The police patrolled only at night to prevent incidents between landowners and peasants. They began to do this after some landowners had driven down the road late one night with rifles, taking potshots at any unguarded signs and banners put up by the peasants. Later, the right-wing Congressman Victor Carmine was able to steal a sign from the occupied farm Los Vertientes. He took it to Congress and displayed it in order to demonstrate the anarchy and the lawlessness of the south for which the government and the MIR were responsible. The sign had slogans of the MIR inscribed on it. No incidents occurred at Rinconada although occasionally passing cars belonging to landowners were stopped and searched for weapons.

The situation in Lautaro was so critical that Minister of Agriculture Jacques Chonchol and the Minister of Land Humberto Martones paid a visit to the county. On December 19 they met with representatives of the occupied farms in the town of Lautaro. Several representatives of Rinconada went to the meeting. Chonchol asked for the occupations to cease since they hindered the government, making it vulnerable to attacks from the right. He promised that the big farms would be expropriated, but said that the smaller ones could not; that they would have to be returned to their old owners. The peasant representatives protested, saying that it was impossible to return any occupied farms.

Now that the land had been taken over, and the landowners at least temporarily checked, the next question for the peasants at Rinconada was how the land was to be worked and what would be its relationship to the state. The peasants were still keeping their distance from CORA. There were even one or two who argued that the land should simply be divided up among all twenty-five peasants and worked individually. But the MIR organizer strongly opposed this plan.

4

The Area: 1970

The dramatic events at Rinconada farm formed only a part of a mass movement of the peasantry in Lautaro County.

Lautaro County has a population of 26,000 people, about half of whom live in the countryside. Of the rural population, about 70 percent is Mapuche. Most of the Mapuches live on reservations. There are 161 reservations in Lautaro County, of which 55 are legally divided (see Maps 4 and 7). Most of these were divided by swindlers who wanted the land, as in the case of the Juan Catrileo Reservation. Many of the undivided reservations are smaller than when they were founded as a result of illegal encroachments by neighboring landlords. The Mapuches wanted to settle some old scores when they took over the farms in Lautaro County.

The forces of the right in Lautaro County are well-organized and powerful. Southern Chile is predominantly agricultural and is known as a stronghold of the right-wing. The landlords were accustomed to having their own way with the unorganized peasantry. Many of the landowners were politically active, members of the National Party. In the presidential elections of 1970, the vote in Lautaro County favored the right. Only 22 percent voted for Allende while 40 percent voted for Alessandri. Nationally the respective figures were 36 percent and 34 percent. Many of the peasants did not vote because they were illiterate. Only after Allende was elected were illiterates allowed to vote. (By the 1973 congressional elections a much higher percentage of the peasantry voted. Ninety-one hundred votes were tallied in Lautaro County in 1973, whereas in 1970 there were only 6600. And in 1973 the left received 42 percent of the vote, similar to the 44 percent it received nationally.)

The Mapuches usually owned a small plot of land on the reservation. Since Lautaro's rural population was predominantly Mapuche, most peasants in the county were small owners. According to the census of 1965, 73 percent of the active rural population owned their own land. Less than 1 percent owned farms larger than forty BIH. Most peasants owned only a few hectares. Twenty percent of the actual rural populations were salaried farmworkers and the remaining 7 percent were inquilinos.

Given this distribution of land ownership, it was only natural that the majority of the peasants, given the opportunity, would be eager to take some of the land back from the big owners. The MIR's agitation and then Allende's election were to provide them with this opportunity.

The peasants began with the fence-running in June 1970. By August enough incidents had occurred so that the landowners in the area had become alarmed. On August 12 a group of landowners visited the undersecretary of the Ministry of the Interior in Santiago to complain. Included in the group were two landowners from Lautaro County, Carlos Taladríz and René García. The latter was a congressional deputy of the National Party. The landowners asked for and got a promise from the undersecretary (Achurra) to see that the fence-runners were evicted. The Christian Democratic government had appointed the governor of Cautín Province, and the undersecretary promised to instruct the governor to throw the Mapuches off the occupied land. The undersecretary never fulfilled his promise. The elections were too close, and higher-ups decided that it was politically unwise to act just then against the Mapuches. So the Mapuches remained on the land. The Taladríz and García families had to accept, at least temporarily, the loss of a few hectares of their farms.

On September 4 Allende won the presidential election, narrowly defeating the right-wing Alessandri. Christian Democrat candidate Tomic ran third.

Shortly thereafter the first congress of the Revolutionary Peasant Movement (MCR) was held secretly in the provincial capital of Temuco. The results of the election were discussed, and plans were made to initiate the occupations of entire farms after Allende's inauguration in November. In the meantime the fence-runnings were to continue.

And so they did, throughout September and October. The landowners were looking for someone to blame. They were sure that some outside forces were helping the Mapuches to organize. One likely candidate was Wilfredo Alarcón, a protestant minister in the town of Perquenco, near Lautaro County. Alarcón's truck had been sighted at one of the fence-runnings and was rumored to have been seen at others. As a result, it was decided to intimidate him. The night of October 13 the mayor of Perquenco and some of his friends drove by Alarcón's house and shot it full of bullet holes. Witnesses were later able to identify the mayor, but he was never prosecuted.

But Alarcón was not responsible for the fence-runnings, and they continued. In early November, Allende was inaugurated, and the farm takeovers began in the county. The first one took place on November 21 at the Huerqueco farm and was organized by the Socialist Party. About one hundred peasants participated. On November 22 the Governor Fernando Teillier visited the farm as did a group of police. Teillier did what he was to do many other times afterwards. He asked the peasants to leave. They refused. The fact that the Socialist Party organized the occupation while the Communist governor opposed it indicated a split in the Popular Unity coalition at the local level. The Communists and Socialists had joined together nationally to form the Popular Unity coalition and had agreed on a common program. But in Lautaro County, as in so many other places throughout Chile, there were disagreements between the two parties. The Socialist Party was notorious for its lack of discipline, and local Socialist committees would often undertake actions which were not approved by higher leadership.

Teillier left the Huerqueco farm and the peasants stayed. The issue was taken up by the courts.

When Allende assumed office the Popular Unity gained control of the executive branch, but the judicial system continued to be controlled by the right wing. The courts and judges became the most stalwart opponents of Allende and the left.[1]

It was a foregone conclusion in Lautaro County that the courts would favor the landowners. With the election over and the different sides well-defined, the courts began to make rulings which would reverse the trend of illegal occupations in the county. In November they ruled, for example, that the fence-running at the Three Pastures farm owned by Carlos Taladríz was illegal. On November 24 they ruled that the occupation of the Laurel farm on November 16 was illegal. They farm was located in Galvarino County, just on the border of Lautaro County. The occupation of Laurel farm was the first farm takeover during the Allende government in all of Cautín Province. In just eight days the courts ruled that the occupation was illegal. The next step was for the police to clear the peasants out. But the police were controlled by the Ministry of the Interior, part of the executive branch. Therefore, the Allende government had to give the order to the police to clear the peasants off the Laurel farm. The governor of the province was Gastón Lobos, a member of the Radical Party who had been appointed by Allende. He declared that he would throw the peasants off the land only at the explicit orders of the minister of the interior.

The chain of command ran from the governor of Perquenco, Galvarino, and Lautaro counties (Fernando Teillier, Communist), to the governor of the whole province (Gastón Lobos, Radical), to the Minister of the Interior José Toha, Socialist. Neither Teillier nor Lobos would order the police in without orders from Toha, and Toha refused to give those orders. It was simply not politically possible for the Allende government, just newly in office, to side with landlords against peasants occupying land. The Allende government was pledged to carry out an agrarian reform in favor of the peasants; so the peasants remained at Laurel farm. The same scenario was to be repeated many times during the Allende period. Chile's government was never set up to cope with a conflict between the judiciary and the executive. Always before they had been on the same side, and any judicial order was promptly fulfilled by the police.

The landowners were later to take their revenge. After the coup, Gastón Lobos was jailed, tortured, and finally murdered by the military in Temuco. José Toha was tortured to death in Santiago. Fernando Teillier was killed by right-wing civilians a few days after the coup.

In November 1970, however, the landowners were worried. On November 28 a group of prominent landowners from Lautaro County left for Santiago where they met with government officials to discuss the fence-runnings and takeovers. They met with Daniel Vergara who was second-in-command at the Ministry of the Interior. The next day Fernando Teillier also left for Santiago to speak with the ministers of interior and agriculture. Teillier and the landowners had met with each other in a stormy session in Lautaro on November 25. Now both sides were taking up the issue with top government officials.

The group of landowners included Carlos Taladríz who had lost twelve hectares back on August 11 to a nearby reservation. This time, while Taladríz was in Santiago, the peasants took over his whole farm. Its name was Three Pastures, and it was taken over on November 30. The peasants put up banners reading "Revolutionary Peasant Movement" and issued a declaration to the press. They vowed to let no one enter the farm except for the governors of the county and province.

Gastón Lobos went out the next day to investigate the situation personally. The peasants proved insensitive to his argument. He explained to them that the courts had already ruled against the fence-running and surely would rule against the takeover as well. The governor concluded, and said so publicly, that the peasants were led by extremists. He authorized police guards but did not order the police to clear the peasants off the land. During his visit the peasants formed columns in semimilitary fashion and paraded, calling themselves militia.

Back in Lautaro the landowners, grouped in the Manuel Rodríguez Employers' Union of Lautaro County, sent a telegram of protest to Minister of the Interior José Toha.

On December 3, Toha set up a three-man commission to study the illegal occupations in the south. Their first step was to go to Lautaro County and visit the Three Pastures farm. They then had a meeting with the Employers' Union, headed by Carlos and Alfonso Podlech. Both men were well known right wingers. Carlos Podlech had just been chosen as a leader of the National Party in Lautaro County in party elections on November 7.

The Agricultural Employers' Unions were set up by county at the same time as the peasant unions (1967). In January 1969 the National Federation of Agricultural Employers' Unions led a protest against the agrarian reform of Frei by blocking major roads with their vehicles for a day. In Lautaro County Carlos Podlech and Alfonso Podlech were active in leading the local Employers' Union snarling of traffic. If the brothers Podlech thought Frei's agrarian reform was bad, their reaction and opposition to Allende's can be imagined. They fought the agrarian reform throughout the Allende period. After the coup, Alfonso Podlech became the chief prosecutor for the military in the trials of members of the MIR in Temuco.

On December 4 the landowners in Lautaro County began a legal process to have county Governor Fernando Teillier impeached for having failed to do his duty when he refused to send the police to clear the Mapuches off the Three Pastures farm. This action proved to be a precedent. In 1972 and 1973 the right-wing majority in Congress frequently impeached whichever officials of the Allende government it disliked. On the same day, December 4, another farm was taken over in Lautaro County by the Revolutionary Peasant Movement. From Santiago, Daniel Vergara held a press conference and announced that all was calm in the south, despite exaggerated reports of peasant violence. Vergara was to issue similar statements during the next several months, despite the fact that it was becoming increasingly clear to everyone that all was not calm in the south.

On December 5 the peasant unions in Lautaro County (controlled by the Christian Democrats) sent a telegram to Toha condemning the illegal occupations and saying that they were led by extremists who were not part of the government. The peasant unions threatned to go on strike if the government did not put an end to the takeovers. This telegram was a curious document. The Christian Democratic peasant unions had many members who were themselves participating in the takeovers. The facts were that the telegram was sent by a few "leaders" of the Christian Democratic unions who did not represent the mass of the membership. In any case the membership was not large to begin with. Only a few hundred of the peasants in Lautaro County belonged to a peasant union; and, as we have seen in the case of Rinconada, the unions, largely paper organizations, did a very poor job of representing their members.

On December 10 Governor Gastón Lobos met with Allende and the other provincial governors. Speaking with the press after the meeting, Lobos said that Allende was against the illegal occupations and that the police would be used when the courts ruled that a situation was illegal. This was a change from his previous position. But despite the statement, the police were not used. Lobos also said that occupied farms would be intervened. Intervention meant, according to the agrarian reform law, that the government would send in an administrator to run the farms until it was decided whether they would be expropriated or returned to their owners. The government representative would take in the profits and pay the salaries as well as make any investments he saw fit. If investments exceeded profits, the intervenor could demand that the owners pay for such investments.

Lobos also predicted that the CORA would shortly announce which farms were to be expropriated in Cautín Province. Such an announcement would, it was hoped, slow down the takeovers because the peasants would realize that the government was going to expropriate many farms in the province. Governor Lobos set up a forty-eight-man team to tour Cautín to carry out a publicity campaign against illegal takeovers. The idea was to prevent any more from taking place.

But on December 11 the Rinconada farm was taken over. On December 16 and 17 more takeovers occurred in the Lautaro County, again led by peasants belonging to the Revolutionary Peasant Movement.

On December 17, while the peasants were taking over the new farms, Allende met in Santiago with forty representatives of the national landowners' associations to discuss the takeovers. The leaders of the National Society of Agriculture and the National Federation of Agricultural Employers' Unions complained to Allende. Allende announced plans to go to Cautín Province on December 20.

Given the climate of insecurity, the landowners began to sell off their cattle at cheap prices, preferring to get rid of their animals rather than to lose them to a peasant takeover. The landowners knew that after the Three Pastures farm had been occupied, the peasants had refused to allow the owner to take his cattle out, despite a court order to do so. Many owners took their cattle across the summer passes of the Andes to Argentina. On December 18 the provincial newspaper reported that cattle prices had dropped 20 percent for steers and 50 percent for cows, in comparison to the previous year.

About this time the Revolutionary Peasant Movement (MCR) sent a declaration to the provincial newspaper. The MCR said that the reaction of the right to the peasant takeovers was to be expected, but that the reaction of the Popular Unity government was not. The MCR pointed out that the peasant takeovers resulted from the real misery of the peasants, not from outside extremists. Therefore, the Popular Unity government should not attack the occupations nor blame them on ultraleftist agitators. This statement was another indication of the polemical debate between the MIR and the Popular Unity coalition, especially the Communist Party. This debate had been going on for several years. The MIR and the MCR felt that the Popular Unity government should push ahead faster. Many sectors of the Popular Unity coalition, on the other hand, felt that the MIR was a small group of students who were extremists without any connection to the masses of the people.

On December 19 the minister of agriculture and land came to Cautín Province, and on December 20 Allende himself arrived. The ministers visited several occupied farms and met with both peasants and landowners. Allende himself spoke to a large crowd of peasants. He explained that the government understood that the peasants had legitimate grievances that caused them to take over the land, but that he wished that they would await the normal procedures of the agrarian reform. The illegal occupations, he said, only created a climate of instability which would offer political advantages to the right. At the same time Allende harshly warned the landowners against any attacks aimed at the peasants. Meanwhile Minister of Agriculture Chonchol said that he would come to Cautín for the months of January and February in order personally to oversee the agrarian reform in the province. He promised large-scale expropriations.

The same morning that Allende came to Temuco, the Revolutionary Peasant Movement took over yet another farm, this time in western Cautín. The farm was called Ruculán and was owned by the Landeretche family. The peasants renamed the farm "Arnoldo Rios" in honor of a student belonging to the MIR who had been killed in Concepción in early

December by students who belonged to the Communist Party. The polemic between the MIR and the Communist Party had moved beyond debate into the realm of physical violence. The killing had shocked the entire left and led to an attempt to patch up some of the differences between the MIR and the Popular Unity. This attempt was temporarily successful, to a limited degree. The sectarianism of both sides was only slightly diminished.

A few days after the takeover at Ruculán, the peasant unions controlled by the Communist Party in Cautín issued a statement condemning the takeovers. The statement said that the L. E. Recabarren Federation (Communist) would seek an alliance with the provincial federation of Christian Democratic peasant unions (Fed. President Frei). The Recabarren Federation would also undertake an active campaign against outside agitators who encouraged illegal takeovers. Such agitators would be denounced to the government authorities. The effort to achieve an alliance with the Christian Democratic peasant unions in Cautín was only a local reflection of a strategy which the Communist Party frequently pursued at the national level, that is, an alliance with the opposition Christian Democratic Party.

While these debates were going on within the left, the landowners in Lautaro County turned to direct action. On December 21 they attacked a group of peasants who had occupied thirty hectares belonging to Tomasa Rivas, one of the big landowners of the area. The peasants were driven off the land. No one was injured. The peasants who were occupying the Ruculán farm were not so fortunate. On December 25 the Landeretche family and a large group of landowners attacked them. The landowners opened up with rifle fire. The peasants fled, leaving three wounded, one seriously, behind. The landowners came up in trucks. The peasants claimed there were about 150 attackers while the Landeretche family claimed only seven. Minister of the Interior José Toha immediately assigned two lawyers to the case. The Socialist governor of the county where Ruculán was located issued a statement condemning the landlords' attack and also the original takeover by the peasants.

The next day José Toha spoke to the press, condemning the violence of the landowners. He spoke of a threat made a few days before by Carlos Podlech. Podlech had told Minister of Land Humberto Martones that, unless the government did something to stop the takeovers, the landowners would make the sound of machine guns heard in southern Chile. Although it is not known whether Podlech himself actually participated in the Ruculán attack, some owners from Lautaro County had. Many of the large owners in the county had several other farms spread out through Cautín Province. Most of the landowners of the province either knew of each other or knew each other personally. So it was natural that friends from Lautaro County would help in the Landeretche's attack at Ruculán. Among the arrested for the Ruculán incident were two members of the Fagalde family which owned land in Lautaro. One of the two was Hernán Fagalde, who had shot and killed a Mapuche peasant on September 15, 1970, for stealing fruit from the family farm, Los Albertos. Fagalde said it was an accident and was never prosecuted. He was to suffer no penalty for his participation in the Ruculán attack either. In both cases the court system freed him.

On this same day, December 26, the government moved to counterattack by ordering a search of eleven farms, looking for weapons in the hands of the landowners. Included in the list of landlords were several prominent ones in Lautaro County, such as José Dattwiler, Carlos Taladríz, Pablo Goebel, and Carlos Podlech. Pablo Goebel was the son of Tomasa Rivas who owned the property in Lautaro that had been retaken by the landowners only five days before. Goebel was a leader of the National Party in Lautaro. He later left Chile for Argentina, after the government expropriated his Muco Alto farm in Lautaro.

No arms were found in the houses of the landowners. As Governor Gastón Lobos admitted several days later, it was likely that the landowners had been tipped off about the raid ahead of time. Probably the police themselves told the landowners.

The final result of the Ruculán incident was that neither the peasants nor the landlords were convicted for any illegalities. The incident did serve, however, to cause the Popular Unity government to place even more priority on land reform in Cautín Province. The peasants themselves eventually did get control of Ruculán, after the government intervened the farm. Finally the farm was expropriated. It is quite likely, however, that since the military coup the Landeretches have once more gained control of the farm.

The Ruculán incident also led to a personal inspection tour by José Toha. On December 30 Toha took a whirlwind tour by helicopter to Cautín and Valdivia provinces. He visited several occupied farms in Lautaro County, conversing with the peasants. Toha hoped that by his presence he would defuse a situation that was nationally polarizing the country. Upon his return to Santiago he once again reiterated that the peasants were armed only with a few old shotguns and that it was the landowners who were advocating and carrying out the majority of the violence.

As the year ended, Governor Lobos continued to threaten to arrest anyone who was caught organizing illegal takeovers. But by now it was clear that such threats would not slow down the takeovers. Neither would friendly persuasion and political education, nor right-wing violence. Only a massive expropriation of the large landholdings could provide a satisfactory solution to the peasants' grievances. Such a massive expropriation was exactly what Chonchol planned to carry out in January. Allende's agrarian reform would begin in Cautín.

The year 1970 had been eventful in Lautaro County. There had been eighteen separate incidents of fence-running and seven farms had been occupied. The fence-running incidents took place for the most part between June and early November. After Allende assumed office on November 3 the occupations of entire farms had begun.

The fence-running incidents had returned 724 hectares to the hands of the Mapuche peasantry. The occuptions of the farms had meant that a further 2,370 hectares were taken away from the big landowners. The average size of the farms that were taken over was 340 hectares. All of the farms were too small to be expropriated under the agrarian reform law. The law called for the expropriation of any farm over eighty Basic Irrigated Hectares (see glossary for definition of BIH). Six out of the seven farms in Lautaro County measuring over eighty BIH had already been expropriated under the Frei government.

A farm of 340 hectares in the county, unless it was located in the infertile land near the Andes, was usually somewhere between forty and eighty BIH. Under the agrarian reform law such farms could be expropriated only if it could be proved that they were either abandoned by their owners or poorly exploited (see Maps 2 and 6).

The Allende government did not have as a priority the expropriation of such farms. It was felt that the first order of business was farms over eighty BIH. The Frei government in most areas of Chile had expropriated only about one-third of such farms, and it was the remaining two-thirds that the Allende government was planning to expropriate. The takeover of smaller farms in Lautaro County caught the government unprepared, forcing it to consider the expropriation of farms not on the agenda.

For the most part, both the fence-runnings and the farm takeovers had been led by the MCR, which was controlled by the MIR. In one case, however, a farm was taken over by a group of peasants organized by the Socialist Party (a member of the Popular Unity government coalition).

The takeovers organized by the MIR reflected the MIR's belief that the agrarian reform law should be pushed to its limits by the Allende government. The MIR felt that the agrarian reform law, a product of the Christian Democratic Frei government, had too many limitations. A new agrarian reform law was needed to carry out the kind of massive change in power in the countryside envisioned by the MIR. Many sectors of the Popular Unity coalition felt the same way, and Allende spoke of submitting amendments to the agrarian reform law to Congress. As it turned out, however, this never happened. As the political situation rapidly polarized, the Christian Democrats in Congress blocked with the National Party to oppose most legislation proposed by the Popular Unity government. Since the Popular Unity controlled only a minority of the votes in Congress, it soon became clear that it was impossible to pass any legislation initiated by the executive. The Frei Agrarian Reform Law would have to do. The debate within the left became a debate about how that law could be most effectively used.

Chapter 5

The Farm: 1971

Intervention turned out to be the solution for the Rinconada farm. The peasants had continued their occupation of Rinconada for over a month. The government still felt that the farm was too small to expropriate, and in any case the expropriation process was a long and bureaucratic one. The tense situation at Rinconada and the other occupied farms in Lautaro County needed an institutional solution, or at least patching up, as soon as possible. The answer proposed by the government was intervention. In cases of labor disputes which paralyzed agricultural production, the 1967 Agrarian Reform Law enabled the government to intervene, that is, to administer the farm in question until the labor dispute could be resolved. The Frei government undoubtedly intended that the interventions were to be used against agricultural workers who went on strike during harvest time. But the Allende government was to use the law to favor the peasants, especially in cases of illegal occupation where expropriation of the farm appeared difficult.

For the peasants intervention was also a good solution. It meant that the peasants were paid salaries. The intervenor used the owner's bank account to continue to pay salaries. In the case of Rinconada he put nineteen new workers on the payroll, so that all those who had occupied the farm were paid. In case the owner did not have sufficient money in his account to pay all such salaries, then the state paid them. The owner would have to pay them back later.

The decree of intervention became effective in mid January or the middle of the summer. At that same time the peasants at Rinconada succeeded in borrowing four pairs of oxen, and they began to work the land. Fernando Schultz had had about 200 cattle on the place (100 cows, 100 calves) and had only farmed about fifteen hectares. Such use of the land was not very efficient. Schultz had not been interested in increasing production. He would have had to make risky investments and hire more labor. He wanted to do neither. The new occupiers of Rinconada were planning to cultivate the land much more intensively. As it turned out, eventually about 150 hectares were cultivated with crops, and there were over 200 cattle.

In January 1971, however, the peasants were not sure how they were going to manage. The intervention brought salaries, a first step forward. Then came the oxen. The neighboring Mapuches who had oxen lent them in exchange for pasture rights. The farm grazed the oxen on its own good pasture which improved the health of the animals considerably.

About the same time both the peasants on the farm and in the area were getting used to the farm's new name. The peasants had renamed it Elicura, after one of the first leaders of Mapuche rebellions against the Spaniards. The name meant "white stone."

The intervention meant that the peasants at Elicura could legally begin to work on the farm, something they had already begun to do anyway. They harvested the fifteen hectares of wheat that Schultz had planted, wheat they had to deliver to Schultz. They also gave up the cattle. After the intervention Schultz went to the intervenor and demanded the right to withdraw his cattle in accordance with the Agrarian Reform Law. The intervenor, a member of the Radical Party named Hernán Gómez, agreed. He told the peasants at Elicura that the cattle had to be given up. The peasants did not oppose this. They felt that now they had the land, they would eventually get their own cattle. Besides, they were beginning to trust the intervenor somewhat. He came out once a week to check on what they were doing, and he made sure that their salaries were paid. When he insisted that Schultz be given the right to withdraw his cattle, the peasants went along with it. To have refused would have meant to have put in jeopardy the intervention and the new salaries. It would have created a situation of conflict that might have destroyed the support the peasants had managed to win from the local government authorities. Loss of that support could threaten the occupation itself. Rather than make an issue of the cattle, the peasants allowed Schultz to withdraw them. The MIR organizer also agreed to this policy.

The most critical immediate problem for the peasants was housing. Only three workers had houses. The remaining twenty-two split into two groups. Those who lived close enough to the farm to walk to work every day did so, while those who lived a long distance away (over two or three miles) got first priority on the miserable shacks and tool sheds which were to serve as houses for the first year. Four bachelors moved in together in a tool shed.

The intervention required that an official survey be taken of all the buildings and grounds. Everything had to be evaluated, including the fence posts and irrigation ditches. Since Schultz had lived in town, there was no fancy house. There were only a few buildings; a shed for the tractors, a barn for the cows, a storage building for fertilizer and seed, and a corral for milking. Everything was written down and evaluated. In addition, an official survey of the previous working conditions was carried out, so that Schultz's failure to pay back wages was recorded.

All this information was available to the Land Reform Corporation (CORA). The mistreatment of the workers and the ill use of potentially productive land indicated that, even though the farm was only about fifty BIH, it was poorly exploited and might on that basis be expropriated after all. Armed with this new information, the provincial head of CORA arrived a few weeks after the intervention and explained to the peasants of Elicura that he thought the farm would indeed be expropriated. The peasants were hesitant. Their leaders were still suspicious of CORA, even though by now Minister of Agriculture Chonchol had arrived in Cautín Province and had begun to expropriate farms right and left. The peasants at Elicura were beginning to have a better idea of what expropriation would mean. Some opposition to expropriation came from one of the older and more influential peasants named Pablo. Pablo's idea was to divide up the farm and work it in individual plots, and he encouraged others to think the same way. Pablo had a few oxen and a pretty good plow. He thought he could get on well enough on his own. But most of the opposition to expropriation was from those peasants who insisted on working collectively but distrusted the CORA. A majority of the twenty-five workers at Elicura did not participate actively in the debate, but listened to the various arguments and waited to make up their minds.

Expropriation would have meant the formation of a partnership with CORA to own the land. At the farm itself a cooperative would be set up. Each peasant would have an individual plot of a half or an entire hectare, and the rest of the farm would be worked collectively. CORA would supply credits for seed, fertilizer, and machinery. Salaries would be advanced in anticipation of the harvest. Any profits would be divided among the peasants. This arrangement was to last three to five years after which the cooperative would be on its own. At that time it could continue to exist as a cooperative.

As the weeks went by, the advantages of this arrangement became increasingly clear. The intervention supplied salaries, but not machinery. Oxen were going to be inadequate to work a large amount of land. Furthermore, seed and fertilizer would be hard to get in sufficient quantity without the backing of the CORA. Both the peasants and the MIR organizer began to view expropriation favorably.

The MIR had feared that forming a parnership with the CORA might limit the political development of the peasant cooperatives. CORA was after all a government bureaucracy which frequently treated the peasants as ignorant workers who had to obey the production requirements of management (i.e., CORA). Furthermore, CORA was filled with many Christian Democrat and even National Party members who were already doing their best to sabotage Allende's land reform. Placed at crucial points in the bureaucracy, such opposition members could simply delay papers or fail to fill out reports in order to make the work of expropriation very difficult. About half of personnel of CORA in the local offices of Lautaro County belonged to the right-wing opposition.[1]

The MIR also feared that the Agrarian Reform Law led to cooperatives which would, after the three-to-five-year transition period, turn into individual small holdings. The large landowners who owned between forty and eighty BIH would then be in a position simply to buy out the best of the small holdings, and the whole redistribution of land carried out under the reform would be jeopardized. Many landowners who had had farms larger than eighty BIH had been given (or would be given) a reserve area to keep, usually the best land on their farms. Such reserves were usually somewhere between forty and eighty BIH. They were also allowed to keep all the machinery and animals on the farm. The result was that a well-capitalized and efficient sector of private farms between forty and eighty BIH had been partially developed under Frei and was to be even more so under Allende. The owners of these farms could buy out whatever small plots they chose when the cooperatives formed on the expropriated land were eventually divided. That is what had happened in Mexico. The Mexican Revolution had brought about a radical division of the big haciendas. But afterwards, the big estates had been reconstituted once again. The former owners had used their wealth to buy up the individual holdings of the peasants.[2]

Several things happened in January 1971 which caused the MIR to look more favorably at expropriation and at CORA. First, Chonchol's arrival in Cautín in early January was soon followed by a massive expropriation program carried out by the Popular Unity government. This program demonstrated the government's strong resolve to change the balance of power in the countryside. Second, the practical problems of running the occupied farms without their expropriation seemed overwhelming. The interventions were a positive step, but they did not solve the problem of credit for machinery and fertilizer. Third, the formation of the Peasant Council took place. It was to be a source of power for the peasantry and was to keep an eye on the bureaucrats in CORA. Several thousand peasants gathered in the town of Lautaro on January 16 to form the Lautaro Peasant Council. All the workers from Elicura were there, and one of them had been chosen a member of the new Council.

These events led the MIR organizers in Lautaro County to favor government expropriation. The peasants at Elicura, and at the other occupied farms, agreed. Their concrete necessities for credit and their continued trust in the MIR organizers combined persuaded them to seek expropriation.

The expropriation of Elicura went through in May. The actual expropriation was done by a point system. CORA sent out agronomists who determined how well the farm had been run by Schultz. Each category of production was evaluated and given a score. The treatment of the workers was also evaluated and awarded a certain number of points. A lot of this work had already been done by the intervenor. The points from all categories were added up; if the total did not reach a certain minimum, then the farm was determined to have been poorly exploited.

Schultz needed a minimum of 300 points, but he only got 240. Of some 300 hectares which were arable on the farm, Schultz had worked only about 125 for crops or pasture, less than the 70 percent required. His failure to pay back wages or to improve the housing of his workers meant that he scored very low in the worker-welfare category. Combining the poor use of potentially productive land and the poor treatment of his workers, Schultz failed.

This meant that this farm could be expropriated by CORA. CORA would not *necessarily* expropriate it since CORA was busy expropriating many larger farms. But because it was intervened and occupied by a group of peasants asking for the expropriation, it was a foregone conclusion that CORA would go ahead. Knowing this, Schultz decided to offer his farm to CORA voluntarily. He did this in order to get better terms in the eventual settlement. He had no chance of getting a reserve area because a farm judged to have been poorly exploited did not qualify for a reserve according to the law. Schultz did hope, however, to get a better cash payment.

It turned out that he was awarded a settlement of about $20,000

(400,000 escudos) for the farm and everything on it. Seventy percent of this payment was for the land. The figure was determined by reference to the tax roles (land value derived from the tax roles was usually slightly less than actual market value). The other 30 percent of the settlement was for the buildings and permanent improvements to the land; fences, irrigation ditches, trees planted.

Of the $20,000, Schultz only received $5,000 immediately. The rest was to be paid over a thirty-year period in equal annual payments. Of this $15,000 balance, only 70 percent was to be adjusted for inflation. It should be remembered that $20,000 was a large sum of money in Chile in 1971. The minimum wage was about $40–50 a month at that time.

The expropriation became effective once it was published in the official government bulletin and the first payment to Schultz had been made. In early 1971 CORA had no difficulty making the payments. Its budget was satisfactory. The policy of large-scale expropriations was not hindered by a lack of money. In 1972 and 1973, when Congress consistently refused to grant sufficient funds, CORA went ahead and spent money it did not have in order to keep the land reform moving. This, of course, contributed to inflation.

The customary delay between expropriation and the actual taking of possession of the farm by the peasants and CORA did not occur in the case of Elicura since the peasants had already occupied the farm. The next step after expropriation was the official constitution of the cooperative: this involved the election of officers by the peasants and the opening of a bank account.

In May the state bank gave the peasants at Elicura credit to get their first tractor, just in time to plant the winter wheat. Many of the peasants could not operate a tractor. They had never before had access to one of their small plots on the reservations where oxen were adequate. But several of the old workers on the farm knew how to run the tractor, an Italian Fiat. The CORA also supplied a sowing machine, and the peasants planted twenty-five hectares of winter wheat. The seed and the fertilizer came through credits by CORA. The cooperative thus began to pile up large debts to the state bank and to CORA. The state bank began to pay the salaries of all twenty-five workers in anticipation of future crops. The salaries were a loan which was endorsed by CORA. Since it would take at least several years before the farm was running at its peak, it was expected that the peasants would be in debt for at least that long, just counting short-term credits (salaries, seed, and fertilizers). Long-term credits for the tractor, new housing, and the land itself would take much longer to pay off. The payments that CORA would make to Schultz for his land ultimately had to be paid back by the peasants to CORA.

Many of these debts were never to be paid off. Some credits were not adjusted for inflation and therefore practically became a gift (such as the credit for the tractor). Production was insufficient to pay even for the short-term loans. In effect the government ended up heavily subsidizing the new cooperatives.

The election of the officers at Elicura was not a complicated affair. The peasants who had already distinguished themselves at the time of the fence-running and the occupation were elected. There was some prejudice against the younger members of the cooperative. While several of the younger men had played very important roles during the takeover of the farm, they were not considered to be capable of running it. Only one of the younger men, Pedro, was elected to a position of leadership. He was also a member of the new Peasant Council. The organizer from the MIR and an official from CORA were present at the voting but did not try to influence the results. The officers were elected for one year and could be recalled at any time.

No women voted, and none were present at the meeting. It was to take a long time even to begin to break down the traditional exclusion of peasant women, especially Mapuche women, from serious community business. This was to be one of the tasks of the MIR organizers in the area. At the time of the election of officers at Elicura farm in 1971, however, the participation of women was not an issue that anyone raised. The MIR organizer did suggest that women attend the meeting, but got no response. His more insistent suggestions in the future were to be met with either silence or rejection by the men. The women for their part began to meet separately from time to time in 1972 and 1973. These meetings would be social gatherings, but they took on an additional political importance because they represented the first time that women in the countryside had gotten together, except for weddings or deaths, on their own initiative. The formation of a cooperative meant that for the first time the peasant women lived close to one another. On the reservations the Mapuche houses (rucas) were spaced far apart, and it was rare that one woman would go on her own to visit another. It took almost two years at Elicura before this traditional isolation began to be overcome.

The MIR organizer was continually, and usually unsuccessfully, to urge the participation of women in the peasant assemblies at Elicura. He viewed their exclusion as a definite problem. On the other hand he was not so concerned about the prejudice shown during the elections towards some of the younger men. He hoped to work with the younger peasant leaders and turn them into politically conscious and disciplined party members. Had they become officers of the cooperative, they might have been too busy for party work. The business of running the farm, what was to be called the battle of production, was considered important by the MIR, but it took second place to the task of building a strong party. This attitude was to cause much debate within the left and was to be extensively criticized by some members of the Popular Unity coalition.[3]

The organizer from the MIR was the same one who had helped with the fence-running and the takeover. He was soon to be replaced since the MIR frequently changed its personnel in Lautaro County. When someone with experience was needed in some new area of conflict, he or she would be pulled out of one place and moved rapidly to another. All members who worked as peasant organizers continued to live in the countryside, except for those few who had jobs in the government agricultural bureaucracy. In early 1971 there were four MIR organizers in Lautaro County. They all lived on different expropriated farms. One lived at Elicura.

While the organizer from the MIR spent most of his time working on new takeovers in Lautaro County, the peasants at Elicura began to dedicate themselves to their work. There was to be no CORA official who lived on the farm and oversaw daily work. Discipline on the job was to be self-discipline. The CORA personnel, although numerous, were insufficient really to oversee day-to-day production on all the expropriated farms.

A lot of people in CORA spent most of their time in the town of Lautaro. Only about one-fourth of the local CORA bureaucracy was actually engaged in the countryside on a day-to-day basis. Even they lived in the city and visited the farms whereas it should have been the other way around.

Theoretically the peasants at Elicura were to be disciplined not only by their political consciousness (the need to supply food to the city and to make a success of the agrarian reform), but also by material sanctions for poor production. If a farm did not produce well, credits were to become harder to get from the state bank and CORA. Ultimately salaries were dependent on sufficient production. Irresponsible behavior on the part of the peasants at Elicura, it was explained, could lead to a cutoff of salaries which were, after all, only an advance on future production.

In practice these material sanctions were not very effective. When they were applied, they led to conflicts between the state bank and the CORA on the one hand and the peasants on the other. If production failed, the state bank and CORA would often blame the peasants. The peasants would frequently blame the state bureaucracy for having failed to deliver the needed seed on time or for having delayed the repair of a vital tractor. The battle of production, which was ideally to be a joint war of peasants and technicians against nature and right-wing sabotage, frequently turned out to be a battle between the peasants and the state technicians.[4]

In mid 1971, however, these future conflicts were not foreseen. The peasants at Elicura had gotten one tractor, and the seed and fertilizer arrived on time. Work was done well, and there were no problems about some working harder than others at the collective tasks. Towards the end of the year, they managed to get another tractor. This one was Czechoslovakian. The Allende government was already feeling the unannounced credit blockade, and the traditional American tractors were being replaced, slowly but surely, with Eastern European equipment. With dollars still relatively abundant and the economy as a whole in 1971 experiencing a boom, the government invested heavily in the new cooperatives. Tractors in Lautaro County multiplied.[5]

New housing was begun as well. Plans were for ten new houses, of the same type that were being built all over the province. The peasant would pay for them over a period of thirty years. Basically they were so cheap that they were practically free. They were to be a vast improvement over the straw huts with dirt floors (rucas) where the Mapuche had traditionally lived. The new houses were to have tin roofs and wooden floors elevated off the ground. A space between outer and inner walls would provide some rudimentary insulation. There would be no running water, heat, or electricity.

Almost every expropriated farm was to have some of these new houses. Perhaps between 100 and 200 were started under Allende government in Lautaro County alone. Unfortunately many were never completed because once the shortages began to affect the supply of construction materials it became increasingly difficult to continue work on the new houses. While waiting for the houses to be completed, some peasants at Elicura began to build new houses of their own, using lumber from the trees on the farm. They took advantage of bank credit to get some nails and tin. These self-made houses were a far sight better than the tool sheds and the barn where many of the workers had to stay for months. But even these houses were viewed as a temporary solution. Every two or three expropriated farms received a full-time carpenter to work on these government-financed houses. The carpenter enlisted a few members of the cooperative to work with him full-time, and little by little the expropriated farms turned into miniature housing projects.

Spring brought renewed work. Thirty hectares of oats, thirty of rape, thirty of intermediate wheat, twenty of spring wheat, fifteen of winter wheat, ten of hay, three of sugar beets, four of beans, and six of potatoes were planted. The total cultivated area was 148 hectares. In addition over 100 cattle had been brought to the farm. The cattle were obtained through arrangements with different government agencies. Forty cows were obtained through CORFO, the state development corporation. The peasants would have to return 100 female calves over the period of seven years. SOCOAGRO, the state cattle agency, supplied steers to be fattened. In two years time the steers would have to be delivered back to SOCOAGRO. Any profits obtained from an increase in weight would be divided equally between the peasants at Elicura and SOCOAGRO.

There was plenty of work to do. The cattle had to be watched constantly, the crops had to be planted, houses had to be built, and the cows had to be milked. The elected officials constantly had to go into town on the one bus a day in order to work out the details of running the farm.

But the traditional social life in the countryside continued. Things were not so busy that time off could not be taken for a soccer game between rival clubs. Wine was plentiful at such games, which were the main social life of the peasants. Most soccer games resulted not only in athletic prowess but also in several drunken brawls which sometimes caused serious injuries. On the other hand young men and women met and talked, and marriages were arranged. Peasants from all the nearby farms and reservations went to the soccer games.

Time was also taken off occasionally to participate in a farm takeover somewhere else in Lautaro County.

Chapter 6

The Area: 1971

Five more farms were occupied in 1971 in Lautaro County. All of them were eventually expropriated. By the end of 1971, twenty-one farms had been expropriated in the country. Of these, twelve had been illegally occupied by the peasants (seven in late 1970, five in 1971).

The fact that twelve of the farms had been taken over encouraged their owners to sell to CORA. The profits of such farms were of course immediately lost to their owners since the peasants who occupied the farms refused to allow the owners to continue production. In case of intervention by the government (seven farms) the owner was forced to pay new salaries and investments made by the intervenor, which even further encouraged his selling to CORA.

Even those owners whose farms were not occupied were affected by the takeovers. The very threat of a takeover pressured them to sell to CORA. The fact of the matter was that the owners were on the defensive, and CORA's task was made easier by the illegal takeovers. CORA itself only moved to expropriate so many farms in the Lautaro County because it was being pressured by the peasants. Unless the government moved rapidly to expropriate, the peasants were almost sure to take over more land. If this were to happen and if the landowners were to respond violently, then the right wing would continue to mount a national campaign calling for law and order. The Popular Unity government wanted to avoid such a campaign. Minister of Agriculture Chonchol had expressly arrived in Cautín in order to make sure no more incidents like the one at Ruculán happened again.

The twenty-one farms expropriated by the end of 1971 totalled 17,000 hectares; this surpassed the 13,000 hectares (six farms) expropriated during the Frei government. The farms which had been expropriated by the

Frei government were generally in the eastern part of the county, nearer the Andes, where the land was not as rich. They were all larger than the eighty BIH limit allowed by the Agrarian Reform Law. Arrangements had been made with most of the owners of the six farms, so that they were offered voluntarily for sale to CORA. The owners thereby got a good settlement. In three of the six cases the owners were given a rich reserve area to keep (see Maps 2 and 3).

Under Allende the farms expropriated were often in the western part of the county where most of the Indian population lived and where the land was better. All but one of the farms were between forty and eighty BIH. The twelve illegally occupied farms totalled 9,000 hectares, or more than half of the area expropriated in 1971. In only two cases out of twenty-one were the owners given reserves. Many of the farms were expropriated because they were poorly exploited, not because of their size. The other farms were expropriated either because the owner offered them voluntarily for sale to CORA, or because the owner had other farms outside the county, so that the total area of all his farms did exceed the eighty BIH limit.

Minister of Agriculture Chonchol arrived in Cautín in early January. On January 22, CORA announced the first expropriations in the province. Twenty-three farms were expropriated, five in Lautaro County. On February 8, another illegal takeover occurred in Lautaro. The Santa Ana farm belonging to Pablo Paslack Weber was taken over by a group of peasants belonging to the Revolutionary Peasant Movement. The farm had 580 hectares and forty-five BIH. A week later Chonchol went to Lautaro County and met with the peasants who were occupying farms. He promised them that more expropriations would take place and that the unemployed peasants (at least twenty-five percent of the work force) would be given top priority to become members of the cooperatives set up on the expropriated land. In a later statement to the press, he claimed that he had avoided twenty-five new takeovers in the county by promising more expropriations. Still, occupations continued. On February 15, just after Chonchol's visit to the county, the MCR took over the farm Puente Largo (456 hectares) and renamed it Che Guevara. On February 17, CORA in Temuco announced the expropriation of fifteen more farms in the province, five of which were in Lautaro County. The list included the Santa Ana farm which had been occupied only a few days earlier. The constant pressure from the peasants led to more and more expropriations.

The peasants chose new names for all the expropriated farms. A few were common names, such as the names of saints (Santa Clara, Santa

Inez); but most reflected the political view of the peasants who joined the new cooperatives. The peasants chose many of Mapuche heros (like Elicura). Soon people were speaking of Lautaro, Colo-Colo, Galvarino, and Caupolicán. The textbook figures who lived in the sixteenth century were reborn in the 1970s. Other names were not based on Mapuche history but on the peasant-landlord conflict. The Land for One Who Works It became the new name for what was before a farm called The Pines. The Victory of the Poor and Peasant Struggle went on the tax roles. Ideological concepts could now be measured in hectares. L. E. Recabarren, the founder of the Chilean Communist Party in the late 1920s, was the inspiration for yet another farm's name. One farm was called Elmo Catalán, named for a Chilean Socialist who had been killed in Bolivia while working with the Bolivian ELN (Che's guerrilla army). Another farm was called Arnoldo Rios, after the member of the MIR who had been killed by Young Communists in Concepción in December 1970 (see Map 2).

All these names were to have a short life. When the military overthrew Allende in 1973, most of the expropriated farms were returned to their former owners, and, of course, all the names were changed once again.

But few foresaw that in early 1971. Chonchol arrived in Temuco with a great deal of fanfare on January 4.[1] In a press conference he described the situation of the peasantry in Cautín, a situation he pledged to change. He explained that Cautín was Chile's fourth most populous province and that it produced 25 percent of Chile's wheat, 18 percent of its meat, and 24 percent of its milk.[2] More than half the population lived in the countryside. The Mapuches constituted 75 percent of the rural population but owned only 25 percent of the land. Chonchol spoke conciliatory words to the small and medium farmers. He explained that in Cautín a farm of eighty BIH had about 550 hectares. The provice had 23,296 farms between 1 and 100 hectares, 2,177 farms between 100 and 500 hectares, and only 250 with more than 550 hectares. Therefore, only 250 owners were subject to expropriation for excess size. Chonchol did not point out, however, that in Cautín many owners had several farms between forty and eighty BIH, and many others had farms in the name of their wives or husbands. Such farms, if they exceeded 80 BIH taken together, were also legally subject to expropriation. And of course, farms of under eighty BIH were subject to expropriation for poor exploitation.

Chonchol also announced that the Ministry of Agriculture was dedicating 10 percent of its budget to carry out an emergency plan in Cautín. The plan included massive expropriations, new housing, machinery to the reformed sector, new roads, and so forth.

1. Peasant rally in Lautaro during the March 1973 elections. The rally was organized by the Socialist Party and the MIR. A sign at the left reads "The bosses are responsible for the black market."

2. Mapuche woman on a reservation in Lautaro County harvests wheat by hand.

3. Typical Mapuche *ruca* (house).

4. Inside a *ruca* on the reservation, a Mapuche woman serves maté.

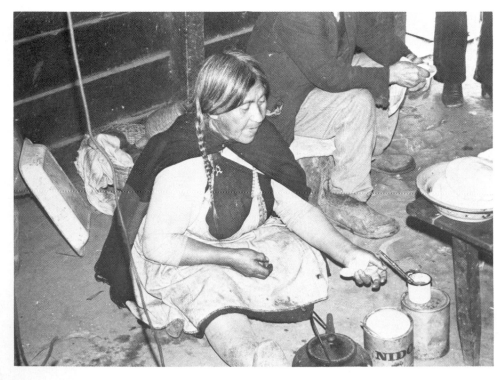

5. Mapuche mother and children, with chicken.

6. Election rally in Temuco in March 1973.

7. Election rally of the Revolutionary Peasant Movement (MCR). The sign says "Here we make the decisions." and "We won't take power with just good intentions."

8. Felix Huentelaf, leader of the Revolutionary Peasant Movement (MCR). He was imprisoned after the coup.

9. Minister of Agriculture Rolando Alarcón (Socialist Party) addresses the peasants in Lautaro County. He took refuge in the Swedish Embassy after the coup, was seriously wounded by a sniper, recovered, and finally went into exile.

10. Right wing demonstration in Temuco. The sign says "No to the Communist yoke."

11. On the way to a demonstration. The poster has a quote from Che Guevara: "We cannot afford the illusion of achieving victory without fighting."

12. Mapuche peasants gather at night for a land takeover.

13. Leftist urban workers demonstrating.

14. Leftist urban workers demonstrating.

15. Author relaxes with peasants in Lautaro County. The faces have been obscured for security reasons.

16. Mapuches in Lautaro County.

17. Older peasant applauds during election rally in Lautaro in March 1973.

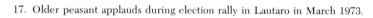

When Chonchol arrived, he brought with him the top government figures connected with agriculture. Together they formed the CORA Council, which had to pass on any proposed expropriation. Rather than have the Council in Santiago where it customarily met, now everyone was to be in Cautín. The CORA Council could meet on the spot, and the expropriation pace would go faster. Chonchol and the CORA Council stayed until the end of February, nearly two months.

The right wing also concentrated their forces in Cautín. Manuel Valdés, head of National Federation of Agricultural Employers, transferred the Federation's headquarters to Temuco, the provincial capital. Throughout Chonchol's stay, Valdés travelled throughout the province meeting with landowners and attempting to block the agrarian reform at every step.

On January 16 Valdés gave a press conference attacking expropriations for poor exploitation. He pointed out that the judgment that a farm was poorly exploited was made by government officials who were often biased in favor of expropriation. Valdés correctly anticipated that the government would expropriate many farms for poor exploitation, and he pointed out that the criteria for poor exploitation sometimes had as much a political as a technical nature. Whereas it was true that most large landholders in Cautín were very inefficient producers, Valdés was right when he claimed that the Allende government would be able to use the Agrarian Reform Law and the poor exploitation clause to its own advantage. The issue here was the same as in the case of the use of police to fulfill court orders. The laws provided a certain leeway. Throughout Chilean history the state had been run by the wealthy and the powerful, and now Allende was to use the state to favor the poor. Naturally he was going to take advantage of any flexibility the law allowed him.

On January 21 Valdés gave another press conference denouncing the illegal occupation. He claimed, again correctly, that most of the occupied farms were under the eighty BIH limit allowed by the Agrarian Reform Law. Valdés demanded that the occupied farms be returned to their owners. He denounced the government interventions as a method to force the landowners to sell out to CORA.[3]

Valdés could rant and rave, but momentarily power was on the side of the peasants. The same day that Valdés gave his press conference, he went out to Lautaro County on an inspection tour. While he and another prominent right-wing landowner were driving past an occupied farm, the peasants stopped his car, forced both men out, and searched them and the car for weapons. The peasants in Lautaro were so unruly that they were capable of humiliating in such a fashion the head of the Agricultural

Employer's Federation. There was nothing the right wing could do about it.

While Chonchol was expropriating and Valdés was criticizing, the Revolutionary Peasant Movement (MCR) held its second Congress in Temuco from February 13 through 16. The first Congress had been held unannounced in September 1970, but this time the event was well-publicized. Delegates from all over Cautín attended, and some came from other provinces. (The MCR had strength in other southern provinces, principally Valdivia.) The conference organizers excluded journalists from right-wing newspapers. The right wing was scandalized that this band of ignorant peasants and extremist guerrillas should be allowed to meet in public. The governor of the province, however, declared that it was a democratic country and the MCR could hold a Congress if it liked. The conclusions reached by the Congress were similar to the previous program of the MIR for the countryside. The principal points were: (1) expropriation of all farms over forty BIH; (2) expropriation of animals and machinery as well as land; (3) no reserve areas for the owners; and (4) no payment for the land. An additional point in the program was support for the newly founded Peasant Councils. The MCR also criticized the Minister of Interior Toha for his recent declaration concerning illegal occupations. Toha had threatened to have those who carried out illegal occupations arrested. If this were carried out on a local level, it would mean that the police would be ordered to throw the peasants off the land they had illegally occupied. A few weeks before Toha had removed a country governor in the province of Santiago for inciting the peasants to take over land.

The issue of police continued to be important in Lautaro County. By mid February thirty-six lawsuits had been begun by landowners against peasants. (The lawyer for the landowners in all thirty-six cases was Alfonso Podlech, the same man who would prosecute members of the MIR in the military trials in Temuco after the coup.) Judges had made rulings in twenty-three cases, and had ordered the arrest of 103 persons. Eighty arrest warrants had been issued. But so far the police had served very few. The governor of the county continued to refuse to order the police to carry out judicial order. In any case the police were not willing to go out into the countryside, against the wishes of the governor of the county, to arrest peasants who were armed and ready to fight the arrests. The arrest warrants did have some affect, however. Some peasant leaders began to come into town much less frequently, for fear of being arrested. They were relatively safe on the farms, but in town some of the local police might spot them and arrest them even without the governor's permission.

The failure to order the police to serve the warrants caused the landowners to be more than ever determined to remove county Governor Fernando Teillier. They had begun a legal suit to have him impeached, and the judicial system was beginning to yield results. On January 19 the Appelations Court of Temuco gave the Senate thirty days to rule on the impeachment of Teillier. If Congress failed to act, then the Appelations Court itself would rule on the question. The Congress did act. By a simple majority Congress voted to impeach Teillier and remove him from office for two years. The government promptly appointed another member of the Communist Party to the governorship. The new governor also refused to order the police to clear the peasants off the land. The right wing had won a political victory, but the peasants continued to occupy the land. And now that Chonchol had begun to expropriate the occupied farms, the arrest warrants were losing significance. The warrants were issued on behalf of the landlords who claimed usurpation of their property, but the new expropriations meant that they no longer owned the property in question.

The landowners were attempting to fight the illegal occupations through the courts, but the executive branch of the government thwarted the judicial. The expropriations carried out by CORA lent an air of legality to the peasant takeovers. The executive branch had effectively dispossessed the landowners of a certain proportion of their wealth, and the legal weapons usually used by the landowners to crush the peasantry were proving worthless. It was becoming clear to the landowners in Cautín, as it would later become clear to other sectors of Chile's ruling class, that it would be necessary to get rid of the executive branch of the government itself. That meant getting rid of the legally elected Popular Unity government. It would do no good for the landowners of Cautín to wait until new presidential elections in 1976. Six years without their land was too long a period. There was no guarantee that the government might not move against new investments the landowners might make outside of agriculture, and there was no guarantee that the Popular Unity might not win again in 1976 at the polls.

The only force that could get rid of Allende was the Armed Forces. The landowners understood this perfectly. In the south the local landowners and the officers of the military were usually close friends. The landowners turned to the military for help. But the military officers said that before they could intervene, a climate of chaos had to be created. One way the landlords could do this was to attack the peasants violently. Another was to disrupt the economy. Both methods would create a climate of disorder which would enable the military to step in.

Some landowners reacted to the expropriation by leaving the country. Those who stayed dedicated themselves to economic sabotage and right-wing terrorism with the eventual goal of helping to provoke a military coup. At first the landowners were alone in these tactics. Wealthy urban interests joined in at a slightly later date, after the Popular Unity government attacked *their* material interests.

The first example of landlord violence in Cautín occurred at Ruculán in December 1970 when a well-armed group drove out the peasants occupying the farm. Subsequent to the successful attack, the government initiated legal action against the landlords who participated. The defense counsel in these cases was Victor Carmine, a prominent right-wing representative to Congress. Carmine, who also owned land in Cautín, had already made himself famous during the Frei government for his vehement opposition to the agrarian reform.

In February 1971 Carmine made the news again. He and a friend cornered some government agricultural men who were helping some peasants with the expropriation of a farm near Loncoche in southern Cautín. Carmine drew a pistol and threatened the government employees. Finally he shot out the tires on their truck and left them stranded. The government began legal action against him, to no avail. Carmine spoke to the press the day after the incident. He asked that Cautín be declared an Emergency Zone due to the prevailing lawlessness. Declaration of an Emergency Zone would mean that the province would be under military control. This same demand had been expressed earlier by other spokesmen for the landowners. The long-run strategy of the landlords was clear: cause as much trouble as possible and call for military intervention.[4]

In April another incident occurred in eastern Cautín. A group of Mapuches had occupied the Carén farm. The occupation itself had occurred without violence. The peasants had built a shelter at the entrance to the farm, where they remained. The owner, Otto Grunner Friedly, was in his house on the farm.[5] The night after the takeover, more than ten friends of the owner arrived. They said they were going to a party which had been planned for some time. The Mapuches made the mistake of allowing them to enter the owner's house. At 5 A.M. Grunner and his friends attacked the Mapuches with pistols, rifles, shotguns, and sticks. The peasants fled. Several were wounded by bullets. The attackers managed to catch one peasant named José Curipe. They began to beat him severely with sticks and the butt of a shotgun. José Curipe's son, Juan

Curipe, fired a pistol at the men who were attacking his father. One of them, Rolando Matus, fell dead.

Rolando Matus became a hero to the right wing in Chile. The youth branch of the National Party organized a paramilitary group called Rolando Matus which was eventually to make itself notorious for its terrorism against the left.

Most of the violence, however, resulted in the deaths of peasants, not landlords. The next major incident occurred in May. The MCR occupied the South Brasil farm, and in the course of the occupation there was resistance. The farm's administrator, who lived on the farm, began firing a rifle at the invaders. The administrator was in his house and was shooting at a group of peasants who were hidden behind the side of the barn. A Mapuche named Juan Huilipán ventured out from behind the barn just at the wrong moment, and a bullet struck and killed him. The administrator finally gave up, the occupation was successful, and the farm was expropriated within a month. Its name was changed from South Brasil to Juan Huilipán.

The administrator resisted alone. The other peasants who were working on the farm joined with the takeover. Perhaps the administrator hoped to hold the peasants off until the owner and his friends could arrive. If this was his idea, he failed. The owner showed up days later.

No one else was killed until late October. At that time a group of forty peasants took over the Chesque farm in southern Cautín, near Loncoche. The peasants were part of the MCR. The Chesque farm had 830 hectares, but only fifteen were cultivated. There were only thirty-two head of cattle on the farm. The workers at Chesque had repeatedly asked CORA to expropriate the almost abandoned farm which measured almost 80 BIH. No results had been achieved, so that the peasants who worked on the farm joined with some of their neighbors to occupy Chesque. At the time of the occupation the owner was not at home. His wife and seventeen-year-old son were in the house. The occupation occurred at 4 P.M. The owner, Martin Doyharzabal, arrived at 4:45 P.M. in his truck. He broke through the barricade which the peasants had erected at the gate and advanced to within 200 yards of the second peasant barricade. Here he stopped and began firing a rifle at the peasants. After several rounds he returned to the town of Loncoche to get some help from his friends. At 5:30 P.M. he returned to Chesque with twelve friends, all heavily armed. The group included the mayor of Loncoche and other well-known landlords of the area. (One of them, Hernán Millan, had been with Victor Carmine during the shooting incident of the previous February). This group initiated a gun battle with the peasants who had only a few pistols and an old shotgun. Three policemen arrived shortly after the landlords. According to the peasants, they joined with the landlords in the shooting. After a short while the policemen left. At 8:30 P.M. peasant Moisés Huentelaf was shot in the back of the head and died instantly. Several other peasants were wounded.

The death of Moisés Huentelaf was well-publicized. The system of justice was seen at its worst in the case. Over twenty peasants were arrested and released immediately. No charges were brought against them.

Among the jailed peasants was Moisés Huentelaf's brother, Felix Huentelaf. Felix Huentelaf was to become one of the major leaders of the MCR and to hold several positions in the Provincial Peasant Council. The military captured him after the coup, and he was imprisoned and tortured.

The last confrontation in 1971 took place at the Huilio farm in western Cautín. On November 22 a group of Mapuches occupied a farm belonging to Antonio Navarrete. The peasants were working with an organization called Netuain Mapu ("We will retake the land"). Netuain Mapu was a Mapuche organization, organized along racial lines, and stressing the solidarity of Mapuches. It was organized mostly by Mapuche students in the city and was affiliated with the Revolutionary Communist Party (PCR), a Maoist party with little strength in Chilean politics, Netuain Mapu never became an important force in Cautín. One reason for this was that they were allied with a weak political force, the Revolutionary Communist Party, which could mobilize little national support to help the Mapuches in southern Chile. Another reason was that the strategy of organizing just Mapuches opposed Mapuche and white Chilean peasants. As the struggle between landlords and peasants grew stronger during the Allende government, most peasants preferred a strategy which united all the poor peasants, Mapuche or huinca, against the wealthy landlords.

A third reason for Netuain Mapu's lack of success was that they failed in several attempts to do just what their name called for, i.e., retake the land. The takeover at Huilio resulted in failure. The promised urban support did not arrive, and the unarmed peasants were unprepared for the landlord attack. The attackers were well-organized and used modern weapons, including automatic rifles. Two brothers named Cheuquelén were killed, and several other peasants wounded. One of the wounded was a pregnant woman, the wife of one of the Cheuquelén brothers, she was wounded in the stomach and lost her baby. No landlords ever had to go to jail for this crime, and the land remained in their hands.

The above-mentioned confrontations were the only ones where deaths resulted in Cautín Province in 1971, but many other similar confrontations occurred where people could have been killed.[6] The shootouts at the Pangal farm near Villarica and at the Boldos farm near Toltén, for example, could have easily resulted in death. Most of the incidents followed a similar pattern. Peasants occupied the land, and the landlords, using modern weapons, attacked them in an organized manner. If the peasants had sufficient guns, they fired back. If they didn't, they retreated. When these cases got to court, the judges absolved the landlords of any guilt and condemned the peasants.

These counterattacks by the landlords served several purposes. First, if they were successful, the landlords achieved the immediate goal of driving the peasants off the land. Second, the threat of landlord violence certainly frightened other peasants from taking over land. Finally, the continual pattern of violence helped create a climate of insecurity which was politically advantageous to the right.

While the landlords were organizing themselves, the peasants were also. In early 1971 the Peasant Councils were formed. The Peasant Councils were organized at a county level and united all the different categories of rural poor into one body. Small owners, temporary wage workers (afuerinos), permanent wage workers who also had rights to a small piece of land (inquilinos), and peasants in the newly formed cooperatives all joined together in the Peasant Councils. In those counties where any given sector of the peasantry was already organized, representatives from that organization would sit on the Peasant Council. This was the case in certain counties where strong rural unions had been developed during the Frei government. In Cautín, however, the rural unions were in most cases weak, and there were few other peasant organizations. As a result the Peasant Councils were first formed by political negotiations between political parties. The different parties in a county would have a certain amount of strength and would try to get a corresponding representation on the Peasant Council. The National Party was, of course, excluded because it had no peasant members. The Christian Democrats sometimes were excluded and sometimes admitted, depending on their local strength and their attitudes in the past toward the land reform. The Peasant Councils were usually formed by the parties of the Popular Unity government and the MIR.

It was planned that, once the Peasant Council was formed, the county would be divided up into sectors. Each sector would hold public meetings and elect representatives. These representatives would then form the new Peasant Council, democratically elected by the peasantry. In practice it later turned out that few county Peasant Councils were actually ever chosen this democratically.

The Peasant Councils were an idea of the Popular Unity government. The government planned a National Peasant Council which would eventually be made up of delegates from Provincial Peasant Councils, the latter being made up of delegates from the County Peasant Councils. The County Peasant Councils would be made up of representatives of already existing peasant organizations. The Popular Unity government had no clear idea what all these councils were to do, except that they were to represent the organized poor peasantry against the landlords. Some saw them as some kind of peasant soviet in revolutionary Chile. Their relationship to the government was not spelled out.

On December 21, 1970, Allende signed a decree setting up the National Peasant Council. When Chonchol went to Cautín, he began setting up both County and Provincial Peasant Councils. As it turned out, the National Peasant Council and many Provincial Peasant Councils soon fell apart because they had been formed from the top down.

In Lautaro the Peasant Council was formed on January 16 with a mass mobilization. It was the first County Peasant Council formed in Chile. On a bright summer day about two thousand peasants marched into the town of Lautaro. Some formed columns and shouted slogans:

Allende, Allende, the people will defend you!

Luciano, Guevara, the countryside is preparing![7]

Peasant, be alert, the reactionaries are watching!

Many of the peasants carried their tools. Banners and flags were common. Some supported the Popular Unity government, others specific political parties. The red flags with the yellow hammer and sickle represented the Communist Party. The red and black flag of the MIR, copied from the flag of the Cuban July 26th Movement, was perhaps the most common.

The peasants gathered in the town square, filling it. Then the speeches began. A member of the Communist Party spoke, then a member of the Radical Party. Then Adrian Vasquez spoke. Vasquez was a member of the Socialist Party and also the head of INDAP, the government agricultural agency which had the principal responsibility of attending to the needs of the small owners. Finally a representative of the MCR spoke. He was a local peasant. He said, among other things, that Che Guevara was the inspiration for the Peasant Councils. He stressed that the Peasant Council would be an organization which was independent of the government, an organization which would play a fundamental role in the carrying out of the agrarian reform. The image presented by the peasant from the MCR was of a Peasant Council that would lead the government agricultural bureaucracy and give it political direction.

Others had different views. Vasquez probably also hoped that the Peasant Council would become a powerful revolutionary voice of the peasantry, that it would keep a watch on the agricultural bureaucracy, and that it would make sure that the agrarian reform moved forward at a rapid pace. On the other hand the representatives of the Communist Party and the Radical Party probably hoped that the Peasant Council would be a fundamental support of the government and would assist (not lead) the agricultural bureaucracy in carrying out the agrarian reform. The differences between the views of Vasquez and the MCR, on the one hand, and the Communist and Radical parties, on the other, were not so marked when the Peasant Council was first founded. Later they would become much clearer.

All four groups (Communist, Radical, Socialist, MCR) had come together to decide on the representation of this initial Peasant Council. Each group was given the opportunity to select representatives on the council as long as they were poor peasants. The MCR was given the right to pick the majority of the new council members because it had predominant influence in the area and because the Socialists gave their support to the idea. Most of the peasants on the council ended up either being small owners or members of the new cooperatives. Most were Mapuche. There were about fifteen members. Two delegates who were Communists came from the local Communist rural labor union (Luis Patrián), which was affiliated to the provincial Recabarren Federation.

The small number of delegates from the rural labor unions was not surprising. The rural unions were weak in Lautaro County to begin with. The stand taken by the Christian Democratic and Communist unions against the illegal takeovers only made the situation worse in a county where most of the peasant movement was involved in the takeovers. The provincial Recabarren Federation had spoken out against the illegal occupations on numerous occasions. The Christian Democratic Union in the county had even organized a demonstration against the takeovers. El Luchador union, which was Christian Democrat, held a demonstration in the town of Lautaro on January 13, only three days before the formation of the Peasant Council. The demonstration was in repudiation of the illegal occupations and in favor of a worker (an inquilino) at the Three Pastures farm who was against the takeover there. This one worker, who was a permanent worker on the farm and who had access to land and pasture there, supported the old owner of the farm, Taladríz. The Christian Democratic labor union was glad to come to his aid because political capital could be made from the situation. Here was a worker on the now famous Three Pastures farm who was against the takeover. The Christian Democrats thereby had found a perfect way to blame the takeovers on leftist extremists who were not really supported by the peasantry. In fact this one worker at the Three Pastures farm was in a relatively privileged position. As an inquilino he had a permanent job and could harvest his own crops on a small piece of land. Even given his privileges, however, he was essentially a poor peasant who did indeed side with the landlord. This was an unusual situation. Most inquilinos joined the takeovers of the farms where they worked, as they had in the case of Rinconada. The Christian Democrats in this one case had found an exception, and they made the most of it. A small number of peasants, about one hundred, gathered on January 13 in Lautaro to support the inquilino at Three Pastures and to repudiate the illegal occupations. The unpopularity of this position was evidenced by the small number of participants in the demonstration. Three days later over 2,000 peasants would demonstrate in favor of the takeovers.

As a result of this attitude by the Christian Democrats, the local left-wing parties in Lautaro simply chose not to invite anyone from the local Christian Democratic peasant union to join the Peasant Council. This same exclusion took place in most of the other County Peasant Councils in Cautín. In some counties where honest peasants, who had fought the landlords, were also Christian Democrats, there was no objection to their membership in the Peasant Council.

In some counties landlords took over the Peasant Councils. They used as their allies small landlords who posed as poor peasants. This occurred in Gorboa, Loncoche, and Pitrufquén counties. (To counteract this, a year later the Cautín County Peasant Council decided that only those who personally worked their land and who did not hire any permanent workers to help them could be members of the Peasant Councils.)

In Lautaro the County Peasant Council drew up a list of unemployed peasants in the area. These peasants were given preference for membership in the new cooperatives to be formed on the expropriated farms. The Peasant Council was placed in charge of assigning the unemployed to the cooperatives. The Council also tried to play a role in determining which farms would be expropriated. A list of farms that the Council considered ripe for expropriation was drawn up by the Council and submitted to CORA. CORA would then argue that only certain farms could be legally expropriated according to the Agrarian Reform Law. The Peasant Council would argue that, unless the farms were expropriated, they would probably be taken over anyway. Some sort of compromise would then be arranged.

The Lautaro Peasant Council also began to develop sectorial meetings to elect a new council democratically. This was a difficult process because most peasants had no experience with public meetings or representative democracy. A beginning was made in 1971 when several sectorial assemblies were set up to meet on a monthly basis.

The Council also represented the members of the new cooperatives in their struggle against the government agricultural bureaucracy. Council members would go to CORA continually to complain about one thing or another. Since most peasants were in the countryside and had limited access to CORA offices in the town of Lautaro, the council worked as a channel for their complaints. The council had an office in town right next to the offices of CORA. However, the council had no money, and it was difficult for council members to get to town for meetings. The president and vice-president of the council came to town almost everyday. They did so with money donated by some of the new cooperatives or by getting a ride with some CORA official. Attempts were to be made in 1972 to develop a continual and reliable source of finances for the council.

The council also supported vigorously the five new takeovers which occurred in Lautaro County in 1971. Council members were frequently present at the site of the takeover and helped negotiate the expropriation of the farm with CORA.

The peasants of Lautaro County found, for the first time, a public voice. The Peasant Council spoke for them. Desperately poor, illiterate, unaware of the complexities of national politics, the peasants of Lautaro were used to the oppression of both landlord and government. Through the Peasant Council they could, at least momentarily, exercise a certain quota of real power. They could even speak as equals with the minister of agriculture. A meeting between Chonchol and the Peasant Council of Lautaro took place only a few days after the formation of the council. An interchange between the minister and a peasant illustrated the strength of the council. Chonchol announced the first expropriations of CORA, which were to become official the next day. Five farms in Lautaro were to be expropriated, but none of the occupied farms were on the list. A new member of the council objected:

We know the land backwards and forwards, and we ourselves want
to decide which farms are going to be expropriated.

Chonchol replied that the Agrarian Reform Law limited what the government could do, to which the peasant replied:[8]

How long are you going to keep telling us about the law, comrade?
The only thing that the law has done for us here is to make sure that
we were robbed, that we were starving to death, that our children
had no schools, while the landlords got richer and got more land.

Chapter 7

The Farm: 1972

Conflict and uncertainty had characterized the years 1970 and 1971 for the peasants at Elicura. The year 1972 was the first that could be described as a "normal" one for the cooperative. The day-to-day operation of the farm had finally become a well-known routine. Questions of prestige and power had been at least partially resolved; the peasants had some idea of where they stood in relation to each other, to the government, to the surrounding reservations. One important way to measure the success or failure of the land reform in Lautaro County is by looking at the everyday life of those who were most affected by it, the peasants themselves.

This chapter is divided into three parts, under the headings of Work, Wealth, and Society. The section on work discusses separately the work of the men and of the women. At Elicura the women did not work on production for the cooperative, and there were no women members of the cooperative. Throughout Lautaro County, and all Chile, only men were members of the cooperatives formed under the agrarian reform.

The section on wealth includes a discussion of the thorny problem of incentives for collective work on the cooperative. By 1972 the peasants at Elicura were making more income from their own private production than they were making from their salaries as members of the cooperatives. Since their salaries were more or less guaranteed, it was natural that any attempts to increase their wealth led to increased emphasis on private rather than collective production. This tendency was counteracted to some degree by threatened government sanctions and also by what might be called social incentives. Decreasing collective production might lead to a cutoff of credit by the state bank. It would also lead to a weakened government which could not control production in the reformed sector. A weakened government, as the peasants well realized, could be overthrown more easily, and in turn, could well lead to losing the farm at Elicura altogether.

The section on society discusses some of the new problems that the peasants at Elicura encountered in the move from individual and relatively isolated producers on the reservations to the cooperative. On the cooperative the peasants had to assume more responsibility to the group. Problems that had affected individuals on the reservation became more serious on the cooperative where they began to affect everyone.

Work: The Men

Every morning the twenty-five members of the cooperative gathered about 8 A.M. in the central area of the farm where the corral, barn, and warehouse were located. The foreman told people where to work during the day. The foreman was an equal, elected from among the twenty-five, and so he did not try to push people around. Every year new elections were held, and the foreman changed. In case everyone was really dissatisfied with the foreman, they could hold a special assembly and vote him out.

There were several categories of workers. The peasants had developed these categories naturally, based on the work that needed to be done and on their own experience.

There were four tractor drivers, a permanent position since tractor driving was a semiskilled job. At any given time two men would be driving; the other two would switch off with them a few months later. Occasionally someone would be demoted out of the tractor-driver category for having an accident which put a tractor out of commission.

There were cowherds and night watchmen, one of each. During the day one man was assigned to watch the cattle and move them from field to field. His duties were taken over at night by the night watchman. Both men had to keep count of the cattle to make sure none was lost or stolen. The night watchman usually was armed when he made his rounds. (The traditions of cattle stealing were very strong in Lautaro County.) In case a cow became sick, these men were to be sure it was reported. If one were available, a veterinarian would arrive. Both cowherd and night watchmen were rotated every month. The job of night watchman was avoided because nobody liked to stay up all night, especially in the cold, rainy winter. On the other hand, being cowherd left one with plenty of spare time to devote to other activities.

There were two officers—a president and a treasurer—who spent a lot of time working on the books, going to meetings in town, and going to the bank. The president was supposed to represent the cooperative in town, to argue with CORA about whether the cooperative could admit new members, or could get another tractor, or was too far in debt, and so forth. The treasurer was supposed to understand, as much as possible, the financial state of the cooperative; he was the one who paid out the monthly salaries and went to the bank to pay for fertilizers, seed, machinery, and other necessities. These two posts were critical ones for the cooperative. The men who held them had to be responsible. They had to be able to carry out business on time, to go into town and do what they were supposed to, avoiding the bars which were the town's main attraction for the peasant men.

The treasurer was perhaps the more important officer. During the three years of the cooperative's existence, the treasurer was the same man, Pancho. The other peasants reelected Pancho because he got the job done and because he had benefitted from what little training in accounting the peasants received from the government. It could not be said that he really understood the exact financial situation of the cooperative. Only the employees of the state bank in town understood that. The accumulation of interests, the inflation, the short-term and long term credits; all of these things were not well understood by anyone at Elicura. Pancho at least knew how much money was in the bank, when major payments were due, who to talk to in case a machine had to be repaired, and how to keep a rudimentary account of the salaries.

Except for officers, tractor drivers, cowherds, and night watchmen, everyone else was just a general laborer. Frequent tasks were separating potatoes, weeding potatotes, carrying sacks of fertilizer and seed to the tractors, fixing the fences, loading hay, harvesting the sugar beets, loading harvested wheat, building a new warehouse, and a multitude of other jobs that had to be done at the farm.

There was no nine-to-five routine at Elicura. Work was sporadic. Hours were shorter in the summer and winter and longer in the spring and fall. In the winter it rained a lot, and more time was spent indoors.

Work usually got underway after breakfast (bread and coffee). But first there was a short meeting. From 8 A.M. to 8:30 or 9 A.M. everyone discussed the jobs to be done that day, as well as throwing in a few comments about the state of the country, the amount of wine Guillermo had drunk the night before, and the possibilities of winning the next soccer game. It was a time for a lot of humor as well as a time when all

members of the cooperative were together and could make serious decisions about any matter that had come up. Conversation went on alterna-
tively in Mapuche and Spanish with a slight predominance of Spanish.
The four white Chileans, or huincas, understood only a little Mapuche.
After the meeting everyone went to their separate jobs.

Work went on until lunch. Everyone who could went home for lunch,
which lasted about an hour. In the afternoon, the men went back to their
jobs without any general meeting. Work went on until around 4 or 5 P.M.
in the winter, 5 or 6 P.M. in the summer.

A major exception to these hours took place during the summer when
everyone went to milk the cows right around sunrise. Most Mapuche
peasants, despite their extreme poverty, manage to make a joke out of just
about anything, and frequently about each other. Milking was a superb
time for jokes, singing, and general carrying-on. After milking everyone
went home for breakfast, taking a pan of fresh milk, a real treat. In the
winter, when the cows did not produce, powdered milk was provided free
by the government. The powdered milk program was one of the Allende
government's most publicized and effective reforms. Like all the rest, it
was later annulled by the military dictatorship.

Another exception to the regular schedule occurred when it rained
heavily, as it did often in the winter. On those days work was restricted to
the inside. Potatoes could be sorted into larger and smaller sizes or
fertilizer could be stacked in the warehouse. But sometimes there just
was not any collective work to be done, and then the peasants simply
went home to work on their own chores. Hours also changed during
harvest time when work frequently extended late into the night.

Beside the work on the cooperative itself, the men at Elicura spent
some of their time working on land outside the farm. This usually meant
borrowing a tractor from Elicura on Sundays and working on a hectare or
two which was either owned by the peasant or sharecropped by him.
Almost invariably grain was grown on these plots and was then sold on the
market.

The men liked their work. They enjoyed being together, despite the
fact that they now had to put up with the barbed humor of the fellow
workers every day. They enjoyed gathering in the morning and deciding
together what needed to be done during the day. Pedro always came to
work smiling, and always found four or five good tricks to play on some of
the other men during the day. Since he was young and newlywed, he was
also a convenient target for laughter. (Sex plays a large part in Mapuche
humor.) The men had known each other for years, sometimes for decades.

They took pride in working together for themselves on the farm where many of them had previously worked for Schultz. It was theirs now, and it was up to them to make a success of it. They felt they could. They had grown up working the land, and they knew all there was to know about it. Now they could apply their experience to a big farm where they themselves were the masters.

Work: The Women

Although the women at Elicura were not officially members of the cooperative and did not work on production, they worked as hard as the men, in order to keep everyone fed and clothed and to take care of the children. Pedro's wife Amalia, for example, got up everyday at daybreak and chopped firewood to prepare breakfast. Usually she had to walk the half mile to the river to get water for drinking and for washing. Amalia washed dishes and frequently had to return to the river carrying huge bundles of clothes to be washed by hand. At lunchtime she returned to the house to prepare food once again. In summer, she might spend the afternoon in the garden, weeding the vegetables. In the winter, when it was frequently raining, she might bake bread. Another common winter task was weaving. The Mapuche women built their own looms and frequently got their wool from their own sheep. The women were responsible for the task of making heavy ponchos and blankets. A large poncho might take many months in the winter. Finally, in the evening, Amalia again prepared and served dinner, and then washed the dishes. After dinner it was usually the women who served the maté. Amalia had to make sure the water was kept at the right temperature and keep the maté circulating around the table.

Child care was another major task of the women at Elicura. This usually involved most work when the children were young since as they grew they were entrusted to the care of their older brothers and sisters. When they got to be about four or five years old, they went off to school for a few years. After that they began to work. But when the children were very little, the mother spent much time with them. All children were nursed, frequently until the next pregnancy. Before the Allende government, most women had their children in the countryside. Under Allende giving birth in hospitals became more common. It is likely that this trend has now been reversed since the military dictatorship has once again made health care unavailable to the poorer sections of the population.

In addition to all the above mentioned domestic tasks, the women were responsible for shopping, a major job. There was only one bus a day into town and sometimes when it passed Elicura it was already full. This meant that the women had to try to hitch a ride into town as best they could. If they were able to get the bus, when they arrived in town a group of merchants was always waiting at the bus stop to buy vegetables and chickens that the women had brought in from the countryside. Surrounded by screaming merchants, many women sold their produce on the spot rather than lug it around town. As a result the prices they got were very low. With the money they received they went through town trying to buy the necessary items like sugar, kerosene, maté, matches, detergent, and perhaps a knife, a broom, or some medicine. By late 1972 many items had become scarce and were available only occasionally at the stores. When they were available, those who were first in line had first chance to get them. The peasants therefore always took second place to the town dwellers who got to the stores earlier. The same thing happened with black-market goods. The peasant women did not have the necessary connections, or the necessary income, to compete with town dwellers for goods on the black market. These difficulties meant that shopping was a very trying task. Frequently women had to carry a small child around with them, at the same time trying to carry all their purchases. Most shopping was done by noon, and then the women had to wait until dusk in order to cram onto the one bus back to Elicura. The bus to Elicura in the evening was literally stuffed with people and packages. At times drunken men would take the places of women loaded with purchases and children, and huge arguments would erupt.

This brief summary can only begin to describe all the chores of the women, which ranged from making blueberry jam to butchering pigs. The men at the cooperative spent most of their time working on production for the cooperative. The women spent most of their time working on vital tasks which were necessary to support the men and the reproduction of labor power at Elicura.

The separation of the work of the men and the work of the women was not resented by the women. No one among either the men or women had sought to have women become members of the cooperative. The business of producing the crops of the farm was something that was traditionally done by the men (with the exception of the vegetable gardens). No one questioned it at Elicura, nor for that matter, did any of the peasants on other cooperatives throughout Chile. Such an idea was still a long way off in Chile. In the meantime, the women concentrated on more immediate problems. They were interested in having a say in how the cooperative worked, in those decisions the men made which affected everyone who lived at Elicura. They were interested in having a say about what the men did with their salaries, in making sure that this new steady income found its way to the purses of the women who did the shopping and not into the pockets of the men who all too often wasted it on wine.

Wealth

The peasants' monetary income was divided into two parts; the salary they received from the state every month, supposedly an advance taken out of anticipated yearly profits, and the money they made from selling their own private production. In 1972 the peasants at Elicura were making almost half of their monetary income from their private production.

The private production was divided into three categories. First in importance was the land held outside the farm. Despite continual encouragement from CORA and from all the leftist political parties, the peasants at Elicura (and the other cooperatives) had refused to abandon the land they had at the reservations. This was usually only a half or one hectare, but the peasants refused to give it up. That small piece of land had been their only source of livelihood before Allende's election, and the peasants felt that it was always possible that their new farm might be taken away from them if things took a sharp turn for the worse politically. In case a peasant, for whatever reason, could no longer work with the cooperative, he could always leave the farm and at least have something, no matter how small, to fall back on.

Almost all the peasants at Elicura had land of their own on the reservations. They frequently also worked someone else's land and received one-half of the crop.[1] Several peasants had added a few hectares to their personal possession during the land takeover at the Juan Catrileo Reservation in July 1970. This land they kept even after they joined the cooperative.

The land that was worked on the reservations was worked with the machinery of the cooperative. Frequently seed and fertilizer were obtained from the cooperative as well. In this way the peasants diverted some of the resources of the cooperative to their own personal production.

Beside the land outside the farm, each member of the cooperative at Elicura had rights to a half hectare on the farm itself. This land was used for a vegetable garden, and its products went for personal consumption. This custom arose because the land on the farm was close by. Vegetable gardens needed constant care. The land outside the farm, on the reservations, was dedicated to grain crops, and the production was often sold in town.

Finally, the members of the cooperative at Elicura also subtracted part of the collective wheat crop for personal consumption or sale. In 1972 about 25 percent of the collective wheat crop was taken by the peasants. This percentage was similar to the figure for other expropriated farms in the county. Like the right to a half hectare of land on the farm, this quota of the wheat crop was a recognized right, approved by the government.

The peasants at Elicura received almost as much monetary income from the sale of products they owned personally as they did from their salaries. In addition they had flour, vegetables, and some meat for personal consumption. Individual peasants were able to use the resources of the farm in order to produce wealth which they themselves personally owned. Such a situation, of course, meant that frequently there was less incentive to work hard for the cooperative. Why spend most of your energy on the oats crop when the oats will be sold to the government, and go to credit the cooperative bank account? The bank account was always in the red anyway, and the sale of products from the farm just sank more money into paying off the various debts which the peasants had with CORA. Some peasants fell into this kind of reasoning, and at some farms peasants even sold some of the cooperative production on the black market, pocketed the profits, and then told CORA that the crop had been worse than expected. Such behavior was the exception, not the rule. Most peasants, like those at Elicura, understood that it was their duty to work collectively and to sell the cooperative produce to the government, so that it would in turn be sold to the workers in the city at low official prices.

Another reason that the peasants at Elicura felt less incentive to work on collective production was that their salaries were practically guaranteed. Salaries did not necessarily correspond to the amount of work performed. Pancho was in charge of paying the men at Elicura. He went to the bank every month, brought the money back to the farm, and paid all the members of the cooperative. In theory each member of the cooperative was to receive the same minimum wage for each day worked. (All peasants in Chile in the reformed sector received the same wage.) At Elicura, Pancho paid everyone for the entire month, but ordinarily several days of the month people did not work. Pancho exerted no pressure through wages against those who did not work the full month. The pressure that *was* exerted was a joint pressure. The members of the cooperative as a whole would begin to criticize someone if he did not show up for work for an extended period of time. In the end everyone got two or three days a month off and was paid for it. Work ordinarily lasted five and a half days a week, with half a day off on Saturday. Sunday was frequently devoted to working the land that most peasants retained back on the reservations.

Salaries added to the debts owed by the cooperative. Elicura owed about $35,000 to CORA. There were long-term debts for the land, the buildings, and the new houses (twenty-five to thirty years). There were medium-term debts for the cattle and the tractors (seven and five years, respectively). Finally, there were short-term debts for salaries, seed, and fertilizer.

It was difficult to keep track of the finances. The galloping inflation which began in 1972 meant that debts had to be recalculated all the time. The value of the dollar continually changed; this, in turn, changed the prices of imported goods. No one knew, for example, exactly how much was owed for the tractors.

Despite these difficulties, some rough estimates can be made. During the agricultural year 1971–72 (May to May) the Elicura cooperative sold about $7,600 worth of products. Expenses for salaries, seed, fertilizer, machine repair, interest, and transportation of produce totalled about $11,600. Therefore, there was a net loss for the year of about $4,000 which was added to the debt owed to CORA. It had been expected that in their first years the cooperatives created through the agrarian reform would suffer a loss, so CORA was not too distrubed about the situation at Elicura. In the agricultural year 1972–73 (May to May) Elicura managed to break even, despite the difficulties caused by the right-wing sabotage of October 1972. (The lock-out by the truck owners caused delays in the arrival of seed and fertilizer during the planting season.) CORA expected that in the future Elicura would begin to show a profit which could go into paying some of the medium- and long-term debts. It would be a long time, however, before the peasants could see the profits coming back to them to be divided up among all cooperative members. As far as they could understand, the sale of the products of the cooperative went into paying a never ending debt. Their only material incentive to maintain production at Elicura was to guarantee that they would continue to receive their salaries. They understood theoretically that increased production would lead over the years to the repayment of their long-term debt to CORA, and that this was desirable. But in practice this knowledge had little effect on anyone's behavior. When the peasants at Elicura worked hard on cooperative production, it was largely from moral incentives. It was because they understood that increased production would help feed the workers in the city and would help defend the government against the right-wing "mummies." (*Momios,* literally mummies, was the word used to describe the reactionaries. It was frequently coupled with the word *pitucos,* to mean wealthy, spoiled reactionaries.) There was also a factor of pride. To some extent the peasants at Elicura took pride in their farm and wanted it to have a good reputation.[2]

The most important product of the farm was wheat. Wheat sales accounted for 46 percent of the value of sales. At Elicura the wheat yield in 1972 was about twenty quintales (100 kilograms = 1 quintal) per hectare, a respectable yield for the county. CORA estimated that the large private producers, who accounted for about one-third of the wheat in the county, had an average yield of about twenty quintales per hectare. The reformed sector, which accounted for about another third of the wheat planted in the county in 1972, had an average yield of eighteen quintales per hectare. Small owners (less than 100 hectares) planted the remaining third of the wheat in the county and had an average yield of about fourteen quintales per hectare. Of course the small owners were usually Mapuches who planted on the hilly and eroded land on the reservations and who used less machinery and less fertilizer.

The second most important product of the Elicura cooperative was cattle, which accounted for 20 percent of the total sales; then came potatoes, which accounted for 15 percent, and rape, a grain sold to make oil, which accounted for 10 percent.

The decisions about which crops to plant were made during negotiations between CORA and the peasants at Elicura. Each year in April, a plan was drawn up. The plan showed how many hectares of wheat would be planted where and outlined all the expenses of Elicura for the coming year. This plan was the guide for the state bank. The bank allowed credits only for expenses outlined in the plan. In practice there was some flexibility since strict adherence to the plan by the state bank might have meant disaster in cases where expenses had been seriously underestimated. Elicura had few serious conflicts with the state bank since their debts were not considered excessive and since their expenses usually conformed to the plan.

In April of 1972 an official from CORA arrived at Elicura and sat down with Pedro (the president), Pancho (the treasurer), and Guillermo (the foreman). Together they worked out the plan for the next year. This plan was later approved by the assembly of all cooperative members. By and large there was little friction between the CORA representative and the peasants concerning the plan. The peasants knew the land well, and the CORA representative knew the financial situation at the state bank and the needs for food production in the county. The only innovation in 1972 was the introduction of three acres of sugar beets. More production of sugar beets was essential as it became more difficult to import sugar due to the dollar shortage. Sugar beets were introduced on a large scale throughout Cautín in 1972. At Elicura they grew well, but the peasants harvested them too late and lost about half of the crop. The only other large mistake made in agricultural production in 1972 was the overestimation of the number of cattle the farm would support. Too many cattle were introduced, and in 1973 a significant number of cattle died from lack of pasture.

All in all, the peasants who joined the cooperative at Elicura enjoyed an increase in wealth. Although no hard figures are available, this author estimates that the income of a number of the cooperative was 30 percent higher than that of a small holder on the reservation. On the other hand the income of the average worker in the city in 1971 and 1972 was probably slightly higher than the peasant at Elicura. By 1973, however, with inflation eating away at the wage gains in the city and with food shortages severe, it is likely that the peasants at Elicura were benefitting from their individual food production and probably had about the same total income as a worker in the city.

Society

One of the most difficult things for the peasants at Elicura was learning to run the farm as a group. On the reservations the peasants had been accustomed to working individually, except on rare occasions when the men got together for a joint planting or harvesting (*mingaco*). But at Elicura, decisions were made by the group. Meetings were frequent. Once a month an assembly was held with a more formal atmosphere than the early morning get-togethers. Frequently a representative from CORA would attend, and the MIR organizer came from time to time. Theoretically official decisions were to be made at these assemblies, but the peasants often found themselves tongue-tied. The informal arrangement between one man and another, or between one family and another, the usual way of doing things prior to 1970, was replaced by the assembly. It took a long time before these meetings were relaxed enough so that everyone was willing to speak up. Even then, when the peasants made a decision, it was often ignored; and everyone went back to doing things as they wished, arranging deals with their friends. At the next assembly everyone would complain and vows would be made to abide by the collective decision. But this in turn was disregarded. The only enforcement mechanism was the pressure that the peasants themselves could put upon one another. Many preferred not to exert that pressure, not to interfere in the affairs of another. Such was the tradition on the reservation. It was difficult to change.

Only a minority of the workers at Elicura understood the necessity of breaking with tradition if the cooperative were ever to succeed. This minority was willing to speak up, to criticize others for failure to abide by the decisions of the group. For example, a decision was made for everyone to return the cooperative's tools to the tool shed. For months work was being left undone because no tools were in the shed. Everyone had them at their own house for personal use. A few men took the tools back right away, but the majority continued to use them at home. Two or three peasants took the initiative of criticizing those who did not bring back the tools. Only by continuous pressure were the tools finally brought back. This incident was relatively minor, but others were not. Pablo, the older man who in 1970 had wanted to divide the land and farm it individually, in 1972 began to rent out the cooperative's old thresher to the surrounding reservations, pocketing the profits for himself. He frequently took off work to do this. Such behavior, if allowed to continue, would certainly have destroyed the cooperative. At Elicura the peasants were able to bring Pablo into line. By continual criticism and by finally bringing it up in assembly, they forced him back to work and made sure the old thresher was used by the cooperative as a whole. Other farms simply disintegrated, and the collective work dwindled to almost nothing. This was true for only about three or four farms out of forty-two.

One farm, which was expropriated during the Frei government, came apart completely. A minority of the peasants withdrew to part of the farm, built houses, and farmed that part collectively. The majority divided up the rest and worked it individually. The treasurer of this cooperative had refused to pay the salaries of the minority, so intense was the animosity between the two groups. CORA was unable to arrange a truce, and the de facto division of the farm was allowed. At yet another farm, expropriated during the Allende government, the peasants spent most of their time drinking. The government paid the salaries, and the peasants farmed subsistence crops and drank. The salaries were temporarily cut off by the state bank, promises of reform were made, but the situation did not improve. This went on for several years. At that farm there were no peasants who had the necessary political consciousness and who could exercise the necessary leadership to improve the situation.

Such cases were unusual, but they did indicate the possibilities. The change from small subsistence farmers to members of a cooperative was a big one, especially where there were few material sanctions for refusing to work cooperatively. The farms where there were MIR organizers (such as Elicura) had an advantage because the Miristas helped to develop the political consciousness of the peasants. But even some of these farms suffered from temporary breakdowns of collective spirit.

One factor which helped maintain the collective spirit on the cooperative farms was that everyone knew each other quite well. In fact in Lautaro County at any given cooperative farm, many of the peasants were related. This was true at Elicura. Elicura was made up of peasants from just two or three reservations, and most Mapuche reservations were just two or three big families. Pancho, the treasurer, was the cousin of Pedro, the president. Pancho's two older sisters were married to Pablo.[3] Pancho's sister was married to Guillermo, the foreman. The only people at Elicura who were not somehow related were some of the huincas who had worked on the farm before the takeover. But even some of the huincas had married Mapuches.

The fact that everyone was related meant that the social life at Elicura followed a pattern similar to social life on the reservation. But unlike the reservation, at Elicura everyone lived practically on top of each other, at least by Mapuche standards. Instead of living a quarter of a mile from their neighbors, as they had on the reservation, at Elicura most peasants lived only several hundred feet apart. In addition to living much closer, frequent meetings meant that everyone had to see everyone else. The principal of staying out of your neighbor's business was abandoned.

The women especially were affected. They began to visit each other with much more frequency and by 1972 had even begun to meet with each other in groups, informally and infrequently, but nevertheless meeting. The more frequent contact among the women was a real departure from Mapuche tradition, and some of the men felt threatened by it. During one assembly one of the men suggested that the women were plotting to take part of the men's salary. Although the idea was rejected, a large number of the men agreed that it was quite possible. The men were paid cash every two weeks and then turned a certain part of the money over to their wives for shopping, usually after much haggling. The men were afraid that the women were planning to get paid a part of the salary directly.

It was pointed out earlier that the women at Elicura never took part in production for the cooperative. Most women at Elicura were Mapuche, and the Mapuche tradition left no place for women in community affairs. Nevertheless, the women at Elicura were strong. They frequently were the force that kept the household together or managed to steer their drunken husbands safely home from a weekend soccer game. Although the women spoke less, when provoked they could more than hold their own in arguments with the men.

Furthermore, although Mapuche tradition excluded women from major community decisions, it also granted them certain rights. For example, traditionally, Mapuche women on the reservations have owned and inherited land just as have the men. They could have the land worked however they liked, and they could keep the profits they earned. They also could will the land to anyone they liked when they died. These rights, concerning the most important property owned by the Mapuche, indicate the Mapuche women have had a share of the power despite male domination.

Both the CORA representatives and the Miristas attempted to get more women involved. One Mapuche woman joined the Peasant Council and became a strong leader. She frequently would be in the lead at demonstrations, or she would demand more responsibility from the other representatives on the council, denouncing drunkenness on the part of one or another representative, or she would make long trips to other cities to buy textiles to be distributed by the Peasant Council, and so forth.

The representative from the MIR was able to recruit several of the younger Mapuche women into the party in Lautaro County, and they were some of the strongest and most disciplined members. They travelled throughout the county speaking to other women, attempting to form women's clubs at several different locations. Such women were exceptions, but they prepared the ground for breaking down the tradition of male chauvinism so common among the peasantry and especially among the Mapuche.

The conflict between men and women at Elicura was not the only point where traditions were strained. Relationships between huincas and Mapuches were strained as well. Several of the huincas were old employees at the farm. As inquilinos, they had been permanently employed and had enjoyed special privileges. Unlike temporary laborers, they had had their own little plot of land and their own grazing rights. In exceptional cases they could even increase their own production and begin to amass some capital. Usually in Lautaro County inquilinos were huincas, and temporary laborers were Mapuches. This had been true at Rinconada as well. Now the inquilinos were part of the cooperative. The were in a minority, and those who had once been temporary laborers now enjoyed the same rights as they did. Most members of the cooperative (twenty-one out of twenty-five) were Mapuche. The old employees at times resented the newcomers. The Mapuches in turn at times resented the huincas. One particular huinca, named Jaime, never was able to accept the Mapuches as equals. When things got tougher, as they did in 1973, Jaime would at times long for the good old days when Schultz ran the farm. Jaime never allowed this feeling to surface openly. It was only when he was very drunk that he would speak in confidence of the problems with the Mapuches at the cooperative. He also never considered leaving Elicura to seek employment with a large landowner. Despite his grumblings, Jaime was considered a peasant like everyone else, and the bitterness between him and the others often melted into friendship at the end of the harvest or after several cups of wine at a soccer game.

Wine itself played an important role at the cooperative. In a country where alcohol consumption is one of the highest in the world, the Mapuche population is known for consuming more alcohol than most Chileans. Occasionally some of the peasants at Elicura would lose a week of their salary at a time by spending it on wine during a long drinking session. Usually, the day after payday, almost everyone at Elicura would load up on the flatbed behind a tractor and go into the town of Lautaro. The women would shop for kerosene, matches, detergent, and perhaps batteries for the radio, but the men would spend a lot of time in the bars. Wine was also bought in two-and-a-half-gallon jugs to take back to the cooperative where for the next few days work was mixed with a good deal of partying. Excessive alcoholic consumption was one of the problems first attacked by the organizer from MIR in late 1970. Because of his influence, drinking at Elicura was a lot less heavy in 1972 than it had been in late 1970. Still, it frequently led to both financial ruin and to bitter, sometimes violent, quarrels. Most of the serious fights, which occurred once every month or two, took place after heavy drinking. Usually a combination of luck and the physical limitations of the combatants limited the number of serious injuries. Members of the cooperative, however, did get involved in several drunken fights at soccer games at other farms, and once or twice suffered knife wounds as a result.

Serious physical injury usually meant a trip to the hospital. Under Allende, health care for the peasants improved. One of the most important steps was the program of free milk for small children. Every month at Elicura the sacks of powdered milk would arrive, and the women from the farm and from the surrounding reservations would gather to receive it. Each woman was guaranteed a liter of milk a day for small children, which meant that the children at Elicura were able to get milk all year. Such an improvement in their diet went a long way to reduce disease among children. Every few months a nurse would come with the milk and would see patients. Serious cases were sent to the hospital. Such rural health care was unknown before Allende and has been eliminated since. Those doctors who actively supported rural health care were attacked by the military junta. For example, Arturo Hiller was a doctor in Puerto Saavedra, a small town on the coast of Cautín Province. He was very active in helping bring medical care to the peasants, often accompanying the ambulance on trips to the countryside at any hour of the day or night. After the coup the military murdered him in Temuco.[4]

Many peasants at Elicura did not go to the hospital in town. Despite the fact that the hospital had been expanded, it was still overcrowded. There was only one ambulance, and it was very difficult to get it to go out to the countryside. At night it was impossible. Instead, peasants had to go on the bus. Once arriving at the hospital, the peasants often spent a whole day waiting for treatment and then were told that there were no doctors available and that they would have to come back the next day. This became expensive because a bus trip in and back cost about one-third of a day's salary. A crowded bus trip was not the best thing for a sick person anyway. Because of these problems, many peasants did not take advantage of the free health care at the public hospitals. It was possible to get around the problem by getting an appointment in advance, but such appointments often had to be made four or five months ahead of time.

Problems of overcrowding were aggravated by the attitude of much of the staff of the hospital in Lautaro. The staff, especially the doctors, treated the Mapuches with contempt and herded them around like so many animals. All four doctors at the hospital were known supporters of the right wing. This situation led to bitterness between the peasants and the hospital, culminating in the violent incident which took place in May of 1972, to be described in the next chapter.

There was an alternative to the hospital. Near Elicura there was a *machi*, or medicine woman, to whom many of the Mapuches went. She applied traditional herbal medicines, and those were frequently successful in healing wounds. Nevertheless, she charged as much or more than a private doctor in town. Despite the prices, many peasants at Elicura preferred the machi to the hospital.

Serious wounds were not the major medical problem at Elicura. The major problems were tuberculosis and diarrhea. Tuberculosis could have been brought in check only by a sustained program for which the Allende government lacked sufficient funds. Perhaps as many as a fifth of the peasants at Elicura had tuberculosis. Diarrhea was even more serious. Common among small children, it led to dehydration and in many cases, death. It was a product of poor diet and unhygenic conditions. Infant mortality among the peasant children at Elicura was very high, about 30 percent. The Allende government tried to carry out an educational program against diarrhea in the countryside, but the problem was so big that it had only just begun to be confronted when the coup occurred.

Mapuche women have a lot of children. The women at Elicura were no exception. An average family had four or five children, and frequently several more had been born but had died. It was considered natural for a woman to go on having children while she was healthy. Birth control was a rumor that was just beginning to be discussed at Elicura. It was poorly understood and probably frowned upon by public opinion although many women showed a lively interest in it. A few women had been in the larger cities of Chile for several years where they had worked as maids or in factories. There they had learned about birth control.

In general the influence of the city is beginning to erode a lot of traditional Mapuche customs. Although most of the peasants at Elicura could not read, almost all families had small transistor radios which continually bombarded them with the ideas of the city. Most peasants at Elicura still believed that spirits existed, traditional spirits like *witranalhue* or *anchimallen,* which were powerful and dangerous.[5] Traditional musical instruments like the *trutruca* were present at Elicura. But the trutruca was used rarely and took second place to the guitar and the harmonica. The traditional Mapuche dance, the *nillatun,* was celebrated very infrequently, but all Mapuches could and did dance the traditional Chilean *cueca.* And the spirit witranalhue was less of a concern than the fascists of Fatherland and Liberty who already in 1972 were shooting at the peasant houses from speeding cars at night.

The change from the traditional Mapuche life and customs, already begun on the reservation, was furthered by the move from the reservation to Elicura. At the cooperative frequent contact with CORA and with the MIR organizer led to new knowledge for the peasants. But there were some important changes in production on the reservation during the Allende years. Credit was made available to the small owner. Deliveries of seed for wheat in Lautaro County to small owners went up six times between 1969 and 1972. Fertilizer deliveries increased three times. In addition a tractor pool was created in Temuco, and small owners were able to hire a tractor at low rates though there were few tractors and not everyone was able to take advantage of this service. The peasants at the reservation had to form a committee in order to qualify for credits, and in this way CORA encouraged the small owners to organize. Despite these improvements, no effective cooperatives, either of production or marketing, were set up on the reservations, and the standard of living there improved only slightly during the Allende years. Much work was still done with handmade wooden plows on eroded slopes. Land remained extremely scarce on the reservations, and unemployment was high. The standard diet was still beans and noodles, homemade bread, and abundant maté. Despite the massive flow of unemployed peasants from the reservations to the new cooperatives formed on the expropriated land, there were still hundreds of unemployed peasants on the reservations in Lautaro County.[6]

The continued poverty on the reservations and the improved life on the new cooperatives led to friction. The reservations surrounding Elicura both admired and were jealous of the cooperative. They respected the workers at Elicura because they had been bold enough to take the land. But now that the members of the cooperative were slightly more wealthy and had steady employment, they sometimes took advantage of the people on the reservation. For one thing they kept the land they had regained during the fence-runnings. In one sense this land served as a kind of insurance against the possibility that the cooperative might some day be taken away from them. On the other hand they were keeping land which was sorely needed by others at the reservation. At the cooperative the workers had salary and had a small plot for themselves. On the reservations many were landless.

Also, members of the cooperative began to hire unemployed men from the reservations to do work at the cooperative. For example, Guillermo would hire someone to chop firewood for him. Guillermo would pay daily wages which were half of what he himself was paid for working a day at the cooperative. Such was the unemployment in the area that Guillermo could get away with paying such wages while his own wages were guaranteed by the government to remain at a certain minimal level.

Members of the cooperative would also sometimes charge money for allowing the reservations to use machinery from the cooperative. One of the tractor drivers at Elicura caused a lot of resentment because he charged money to people on the road to town when they asked for a lift on the empty flatbed. Another example was Pablo's attempt to charge high rates for use of the thresher. At one point members of the committee formed on the three reservations surrounding Elicura refused to attend a meeting with CORA and the cooperatives because they were so mad at the people at Elicura.

The desperate economic situation was of course the cause of the strain between the reservations and Elicura. The organizers from the MIR continually pointed out that the agrarian reform had not been completed in 1972, that there were many unemployed on the reservations, and that many large farms had not been expropriated. They attempted to promote unity between the cooperatives and the reservations by enlisting the help of members of the cooperatives for new land takeovers which benefitted the unemployed on the reservations. At Elicura the MIR organizer continually warned against forgetting those less fortunate who still had no land on the reservations. Such talk was not in vain. Many peasants at Elicura helped out in land takeovers in 1972 and also in 1973 when it was more dangerous. There were also some peasants at Elicura, a very few, who said that they had given up the use of their land on the reservations in order to help out someone who had no land. If necessary, they would be able to go back to that land because they still retained ownership. But they allowed others to work it and keep the profits.

It could be said that the peasants at Elicura were more willing to risk their lives in a land takeover in order to help others than they were to give up their land on the reservations. The attitude of the peasants at Elicura was that land takeovers were risky, but also that they were quite a bit of fun. After all in most cases no one got hurt. A cow was slaughtered and eaten in celebration and more land was available for the unemployed on the reservations. Of course there were cases of gun battles and right-wing attacks, but the peasants were brave when it came to personal danger. They were militant when it came time to take land away from those who had exploited them. They were conservative, however, when it came to their own land on the reservations. Tradition weighed heavily on the peasants at Elicura, and its effects were contradictory. Generations of poverty had bred revolutionaries, but the dependence on scarce land for subsistence had bred conservatives—within the same people.

Chapter 8

The Area: 1972

In 1972 the right wing in Lautaro County grew more powerful while the peasantry was only able to maintain its previous strength. One of the reasons for this was that the right wing was more unified than the left. Many of the major incidents in 1972 in Lautaro County reflected the division among the left, a division that would grow stronger over time.

The division of the left was both theoretical and practical. On the theoretical level one part of the left believed that socialism could be achieved gradually through the electoral process. The idea was to gain more and more votes and eventually be able to control the state; not just the executive branch, but also the Congress, the courts, and most important, the military. During the process there would be strong tensions in the military, but the military would not intervene if the left maintained itself within the framework of the Chilean constitution and law and order. This sector of the left believed that the legal framework was broad enough so that substantial reforms could be carried out through the executive branch and that these reforms would gather enough popular support so that eventually the left would gain total control of the state. At that point it would be possible to attain socialism. These views predominated in the Popular Unity government and were most consistently presented by the powerful Communist Party.

On the other hand, part of the Socialist Party and two smaller parties (the MAPU and the Christian Left) dissented from these views and argued against them within the government coalition. The MIR also disagreed and fought against these views from outside the Popular Unity. These forces believed that extensive reforms would result in a military intervention to overthrow Allende and that a peaceful road to socialism was impossible. The right wing would never permit the left gradually to get control

140

of the state but would instead sabotage the economy and urge the military to take over the government. A military takeover would also be supported by the CIA and the U.S. government. This perspective claimed there were two choices: (1) sacrifice the reforms of the system; (2) deepen the reforms and prepare the supporters of the left to resist a military coup. The former choice was unacceptable. The latter choice implied agitation among the rank-and-file soldiers to divide the military and preparation of the workers and peasants who supported Allende for an armed confrontation.

By 1972, as the political situation deteriorated and tensions in the military increased, these different perspectives led to two different practical tactics. On the one hand the Communist Party and the majority of the Popular Unity coalition called for a retreat. It was time to consolidate the gains won. Further advances would result in a military coup. Popular mobilizations for further social change were to be discouraged. On the other hand part of the Socialist Party, the MAPU, the Christian Left, and the MIR called for deepening the reforms, encouraging further popular mobilizations to call into question more and more of the existing system.

This is a broad description of a situation which was extremely complicated, but as a rough outline it is accurate. In this chapter we will try to describe how these divisions weakened the left in Lautaro County in 1972 and how the correlation of forces changed in favor of the right. (It must be pointed out that, although cleary discernible in 1972, the differences within the left were not yet so clearly defined as they would be in 1973.)

One point needs clarification. The Mapuche peasants did not yet clearly favor one line or another in these disputes. The peasants looked to their immediate interests furthering the land reform and improving the reformed sector. The peasants had learned a lot in two years of agrarian reform, and they would press their demands further. These demands coincided with the practice of one part of the left, then the peasants would support that part of the left. If the demands of the peasants were met by both of the political lines in contention, then the peasants would remain neutral. The criteria for the support of the peasants was a practical one, and the different political lines of the left would be judged by their practical consequences. This was only logical. In this chapter we will try to show how the practical needs of the peasants fitted into the framework of the political struggle going on nationally.

The number of expropriations decreased slightly in 1972 as did the number of illegal occupations. CORA expropriated fifteen farms in the county, compared to twenty-one in 1971. Of these the peasants had occupied only four. In many cases CORA expropriated farms after lengthy negotiations which resulted in the landowners being granted a reserve area. This occurred in six of the fifteen cases, reflecting a lack of peasant pressure at the farms in question.

There was some violence at the four occupied farms that were eventually expropriated. At the Fernando Teillier farm (named after the impeached county governor) there was shooting during the occupation, but no one was seriously hurt. At the Camilo Torres farm, isolated right-wing attackers shot at peasant barricades from speeding cars in the weeks following the takeover. But most of the violence occurred during three unsuccessful occupations when the right wing organized well-coordinated attacks against the peasants. In all cases the peasants retreated in the face of overwhelming force. The right wing organized caravans of between twenty and thirty cars, carrying sixty or seventy people, all armed. The attackers approached shooting. The incidents occurred on February 17 and 18, and May 17. On February 17 at the Santa Ana farm the police were present when the incident took place but did not try to intervene. The police officer in charge was a friend of the attackers and had informed them previously about the strength and position of the peasants.

The attack on May 17 at the Muco Bajo farm had serious consequences. Five peasants were wounded, three seriously. All ended up in the hospital. Others were wounded but preferred not to go to the hospital, afraid of arrest. The attackers arrived at 3 P.M. in about twenty vehicles and began firing one hundred yards from the entrance to the farm. After the peasants fled, so did the attackers. They left a foreman in charge of the farm, and he was arrested by the police. The peasants were able to identify many of their assailants, but none were ever jailed. The foreman also went free.

These incidents indicated that the right wing had reached a new level of organization. The fascist paramilitary group called Fatherland and Liberty (Patria y Libertad) was surfacing in Lautaro County, spreading its slogans on the walls of the town. Its symbol, which looked like a cross between a swastika and a spider, showed up on several public buildings. Its members were mostly wealthy young men, sons of the landowners. They used their money to buy arms and communications equipment and, if necessary, to hire thugs to do their dirty work. In early 1972 in Lautaro County, Fatherland and Liberty was still an immature organization made up of well-to-do young people playing with politics. Nationally, however, the organization was almost certainly manipulated (and possibly created) by the CIA, which had important future plans for the fledgling terrorists.[1]

In Lautaro, Fatherland and Liberty joined the leaders of the National

Party to carry out paramilitary operations. The confrontations of February and May were to be followed by the more serious national offensive of October when terrorism and sabotage became the order of the day.

Meanwhile the peasants were busy attending to other matters. A major problem arose in March, and the peasants in the reformed sector mobilized to solve it. The problem was a salary cutoff. The state bank had decided that the debts of a number of cooperatives were too high, and they stopped the payment of salaries to about one-third of the cooperatives in the county. The peasants at the cooperatives affected believed that they were not at fault for the high debts and low production. They felt that they had been working hard. They claimed that delayed deliveries of machinery, seed, and fertilizer had caused problems the previous spring and that CORA was responsible. Furthermore, they wanted CORA to move faster on expropriating land. The huge four-farm La Peña complex, which had belonged to the Velasco brothers, had been occupied by the Revolutionary Peasant Movement. The peasants renamed the farm Camilo Torres, and it was to employ forty or fifty peasants on about 1,600 hectares. But CORA had still not expropriated it, and in the meantime right-wing attacks were increasing. Other farms in the county had been expropriated months before, but the peasants had been unable to take possession of them due to bureaucratic slowness.

Annoyed by this situation, in early April about sixty or seventy peasants, led by several Miristas, occupied the offices of CORA in Lautaro at 9:30 A.M. At the same time another sixty or seventy took over the CORA offices in the provincial capital, Temuco, about twenty miles away. The occupations continued until about 9 P.M. at night and ended in success for the peasants.

The major decisions took place in Temuco. There the peasants met with the heads of CORA in Temuco and Lautaro. The demands made were an end to the salary cutoff and to the bureaucratic delays in expropriations. The CORA chiefs informed Santiago of the situation. Perhaps the top officials in Santiago were particularly sensitive to peasant demands because of the recent mass movement in the southern province of Nuble where over 300 farms had been occupied.[2] In any case in the late morning a phone rang in Temuco. Adrian Vasquez, the vice-president of INDAP (one of the major government agricultural agencies) and an important figure in the land reform program, was calling. Vasquez was a member of the Socialist Party and a strong supporter of the Peasant Councils and peasant mobilizations in general. His call was answered by one of the Miristas, and negotiations began. It should be kept in mind that although the office takeovers resulted from the anger of the peasants, they were led by the MIR. It was the MIR organizer who helped phrase the peasants' demands and who negotiated them with the government. Again, there was no evidence of manipulation here. The peasants trusted the leadership of the MIR.

Adrian Vasquez began by agreeing that the peasants had a good case. He said that he would call back in a few hours after discussing the situation with Chonchol (minister of agriculture) and Baytleman (head of CORA) with whom he had already had a meeting. Several hours later Vasquez did call back. He promised that the salaries would be paid the next day. The local state bank officials in Lautaro, who in the majority were members of the right wing, were overruled. The organizer from the MIR asked for the number of the check which was to be sent from Santiago to Lautaro and for the amount. Vasquez supplied both figures a half hour later.

As for the expropriations and the formal taking of possession, Vasquez said the holdup was not in Santiago but in Temuco. The papers were still in Temuco, and Vasquez promised that they would be processed rapidly once they arrived in Santiago. Equipped with this information, the peasants promised to reoccupy the CORA offices in two weeks if the agreement were not fulfilled. This proved unnecessary. When pushed, the bureaucracy could move rapidly. CORA expropriated the Camilo Torres farm, and the peasants took possession of several other farms.

All this provided yet another lesson to the peasants about how to get things done. Direct action had gotten them what months of petitions and requests had not. But not all direct action was successful. The next major peasant mobilization failed and also contributed to a serious national polemic within the left.

On May 16 over one hundred peasants marched the few blocks from the Peasant Council office to the hospital through the town of Lautaro. They were marching to protest the hospital service. The major complaint was that women arriving in Lautaro on the bus from the countryside could not get to the hospital until 9 or 10 A.M., but the hospital began giving out tokens at 8 A.M. The tokens determined who got attended to first at the hospital. Through this system the hospital staff was in fact keeping women from the countryside from receiving hospital care.

The march was a peaceful one. It was organized by the Peasant Council, especially by the one woman represented on the Council, and by several of the young women who were members of the MIR. When the peasants got to the hospital, a delegation led by these women went in to talk to the director of the hospital. While they were inside, a group of about thirty police and detectives watched the peasants who remained outside. Suddenly, they began firing their weapons at and charging the unarmed peasants. Some police went into the hospital. The director of the hospital protested as police beat and arrested the delegation talking with him. Outside, six peasants received bullet wounds. The crowd fled, throwing stones at the police as they ran. Seventeen peasants were arrested and held in isolation.

The police and detectives claimed that the peasants had occupied the hospital, taken it over with the idea of shutting it down. The governor of Lautaro County, Alonso Neira (Communist Party), denied having given the police the order to attack. He said he had not been consulted by the police. The Popular Unity coalition in Lautaro issued a declaration backing him up. The Peasant Council, on the other hand, claimed that the governor, believing that the hospital had been taken over, had indeed given the order to the police.

At a national level the Communist Party used this incident in a campaign against the MIR. Undersecretary of the Interior Daniel Vergara (Communist) claimed that the MIR had attempted to occupy the hospital, and that the police had been forced to intervene against armed peasants. The Communist Party took out ads in all major newspapers:[3]

> The MIR takes over the hospital in Lautaro. What do they want? Another medical strike? A bloody confrontation? No revolutionary will be confused! Provocation is counterrevolution! [signed] Chilean Communist Party.

During this period the Communist Party had launched a propaganda campaign against the MIR. The MIR had recently been successful in forming alliances with other parties of the Popular Unity coalition for certain specific goals, and this irritated the Communist Party. In March the Socialist Party and the MIR cooperated in the wave of peasant takeovers in Ñuble. In April the MIR and the MAPU worked together in an important peasant offensive in Melipilla, near Santiago. But most dramatically, in early May the Socialist Party, the MAPU, and the Christian Left cooperated with the MIR in a march in Concepción, Chile's third largest city. The Communist Party refused to participate in the march which was meant to counteract a major demonstration being organized by the right. The governor of Concepción, Vladmir Lenin Chavez (Communist), claimed the left-wing march would be a provocation. He eventually ordered police to repress part of the march, and a Mirista student was

killed. This happened on May 12, and that same day conversations between the MIR and the Popular Unity leadership were broken off at the
insistence of the Communist Party.[4] Immediately thereafter the Communist Party stepped up its propaganda blitz against the MIR.

Given this background, it was predictable that the news from Lautaro
would be used by the Communist Party to attack the MIR. The Socialist
Party, on the other hand, correctly reported the facts about the hospital
incident in its afternoon Santiago newspaper, *Ultima Hora*. In Cautín the
County Peasant Councils of Freire, Perquenco, Villarica, Galvarino,
Cunco, and Lautaro put out a joint declaration asking for: (1) removal of
the chiefs of Police and Detectives in Lautaro; (2) an investigation of
Governor Alonso Neira's performance during the incident; and (3) the
right to elect county governors locally rather than accepting appointed
ones. None of these requests were granted.

Nothing further happened. The peasants were finally released from jail
and were never tried, but the charges were kept hanging over their
heads. Some would not go back into town after the incident. All the
wounded recuperated and left the hospital. Hospital service improved a
little but not much. The token system remained basically the same. Yet
another example was provided of the cost of the division among the left.

The next important event for the peasants of Lautaro did not take place
in Lautaro, but in Temuco. In July all the County Peasant Councils in
Cautín met in Temuco for a three-day Provincial Congress. Two hundred
and six representatives from sixteen County Peasant Councils attended.
Forty-six peasants from County Peasant Councils outside Cautín came as
observers.

This conference was qualitatively different from the one held the year
before. In 1971 the Provincial Congress was largely run by the government agricultural agencies, from the top down. The peasants who attended by and large followed directions. In 1972 the only representatives
of the government agricultural agencies who attended were those who
were specifically invited. The Peasant Councils in Cautín had made a lot
of progress in a year and a half. They were now self-reliant, and many had
been democratically elected through local assemblies in their counties. In
Lautaro County, for example, the Peasant Council divided the county
into eight sectors; each sector was supposed to meet regularly and to elect
its representative to the Peasant Council. These representatives then
joined with the representatives of rural unions to form the Peasant Council. Although in practice many local assemblies were not meeting regularly and two or three had not met at all, some progress had been made in

forming a truly representative Peasant Council. Similar experiences occurred throughout Cautín.

Cautín was seen as a leader in the organization of Peasant Councils. In comparison with other provinces, the Peasant Councils of Cautín were stronger and more democratically chosen. For this reason the Provincial Congress in Cautín was considered an important event. This attracted national attention. For those on the left who hoped the peasantry would be organized into strong, independent councils which would take the lead in the agrarian reform, Cautín represented progress. Many leftists fought for councils that would be independent of government agricultural agencies and would exercise real power in the countryside. Others on the left, however, differed with these views. Some felt that the rural unions, not the Peasant Councils, should lead the peasantry. Others objected to the councils' independence of the government and attempted to block any moves which gave the councils more power.

These differences on the left were reflected in the elections for officers of the Provincial Peasant Council. At the end of the Congress seven peasants were elected as officers, three from the Socialist Party, two from the Revolutionary Peasant Movement (controlled by the MIR), one from the Christian Left, and one from the Radical Party. The Communist Party withdrew from the Congress because it had demanded that two of the officers be Communists, but only one was elected. The Communists demanded that one of the representatives from the Revolutionary Peasant Movement withdraw in favor of a second Communist officer. When this demand was rejected, the Communist peasant officer (who was from Lautaro) withdrew, and the Communist Party refused to participate in the Provincial Peasant Council.

One of the representatives of the Revolutionary Peasant Movement was Felix Huentelaf. Huentelaf had just been released from seven months of prison. He was in jail as a result of the Chesque incident of October 1971 when landlords killed his brother Moisés during a farm takeover. By the time of the Congress he had already become one of the most active and most respected peasant leaders in Cautín. His militancy was to cost him dearly. Just slightly more than a year after the Congress he was to be jailed once again.

The Communist Party withdrawal from the Congress was prompted not just by a power struggle over the number of officers allotted to each party, but because of political differences. The Communists did not like the political views of most Congress participants. They objected to the emphasis on Peasant Council independence from and control over government agricultural agencies. The views of the Congress can be summarized by the following list of the most important resolutions of the Congress which are taken directly from the text.[5]

In the first place, the Councils must become powerful tools of the peasantry. The County Councils must be the INSTRUMENT OF POWER of the peasants in their struggle against the power of the landlords. It is necessary that the Councils be independent of the state bureaucracy.

In the second place the County Councils must directly represent and actively mobilize all the peasants in the county. Therefore, the County Councils must be the unified organization of all the peasants.

In order that the County Peasant Councils be representative, it is necessary that they be truly democractic. That means that their members must be elected in rank-and-file assemblies throughout the county and by the rank and file in each peasant organization in the county.

We propose the following program for the County Peasant Council:

—Struggle to expropriate all the farms above 20 BIH. Redefine the meaning of Basic Irrigated Hectare in Cautín.

—Struggle to expropriate all farms with all their animals and machinery intact, and without giving any reserve area to the landlord. That is, struggle for a new agrarian reform law.

—Struggle for the immediate taking of possession by the peasants of all expropriated farms.

—Struggle for the rapid restitution of land stolen from the Mapuche reservations.

—Support the social and economic struggles of the workers organized in rural unions.

—Struggle for the rapid delivery of credits and resources to both the small owners and the peasants in the reformed sector.

—Organize the nomination of new workers in the reformed sector, a privilege now in the hands of the state bureaucracy.

—Struggle for more women members in the County Peasant Council.

—Control the commercialization of products from the city to the peasant of the reformed sector and to the small owners.

—Struggle to create Rural Supply Centers in order to make products cheaper and take away the profits of the big middlemen.

—Control the work of those who work for the government agricultural agencies and control the use of government vehicles.

—Seek out and propose concrete ways to finance the Councils.

These resolutions were directed at the most important problems of
peasants and of the Peasant Councils. The main problem of the Peasant
Councils was that they had little actual power. The Congress was an
attempt by the Councils to change that situation.

Other resolutions concerned specific details. For example in two counties, Gorbea and Pitrufquen, landlords had managed to get control of the
Peasant Councils by posing as small proprietors. For this reason the
Congress spelled out who could be a member of a Peasant Council.
According to the Congress, any peasant could be a member of a Council.
A peasant was defined as any wage earner, and any small owner who
worked his own land with the help of his family and who hired outside
labor only during the harvest season. This definition was meant to exclude
landlords from the Peasant Councils. The recommendation that all farms
above twenty BIH in Cautín be expropriated was another. In Cautín
twenty BIH usually corresponded to 150 or 200 hectares, and the Congress felt this was as large as private landholdings should be. The Congress judged Cautín to be an exception because of the high number of
Mapuche peasants on the reservations who had no land or only one or two
hectares. For the rest of Chile the Provincial Congress recommended that
the maximum permissible holding be forty BIH instead of the eighty BIH
fixed by the Agrarian Reform Law.

Another specific resolution concerned financing, a major problem for
the Peasant Councils. The Congress recommended that 1 percent of the
budget of each of the many agricultural agencies be given to the Peasant
Councils that were receiving no government funding. Other resolutions
detailed problems with CORA. The Congress pointed out that there were
fifty-five expropriated farms in Cautín which had not yet been occupied
by the peasants and which were being rapidly dismantled by the landlords
in the interval. Two hundred and fifty farms in the province over forty
BIH remained to be expropriated under the existing Agrarian Reform
Law. Only 7,300 hectares of land stolen from the Mapuches had been
returned, out of an estimated 82,000 hectares in the province. The delegates to the Congress were mostly Mapuches (about 90 percent), and they
were acutely conscious of this problem.

Yet another resolution analyzed the cost of producing wheat versus the
cost of importing it and concluded that the government should pay a
higher price for wheat and import less of it. The peasants also analyzed

the costs of renting machinery in detail. These questions were of crucial importance to the country at a time when food shortages were beginning to be noticed and when the cost of food imports was becoming a major drain on foreign reserves.

In addition the Provincial Congress made recommendations about national politics. These recommendations reflected the political views of the Socialist Party and the MIR, the two parties which had the most influence over the Congress. It is probable that many of the peasants at the Congress did not fully understand the polemical nature of the political resolution. Nevertheless, enough did so that it was proposed and adopted. The resolution read as follows:

1. It is necessary to advance in a revolutionary process without entering into transactions with the bourgeoisie. It is necessary to reject the constitutional reform proposed by the bosses in Parliament. The proposed arms control law must be rejected, since it is a disguised form of repression against the working class. Negotiations behind the backs of the workers can not be permitted.

2. It is necessary to replace the bourgeois parliament by a people's assembly with the decisive participation of the workers' organizations. This means the County Peasant Councils in the countryside and the worker councils which must be created in the city.

3. The reactionaries and the facists must be combatted by the permanent mobilization of the masses.

4. The initiatives of the popular government which permit the access of the working class to power must be supported.

5. The bosses' justice, administered by the Judiciary, must be destroyed and replaced by workers' courts.

6. All workers persecuted by the Judiciary must be supported. Concretely, in the case of Cautín, combative support must be offered to the peasant comrads in prison or on trial in Lautaro, Toltén, Carahue, Puerto Saavedra, Loncoche, Pucón, and Cunco.

7. It is necessary to support all government workers who commit themselves to the defense of the revolutionary interests of the workers. Immediate support must be offered to those government workers who are persecuted by the courts or by the bourgeois Parliament.

8. All people who are struggling for socialism around the world must be supported.[6]

Point 7 about the support for certain government officials was exemplified at the Congress itself. Adrian Vasquez, one of the top three or four officials concerned with land reform, was especially invited to the Congress and gave an important speech which was published by the Congress. Vasquez strongly supported the Peasant Councils, but was under attack by some sectors of the left who wanted him removed from his job. Despite the support of the Congress, Vasquez eventually was transferred to another post. He became head of the government sugar company, a much less politically significant job.

On the whole the Congress was a success. The Peasant Councils were strengthened.[7] The Peasant Council in Lautaro went back home encouraged. Still, the Council in Lautaro, like the others in Cautín, would have to continue to wage an uphill battle. Over the next year the Peasant Council in Lautaro remained in a weak position, and most of the problems outlined at the Provincial Congress remained unsolved.

The Provincial Congress had once again brought the peasants from Lautaro face-to-face with national political questions. The next major event in Lautaro County in 1972 was to do the same. In October the right wing launched an offensive throughout Chile. The owners of trucks took them off the road, store owners closed their stores, and professionals like doctors and lawyers went on strike. The right wing attempted to paralyze the Chilean economy. The left tried to keep it going. The result was a stalemate which lasted twenty-six days. Finally a political compromise was reached. The military entered the cabinet, and a truce was arranged until the March 1973 congressional elections.

In Lautaro County the planting of crops was seriously affected. Many crucial tasks were delayed for weeks because of shortages of seed, fertilizer, and fuel. The peasants on the cooperatives tried to use their tractors and trailers to take the place of the trucks but were only partially successful. The tractors were needed in the fields, and fuel was in very short supply because of fuel rationing.

The military was in charge of public order, and increased patrols went down country roads. A military checkpoint was established on the bridge into the town of Lautaro. Right-wing sabotage was carried out on a large scale, and the military did little to stop it. Investigations were cursory. This was logical since most of the top officers in the regiment in Lautaro were close friends of those who were carrying out the sabotage.

The most common trick was to put bent nails (called miguelitos) on the road to prevent transportation. The right wing manufactured miguelitos by the millions. They were twisted in such a way that they always had a sharp point turned upward to penetrate a tire. Frequently saboteurs would strew miguelitos on only one side of a country road. The right wing would be informed, and their vehicles were always driven on the opposite side. Soon the left caught on to this trick. Other forms of sabotage were the destruction of railroad tracks and power lines. In Lautaro County a number of operations of this nature were carried out.[8]

Despite all this, the peasants managed to keep the farms running. The right's appeal to the peasants to go on strike was ignored throughout the county. Even those few peasants who supported the right, refused to stop working during planting season. (They didn't receive subsidies from the CIA as the truck owners almost surely did.[9])

The paralyzation of transport had an effect, however. The 1973 harvest was to be less than hoped because the area planted was less than anticipated. The right-wing offensive had another effect. The peasants were provided with a graphic lesson in the economic power of the right, and they saw that the military was not likely to repress its own allies, the wealthy landowners of Lautaro. The peasants remembered these lessons in 1973.

Another effect of the crisis was a beginning effort by the peasants to organize their own distribution system. The head of CORA in Lautaro initiated a distribution center in order to get products to the cooperatives. Oil, detergent, sugar, and matches were included in the list of items distributed. Most of the cooperatives in the county put in a certain amount of money, and the state distributing center (DINAC) provided the goods. A peasant represented on the Peasant Council took charge of the operation, which was called the Rural Supply Center (Centro de Abastecimiento Rural, or CAR). This peasant was a member of the Communist Party, a fact that was to have important consequences later when a struggle developed over the Rural Supply Center. One immediate problem was that the Center had too few products and not enough of them even to begin to supply all the cooperatives. The number of items carried was limited to those products produced by the expropriated factories, and many crucial items were unavailable. Another problem was that government employees in the agricultural agencies also had rights to buy from the store, and they bought much of the merchandise.

The Rural Supply Center got started after the October crisis had been resolved in order to confront a possible repetition of food shortages if another transport shutdown occurred. But soon the peasants needed the Center even in normal times. In 1972 inflation reached 165 percent, and a large black market sprang up to avoid official prices. The peasants' income did not keep up with inflation, and they could not afford to buy black-market goods. They had to depend on goods sold at official prices, and that meant that they began to depend more and more on the Rural Supply

Center, inadequate though it was. The private store owners usually claimed they were out of most items unless, of course, you had a few personal friends in the right places and you could afford to pay the high black-market prices.

The October crisis simply accentuated a general economic crisis from which the peasantry was not exempt. The situation was to get much worse in 1973.

Chapter 9

The Farm: 1973

Early 1973 at Elicura farm was the time of the wheat harvest. First came the winter wheat which had been planted the previous winter and was now being harvested in late summer. Harvest time was busy. Every day the big combine would work from sunrise to sundown. The combine cut the wheat, threshed it, and then poured the kernels into burlap sacks. The peasants were responsible for getting the heavy sacks to a central location and then loading the sacks on trucks to be taken to town. The central location was round the only tree which was still left in the middle of the wheat field. The ground near the tree was quickly trampled down by the boots of the peasants and the weight of piles of 176-pound sacks of wheat. Everywhere the kernels of wheat spilled out and the whole area round the tree was sprinkled with them. The smell of the grain was strong. It was in this area at the end of the last day of the winter wheat harvest that the peasants gathered. The harvest had gone on until after dark, but rather than head for home it was traditional for everyone to gather around the harvest area to drink wine and eat bread. The summer night was and clear. The peasants stayed until late into the evening, telling jokes and drinking, letting their tiredness gradually subside. Several women came out to join the group of men workers, bringing more food and wine and staying for the party. It was at this time that the peasants at Elicura felt best about the farm. The product of their labor, the wheat, had been harvested in abundance and sent off to town. They felt like they had done a good job. The big combine had disposed of the extensive fields of winter wheat in only a week, and this time it was the peasants themselves who were controlling the combine. Before, they had only watched it from the hills of the nearby reservations. They themselves

154

had had to settle for harvesting only a few hectares of wheat. If they were lucky, they had been able to get their wheat cut by paying someone who had a tractor and a harvester. Then they had had to bundle the wheat up by hand and get it to a thresher owned by someone else and surely located some distance away. Usually the wheat had to be taken to the thresher with a cart and oxen. Then the threshed wheat had to be taken to town by that same cart and oxen.

Sometimes the terrain had been so hilly, or the family so poor, that a tractor was impossible. Then the wheat had to be cut by hand. But those times were gone. Now the peasants were in charge of huge fields and had the use of a modern combine. There was good reason for pride.

But Chile was in crisis in 1973. The economic deterioration which occurred throughout Chile in 1973 helped the right wing mobilize support and set the stage for the September coup. The outstanding characteristics of the economic crisis were the inflation and the shortage of consumer items. These two characteristics affected the whole of Chile. The Elicura farm was no exception.

Take, for example, the case of Pedro and Amalia. Having been married for several months, they began to discuss the possibility of having children. One night in June of 1973, while drinking maté after dinner, they figured out their budget. The discussion was prompted by Amalia's complaint that the kerosene lamp was giving too little light and too much smoke, and that she wished they could afford candles. Pedro said that his salary was worth less and less.

Back in October 1972 all peasants in the reformed sector had seen their salary jump from thirty escudos a day to sixty to compensate for the serious inflation which had begun in early 1972. Inflation for the year of 1972 had been 165 percent for the whole country, and the October salary increase had almost evaporated by the end of the year. Inflation continued in 1973 at an even higher rate. The government attempted to grant salary increases to all peasants in the reformed sector to compensate. In June of 1973 salaries had gone from sixty escudos a day to 110 escudos a day. The traditional family allowance yielded an additional 200 escudos a month for a wife and 500 escudos a month for each child.

Pedro calculated that he would make about 3,200 escudos a month. Sales of animals and vegetables yielded another 3,000 escudos. The total salary was therefore 6,200 escudos per month. Amalia calculated that food, matches, kerosene, detergent, and all the other necessities cost about 6,000 a month. It would have been less except for the fact that

Pedro's eight-year-old nephew Herardo was living with them, and extra food had to be bought. In any case there was no extra money to buy anything.

Amalia then commented about the prices in town. A pair of work shoes cost 2,000 escudos or about a third of the monthly wage. Good shoes cost 3,500 escudos. A mattress cost 6,000 escudos, completely beyond the reach of the peasants. A large frying pan cost 600 escudos as did a large pot. A teapot was 1,200. A small portable radio was 6,000 or 7,000 escudos. A workshirt was 800 escudos, and a good shirt cost 1,200. A cheap sweater was 1,500, a cheap blanket was 2,000, and a broom was 250. These were items the peasants liked to buy whenever they could accumulate a little extra money. The fact that these items had become scarcer and more expensive was very much apparent to the men and women at Elicura who were reduced to a subsistence economy by the inflation. Nevertheless, their standard of living was still better than it had been on the reservation.

Some items were of course even scarcer. Many peasants wanted a small kerosene heater to supplement the heat of their stoves. Heaters were also a prized item in the city, and they were scarce. When they were available, they could only be bought at black-market prices. They cost 20,000 escudos.

Pedro and Amalia concluded that they couldn't have a baby until they were able to save some money. Although they said that the right wing was to blame for the economic crisis, they could not completely avoid putting some of the blame on the government. After all, Pedro was paid by the government, and the money was too little. Both Pedro and Amalia, like all the other peasants at Elicura, were increasingly anxious about the future. It looked more and more as though the Allende experiment was not going to last.

The economic facts of life on the reservations were even worse. In March 1973 peasants from the reservations met in the one-room school near Elicura to discuss loans from the government for the coming agricultural year (May to May). The peasants came from four Committees of Small Farmers, each one based on a reservation. The four reservations surrounded the Elicura farm. At the meeting the peasants filled out forms which listed their assets and debts. The average peasant there had about eight hectares of land, of which four were sown with crops, usually wheat. (Generally these eight hectares included the land which belonged to the peasant's wife.) From the four sown hectares the peasant would harvest about fifty sacks of wheat (one sack equals about 176 pounds). Half of these would be sold on the market, and the other half ground up for flour for personal consumption. In addition the peasant usually owned some animals; an oxen, a cow, some sheep, or some pigs. Some of these animals would be sold during the year, and the income from the animals was often more than the income from the sale of wheat. All in all, the average assets for a peasant at the meeting were about 30,000 escudos, excluding land. Debts averaged between 5,000 and 10,000 escudos. The debts were owed to the state bank for credits for fertilizer, seed, and rental of tractors.

Most peasants were asking for more credit for fertilizer and seed for the coming year. The government was prepared to allow a maximum credit of 20,000 escudos. This amount would cover seed and fertilizer, and perhaps a small animal. It would not cover an oxen or a piece of agricultural machinery. Most peasants asked for a few sacks of seed and a few sacks of fertilizer, both nitrate and phosphate. The nitrate was produced in Chile and would be available. The phosphate was imported, and many peasants asked for it while realizing that it might very well not arrive.

The government had been able to help the small peasant to survive, but the committees were not being turned into production cooperatives. The small peasant economy of subsistence continued to dominate the reservations around the Elicura farm. The poverty on the reservations was great. In comparison, despite the inflation, life on the expropriated farms was much better.

Nevertheless, the peasants on the Elicura farm remained reluctant to give up their small pieces of land on the reservation. They generally had only one or two hectares, less than what most peasants on the reservation had. It was this fact that led them to form the cooperative on the expropriated farm in the first place. Those who joined the cooperative at Elicura were those who were the worst off on the reservation. But they still hung onto their reservation land, small as it was, in case they should lose their position at Elicura. The government tried to dissuade them. In July CORA called a meeting of four cooperative farms, including Elicura, to discuss the question of land on the reservations as well as the internal functioning of the cooperatives in general.

The meeting was attended by three representatives from Elicura; Pancho, the treasurer, Pedro, the president, and Guillermo, the foreman. They agreed with the other peasants about most of the questions discussed.

The meeting concluded that there was no point in attempting to get the peasants at the cooperatives to give up their land on the reservations until the Peasant Council offered some moral leadership. Several peasants on the Peasant Council who were members of a cooperative continued to hold land on the reservations. This was common knowledge. Until the leaders set an example by giving up that land, it was felt that little could be done with the rank and file. A resolution was passed to this effect.

The other points discussed concerned the internal life of the cooperatives. CORA wanted the peasants themselves to come up with some internal rules to check obvious abuses. Penalties for breaking the rules were to be decided later by the assemblies of each cooperative.

The rules which were drawn up at the meeting were as follows:

(1) No payment would be made for days not actually worked. This rule was supposed to be in effect already but was widely ignored.

(2) Tractor use was to be regulated. It was prohibited to take tractors into town on week days when they were needed at the farm. This was a common abuse. Furthermore, strict penalties were to be set up for those who through negligence destroyed machinery. All too often drunk tractor drivers coming back from town had had accidents.

(3) No wine was to be sold inside the cooperative. Too many peasants bought large quantities of wine in town and sold it at speculative prices on the farm during impromptu parties.

(4) Physical assaults by one peasant on another were to be penalized with expulsion from the cooperative if it became apparent that such behavior was unprovoked and continual.

(5) Theft inside the cooperative was grounds for expulsion.

This minimal code attempted to correct the most obvious abuses at the cooperatives. Unfortunately the rules represented more good intentions than future reality. None of the four cooperatives present at the meeting were able to set up concrete penalties for infractions before the coup in September. Indeed, the internal life at the Elicura cooperative was not seen as such a pressing problem by the peasants there, given the national policy crisis which was having its effects in Lautaro County.

When the peasants at Elicura woke up on June 29 and switched on their radios, they heard machine gun fire from Santiago instead of the expected mixture of Mexican and Chilean folk music. The attempted coup was being broadcast live. Meanwhile the regiment in Lautaro was considering joining the military rebellion. Around noon a military jeep was sent out to reconnoiter the countryside. The peasants at Elicura had a prearranged plan about what to do in case of a coup. Eight men left Elicura with saws and axes and went to cut down trees at strategic points along the road. Meanwhile at the farm itself weapons were hidden. Those peasants who were most active made the necessary arrangements to hide in case the military came. Leftist literature was hidden.

When the lone jeep came down the road the peasants let it go by. After it had passed they began cutting down small trees and building a barricade. The jeep, however, returned quickly, before the peasants had finished. As it approached the barricade, the driver made the decision to try to break through the barricade instead of stopping or retreating. He must have felt that it would be better to risk a crash than to be left at the mercy of the peasants. He gunned the motor and crashed into a small mound of trees and brush. The peasants watched as the jeep barely managed to break through and then continued back to the town and the safety of the regiment. This was the first encounter between the peasants at Elicura and the military. The June 29 coup failed, and the peasants at Elicura had to spend several hours at various roads in the countryside clearing the trees they had cut down. Some roads remained impassable for more than a week.

The next time the peasants at Elicura met the military was in August at the two attempted takeovers of the San Ramón farm. The San Ramón farm was owned by Sergio Madrid, a retired military officer. The farm was forty-four BIH and was one of the few farms that had been expropriated by CORA earlier in the year, a holdover from the expropriations in 1972. But many months had passed without the legal authorization for the peasants to take possession of the farm. The land was lying fallow with only three men employed to look after a small herd of cattle. Sergio Madrid himself did not live on the farm. The peasants involved in the takeover were eager to begin working the farm. Many of those who participated in the takeover were unemployed peasants who would actually be working the land if the takeover were successful. They received help from the peasants from the cooperatives, such as Elicura. The Peasant Council was aware of the takeover and supported it. But it was a difficult time to attempt a takeover. The military was practically in charge of the county after the unsuccessful coup attempt of June 29th. The left on the whole was on the defensive, and many leftists would later say that the attempted takeover was provocative, doomed to failure, and eventually only of benefit to the right wing.

Nine peasants from Elicura joined the first takeover attempt. They set out one cold evening about midnight, riding on a cart pulled by a tractor. The tractor drove without lights so as not to attract attention. Everyone was in high spirits. Before boarding the cart a MIR militant had led the group in a series of exercises in order to increase discipline and offer some kind of paramilitary training. The peasants were armed with sticks. The MIR militant and one of the more active peasants who was being recruited by the MIR carried pistols.

Along the way the tractor stopped to pick up small groups of peasants who were waiting at the side of the road. An hour and a half later the tractor arrived at another cooperative, the staging area for the takeover. Here four other tractors had arrived carrying peasants. After about one hour of marching around and much discussion, the whole column took off on foot down the road.

On the rare occasions when a vehicle came down the road, the entire column of about seventy-five people would disappear off the road, stumbling over barbed-wire fences and into ditches. There was an effort to march in order and to keep down the noise, but too often one joke would elicit laughter throughout the column. Eventually the column moved off the road and towards the farm. Again silence was impossible as the peasants laughed every time someone fell into the many deep puddles of water in the fields. The leaders of the takeover were not too concerned about the noise, however. They were fairly confident that there had been no preparation against the takeover by those at the San Ramón farm. This was in fact the case, and the administrator at San Ramón was easily disarmed shortly before daylight. The two other workers supported the takeover.

No women had come from Elicura although Pedro's wife had almost come. In the end Pedro discouraged her. The only women in the takeover were those who were recognized as working with the MIR. The MIR had several sympathizers who were supposed to take orders and show their committment but were not allowed to attend meetings or really know too much about what was going on. Then there were candidates who had all the duties of a member but none of the privileges. They attended all meetings but could not vote. After a period they were incorporated as full members. The women who accompanied the takeover were candidates. Their special status with the MIR was recognized by the other peasants who accepted them as participants in the dangers and enjoyments of the takeover.

After disarming the administrator, the peasants then set up barricades by cutting down trees. Around 11 A.M. vehicles from CORA arrived, and a short discussion with the peasants took place. The people from CORA did not try to encourage the peasants to get off the land, given that the farm had been expropriated anyway and that such encouragement would have been useless. The governor of the county, who opposed the takeover, also drove by but didn't stop to talk.

About two hours later three or four trucks loaded with soldiers pulled up at the barricades. The soldiers jumped out with sub-machine guns and began firing over the heads of the peasants on the other side of the barricades. The peasants broke ranks and ran. The soldiers ran after them and managed to capture many, commanding them to halt or be fired upon. Then the commanding officer staged a show. He hung several peasants by ropes from the rafters of the warehouse and beat them, demanding information about who had organized the takeover. Finally the officer released all but two peasants. Those two were arrested for insolence and for having a weapon. While most peasants had been able to hide or dispose of what few weapons there were, one was caught with a Colt revolver. He claimed that it was the revolver taken from the administrator. The other peasant was arrested for insolence because he had talked back to the officer in charge of the troops.

A militant from the MIR, the same one who lived at Elicura, was almost also arrested for insolence. The military was unaware that he was a member of the MIR. The officer simply assumed he was another peasant. It was the MIR who had helped organize the takeover. Many peasants had been asking the MIR militants in the county to do so since the farm had been already expropriated and they were eager to begin work on it. The organizers from the MIR had agreed, but this time they did not publicize their participation. There were no armbands reading Revolutionary Peasant Movement, and no banners were set up. The MIR militants (as well as the peasants) had been aware that the military might intervene, and they wanted to minimize the repression which would take place if that occurred. One way to do this was give no indication that the MIR had organized the takeover.

When the military arrived, one MIR organizer had stayed with the peasants to face them. Two others had hidden themselves, according to a prearranged plan. When the officer in charge had begun tying up and beating the two peasants, the Mirista spoke up in protest. The officer then grabbed him and asked him who he was taking orders from, perhaps one of those Miristas in the CORA bureaucracy. The MIR militant replied that he was not taking orders from anybody but that the military officer certainly was, probably from some of those reactionary colonels back in the regiment. At this, the officer told the Mirista he was under arrest, but in the later confusion the military neglected to take him in.

The pretext for the intervention of the army in repressing the takeover was the Arms Control Law. Theoretically they were there to look for illegal arms. In fact, of course, they were there to end the takeover. This was the first time that the military had intervened in a takeover in Lautaro County. The soldiers who did so were a special group who had been selected because they would follow the orders of the officers. They were among those soldiers who were known to oppose the left and who did not come from the county originally.

Only a few days after the unsuccessful takeover at San Ramón the peasants tried it again. This time they expected the military to throw them off, but they took over the farm anyway just to make the point that they were not afraid of the soldiers. They also wanted to expose further the military's role in support of the landowners. All the peasants around the San Ramón farm knew that the farm had been expropriated and should have been already in control of the peasants. The military was keeping the peasants from taking possession of what was already theirs.

The same seventy-five peasants carried out the second takeover, and the same nine people from Elicura participated. This time, however, the MIR militant from Elicura did not go since he had already come danger-ously close to being arrested the time before. Two other Miristas went.

The peasants did not celebrate by killing and eating a steer, as they had the first time, but set up the barricades and posted lookouts, waiting for the military. They didn't have to wait long. The same soldiers arrived. This time they were not so aggressive. They cleared the farm of peasants, but they did not beat anyone or arrest anyone. The peasants were better prepared and were able to conceal all weapons. There was no thought to resist the soldiers. The weapons that the peasants brought along were necessary only in case of attacks by right-wing civilians.

After the second attempt, the peasants and the MIR did not try again. Of the two peasants arrested during the first attempt, one was released. The one who was arrested for carrying a weapon, however, was kept in jail. Peasants throughout Lautaro County learned a lesson from the two attempts. That lesson was that the military was prepared to back the landowners unconditionally and that the military acted with a discipline and superior force that the peasants were not prepared to resist. What happened at San Ramón, it was generally acknowledged, might well hap-pen at already established cooperatives in the case of a successful military coup. The peasants involved in the takeover did not feel that they were wrong in attempting it. It had been they themselves who were eager to work the land at San Ramón and who had urged the MIR to organize the takeover.

After these incidents the people at Elicura changed their attitude towards the military. On Saturdays when raw army recruits from the reservations returned on a weekend pass, they frequently got off the bus in front of the Elicura farm. Often there were groups of peasants from Elicura near the bus stop. After the military intervention at San Ramón the peasants would heckle the recruits, shouting insults at them, and asking them if they were there at San Ramón. None of them had been since the troops at San Ramón were especially selected for their right-wing political views and because they specifically did not come from Lautaro County. The peasants at Elicura knew this, and their heckling was not very hostile. It served to put the recruits on warning that they should not be used in the future against their own relatives and friends.

Chapter 10

The Area: 1973

Ya se fué el verano
ya viene el invierno.
Dentro de muy poco
caerá el gobierno.

The summer has already gone
winter is coming soon.
It won't be long before
the government will fall.
                              "Que turu ru ru ru," song from the Spanish Civil War

The land reform in Lautaro County came to a standstill in 1973. Two or three farms were expropriated but the peasantry did not take possession of them before the coup. There were two unsuccessful attempts at illegal takeovers of one farm which had already been expropriated. These takeovers were designed to speed up the legal process that for months had kept the unemployed peasants from occupying the land. Both attempts were repressed by the military, which, for the first time, directly intervened.

Instead of more expropriations, the struggle was often confined to preserving the gains that had been won. The balance of forces had changed dramatically in favor of the right. The economic situation deteriorated at an alarming rate, and the distribution of common consumer items took on ever increasing political importance. In a period of economic disruption Chileans in Lautaro County, as in the rest of the country, soon found themselves in two opposing camps. There was little middle ground. The right wing openly appealed to the military to overthrow Allende while in many cases the left demanded that the government take drastic steps to fortify the workers and peasants. Some sectors of the left called for rationing to solve the distribution problem and arms to the workers to prepare for any possible military intervention. The government was caught in the middle, attempting to thwart sedition using increasingly inadequate legal methods. On the other hand the government was not prepared to implement rationing or distribute weapons to its supporters. The left itself was divided on these issues, and this division eventually became a fatal weakness.

In Lautaro County, as in the rest of the country, events moved so rapidly that it is best to describe them chronologically, month by month.

January:

The Lautaro County Peasant Council submitted a list of farms which it wanted the government to expropriate in 1973. The number of farms on the list was almost 200. The Peasant Council included many small farms belonging to the same owner, which when taken together, came to more than forty BIH. They also included many small farms which had been completely abandoned and were therefore eligible for expropriation, regardless of their size. Also included, of course, were farms over forty Basic Irrigated Hectares considered by the peasants to be poorly exploited. This included most of the sixteen farms over forty Basic Irrigated Hectares still left in the county. (All farms over eighty BIH had already been expropriated). Most of these farms were indeed underworked. Their owners preferred not to make risky investments. A few landowners, on the other hand, were willing to take the risk of new investments because of the high profits to be obtained by selling produce on the black market. In Lautaro County there were only a small number of such landowners, due to the pressure of the peasantry for the land. In other parts of the country where peasant pressure was not as intense, more and more landowners were no longer allowing their farms to stand abandoned but were enthusiastically sowing crops in order to profit from the black market. The inefficacy of government control of the black market meant that crops could be sold with impunity at astronomical prices.

The question of how to control the marketing of agricultural produce had become a crucial political issue by 1973. On January 10 Fernando Flores, who was the minister of the treasury and a member of MAPU (a political party which split away from the Christian Democrats in 1969 and joined the Popular Unity coalition), announced that the government would put into effect a very limited form of rationing. The plan involved a greater coordination between the small retail grocery stores and the neighborhood JAP (Junta de Abastecimiento y Precios). The JAPs were community groups formed throughout the country to denounce black-market sales and oversee the sale of food in their area. Created in 1971, there were over 2,500 JAPs by 1973, and they had earned the hatred of the right wing. Flores proposed to make sure that each local retail store received no more food than it could reasonably sell to the population in the area. The JAPs were to determine how much food the store should get and make sure that it was sold at official prices. This proposal was attacked immediately by the right as a plot to control the population through rationing. In fact it was a timid attempt to begin the necessary process of control over the distribution of food. By 1973 many consumer items were being funnelled to the black market, and the poorer sections of the population were unable to buy what they needed. The political storm created by Flores's proposal caused the government to retreat, and the rationing plan was implemented only in those areas where local pressure from the left was sufficient to force it through.

The fact that the government controlled only about 30 percent of the distribution of popular consumer items by 1973 meant that any rationing scheme had to be limited. In addition attempts by the government alone to oversee the sale of consumer items controlled by private merchants were hindered by a very ineffective bureaucracy. That is why Flores wanted to give the JAP a greater role.

In the city of Lautaro, for example, there were only two inspectors to check for official prices, and they were easily bribed. As for the JAPs, they were well-organized only in the poorer neighborhoods of the city of Lautaro. These JAPs exercised control over some of the smaller stores, but the bigger stores in central Lautaro were free to do as they pleased, which meant deal on the black market. In the countryside, of course, there were neither JAPs nor stores.

February:

As pointed out earlier, during the October 1972 crisis when transportation broke down, a store had been set up in Lautaro County to sell food to the cooperatives. This store did not sell to peasants who were small owners or who worked for large private owners. Only members of the cooperatives benefitted from the consumer items sold by the store at official prices. The only exception was a number of white collar workers in the agricultural bureaucracy who began buying goods at the store. In February the Peasant Council developed a plan to turn this store, called a Rural Supply Center, into a large operation which would sell to all the peasants in the country. A struggle developed over control of the store. José Fuentes, a member of the Peasant Council and of the Communist Party, was running the Rural Supply Center in early 1973. He had gotten together with the people in CORA who had set up the store the previous October. He resisted using the Rural Supply Center to sell to any peasants except those in the cooperatives. The cooperatives had originally put up the money to buy the initial goods of the store. The sales of the store were sufficient to resupply it and also to pay the salary to its manager. The Peasant Council wanted to enlarge the operation of the Rural Supply Center and bring it more directly under control of DINAC, the state distributing company that was setting up Rural Supply Centers throughout the country. The Peasant Council also had plans to make trips directly to the factories in Concepción that sold nails and cloth in order to buy them directly and sell them through the Rural Supply Center. DINAC did not have those items, and both were desperately needed in the countryside.

The Peasant Council was of course supported by the small farmers throughout Lautaro County who would benefit from having access to the Rural Supply Center. On the Peasant Council, itself, half of the fifteen members were small owners. The other half came from the cooperatives. But all were united behind the plan to enlarge the operation of the Rural Supply Center. The conflict inevitably took on political overtones, because José Fuentes was a Communist while most of the Peasant Council worked with the Revolutionary Peasant Movement controlled by the MIR.

A meeting was held in the town of Lautaro in early February to resolve the problem. Charges and countercharges flew. The Communist mayor of Lautaro supported José Fuentes against the Peasant Council. The Peasant Council denounced Fuentes because it claimed he was personally pocketing profits from the Rural Supply Center. Fuentes responded by saying that the Peasant Council was just trying to take away his job because under the new scheme DINAC would train and hire two new people to manage the store. At the end a vote was taken among the 120 peasants present. About half of the peasants were excluded from voting because they were small owners. Fuentes, who was running the meeting, arbitrarily ruled against them. Only members of the cooperatives could vote. Fuentes won a vote of confidence by a slim margin. For the moment the

Peasant Council as a whole had lost a battle against one of its members for control of the Rural Supply Center.

Also in February the government announced that it would be the sole buyer of wheat. The crop was just coming in, and the government decreed that it would be the monopoly buyer in order to stop sales of wheat to the black market. It will be remembered that Chileans depend on bread as a staple and that wheat is *the* crucial agricultural product. In previous years the government had bought some wheat and controlled its distribution, but in 1973 the idea was for the government to buy *all* the wheat. Lack of bread on the market was becoming a serious problem nationally, and the government had been forced to import huge quantities of wheat with scarce foreign exchange. The amount of wheat imported jumped four times between 1970 and 1973. One of the reasons for this increased importation was that so much of the national production was going to the black market, thereby being unavailable for poorer consumers. This meant that the government had to import more wheat or else succumb to the fact that less and less bread was being sold at official prices. In February the government began a massive publicity campaign designed to convince producers to sell to the government. The right responded by denouncing a tyrannical government which was forcing the producer to go broke by selling wheat to the government at less than its market (black-market) value.

March:

The congressional elections took place throughout Chile in early March. These elections were extremely important. The crisis of October 1972 had been resolved by the entry of the military into the cabinet and a truce until the March elections. The March elections would measure the strength of each side. Both the right and left had united behind their respective candidates.

The elections were preceded by a massive dose of advertising in the newspapers and radio. Dozens of demonstrations and speeches took place in Lautaro County. The right wing had overwhelming control of the radio and newspapers, the most important means of communication in southern Chile where televisions were relatively rare. The left, which was committed to the electoral struggle, fought back with an intense grassroots mobilization. Some leftists questioned the value of the elections and doubted that so much energy should go into them. Nevertheless few leftists were willing entirely to abandon the electoral arena to the right. The MIR, for example, did not run candidates; but it did call on its supporters to vote for specific candidates in the Socialist Party with whom agreements had been reached.

As it turned out, the left got 44 percent of the vote nationally (higher than anticipated but down from the 50 percent obtained in the municipal elections in April 1971. Allende had gotten 36 percent when elected.). The results strengthened the left, but they also convinced the right that Allende could not be removed electorally. Indeed, it was possible that by 1976 the left would have continued gaining votes and would be able to gain a majority in the presidential and congressional elections of that year. This possibility finally caused the entire right to support a military coup.

In Lautaro County voters chose who would represent Cautín Province in Congress. The left ran such figures as Rosendo Huenumán, a Communist Mapuche who ran for deputy. Huenumán gave speeches in Mapuche to his audiences. (He was murdered by the military in Temuco shortly after the coup.) Another figure was Jaime Suarez, a popular Socialist who ran for senator. Both men won.

The left as a whole received 42 percent of the vote, and the right 58 percent in Lautaro County. About 9,100 people voted. These figures show that the right had slightly more strength in Lautaro than it had nationally. But in 1970 Allende had received only 22 percent in Lautaro County, compared to 36 percent nationally. Lautaro's vote was much more heavily weighted to the right in 1970 than in 1973. The reason for this was that in 1970 only 6,600 people voted. Between 1970 and 1973 many illiterate peasants gained the right to vote and most voted for Allende, undoubtedly because they had benefited from the land reform. The electoral results in Lautaro County showed that even in notoriously right-wing southern Chile the left was making gains.

More men than women voted in Lautaro. Fifty-seven percent of the voters were men. The men voted for the left more than did the women. Thirty-seven percent of the women supported the left, while 47 percent of the men did. This difference undoubtedly stemmed from the fact that proportionally fewer working class and peasant women voted than did upper-class women, in comparison to the situation for men. It also was a product of the fact that women were often confined to the home where they received a steady barrage of right-wing propaganda from the media. They did not have the experience of the work place where employees were pitted against the boss. It is also true that throughout Chile the right wing was more successful than the left in its appeals to women. By 1973 the right was calling on the women of Chile to come forward and save the country from the Marxist hordes which were destroying the family, indoctrinating children in the schools, and causing food shortages. Although this propaganda convinced very few working-class women, the right was able effectively to mobilize middle- and upper-class women.

While all the hoopla of the elections was going on, the peasants continued to face the pressing problems of agricultural production. One of the most serious was the lack of machinery. In Cautín a new experiment was taking place with agricultural machinery. Rather than sell scarce machinery to cooperatives and to small farmers, the government in Cautín decided to create a rental machinery pool to serve the entire province. In this pool were large combines, which harvested the wheat for the cooperatives, and also tractors, which were rented largely to the small owners who were organized in committees. (The cooperatives usually had their own tractors since they needed them on a year-round basis to work their large tracts of land.)

The idea of the machinery pool was a good one. Rentals were low, and the peasants were able to avoid paying high prices to private owners of machinery. Unfortunately, there were not enough machines in the pool, despite the fact that the government had more than doubled the amount of agricultural machinery in Cautín. Much of the new machinery had gone to the cooperatives. (For example, there were 100 tractors on cooperatives in 1970, and 650 at the end of 1973.[1]) The committees of small farmers still lacked machinery, and they were to benefit from the pool. In the three-county district which included Lautaro, Perquenco, and Galvarino counties, there were some 104 committees of small farmers (fifty-seven in Lautaro County). These committees had requested 7,500 tractor hours from the pool. But there were only twenty tractors assigned to the district, and they were not enough. In addition the few combines assigned to the district were insufficient, and the cooperatives were having to rent these machines from private owners.

As a result, a demonstration was arranged. Repeated requests had not solved the problem, so more direct action was taken once again. This time the white collar workers in the agricultural bureaucracy who were members of the Socialist Party organized the demonstration. With only a few days notice they asked the peasants throughout the district to come to a meeting on March 12. Seventy people, largely from cooperatives and committees where the Socialist Party had influence, met in a warehouse in the town of Lautaro. After meeting for two hours, they resolved to go to Temuco and occupy the offices of SEAM, the organization in charge of machinery. Clearly, the move was prearranged. A bus had been rented ahead of time, and it loaded up most of the peasants. The others took off in pick-up trucks provided by the agricultural agencies. Half an hour later they occupied the offices of SEAM in Temuco where the machinery pool was based. In addition to the seventy peasants, there were about twenty white collar workers from the agricultural agencies in Lautaro and Temuco. Most of them were Socialists.

The sit-in at SEAM lasted two hours. The peasants had to wait at the beginning because the head of SEAM was out to lunch. After he came back, he suggested that the demonstration move to ODEPLAN, the agricultural planning agency for the whole province. SEAM's chief said that he just took orders from the head of the province whose offices were then occupied. By 4 P.M. negotiations were concluded, with the promise that seven more tractors and two more combines would be sent to Lautaro County right away.

Although the sit-in was successful, it had repercussions. That same afternoon the head of the agricultural agencies in the province called in the head of CORA in Lautaro County for a meeting in Temuco. The head of CORA in Lautaro, Jaime Sepúlveda, was a Socialist who had given consistent support to peasant mobilizations and who represented the left-wing of the Socialist Party. He had not been present at the demonstration in Temuco, but he was blamed for it anyway. The head of CORA in the whole province heatedly criticized Sepúlveda for having led the demonstration, a charge Sepúlveda denied. Nothing further occurred, but the incident was used in what was to be a mounting campaign against Sepúlveda led by the right wing of his own party.

April:

On April 5 an important meeting was held by the Peasant Council in Lautaro to discuss several issues. About fifty peasants attended the meeting, as did the president of the Provincial Peasant Council and a representative from DINAC, the state distributing company. The first point covered was the Rural Supply Center. The Peasant Council had decided to go ahead and set up its own Rural Supply Center, despite having lost the vote of the previous January to José Fuentes. For three months two Rural Supply Centers existed side by side. One was run by Fuentes and worked exclusively with the cooperatives, and the other was run by the Peasant Council and served all the peasantry. The state distributing agency,

DINAC, eventually decided to favor the Rural Supply Center set up by the Peasant Council because it served the entire peasantry. This decision meant that José Fuentes's Rural Supply Center found it increasingly more difficult to get supplies.

At the meeting on April 5 Fuentes, the representative from DINAC, and the Peasant Council once again publicly aired their views. The representative from DINAC pointed out that nationally DINAC only controlled 28 percent of the distribution of common consumer items. Only 10 percent of that 28 percent went for the Rural Supply Centers. The countryside was worse off than the city. The government justified this inequality by pointing out that the peasants at least would be able to get important amounts of food from their own production, unlike workers in the city. Nevertheless, the peasants had to depend on the state for items like sugar, maté, matches, textiles, shoes, and candles. These items were handled by the Rural Supply Center and were unavailable in private stores except at black-market prices. The fact that the Rural Supply Center had so few of these necessary items meant that it was all the more important that they be distributed evenly. For this reason DINAC backed the store set up by the Peasant Council instead of the one run by Fuentes.

Two more points were discussed at the meeting. A delegation of peasants was being formed by the Provincial Peasant Council to go to Santiago and meet with the minister of agriculture. The president of the Provincial Peasant Council, José Purrán, wanted the meeting to elect two representatives from Lautaro County. This was done. Then the head of the county Peasant Council made an appeal for peasant support for a demonstration that evening by people in the town of Lautaro concerning food distribution. The demonstration was to pressure the governor of Lautaro County to bring food to Lautaro directly, to be distributed by the government to those who were organized and who had signed up. This system of direct food distribution was taking place in other parts of the country. Each person who signed up got a basket of products, all of which were sold at official prices. Such a system bypassed the privately owned stores which were increasingly repudiated by the poorer segments of the population because they sold most of their products at black-market prices. The system of food baskets was a kind of city counterpart of the direct distribution of goods to the countryside through the Rural Supply Centers. The Peasant Council, in calling for support for the food baskets, was attempting to unite the peasantry and the townspeople in a common struggle for a just distribution system. Of course with such limited supplies to begin with, the state distributing agency (DINAC) was unable to fulfill the needs of the workers and peasants who could not buy the things they needed at the established private stores. But it could do something, and increasingly people were organizing to pressure DINAC to adopt the forms of distribution which most fitted their needs. While those who were planning to demonstrate for the food baskets did not oppose JAP committees, which oversaw the marketing of goods in the stores, it was felt that the JAPs were not effective or widespread enough to solve the pressing problem. Instead it was proposed that at least a portion of DINAC's merchandise be marketed directly to the organized public.

The demonstration for the baskets was held as planned at 7 P.M. There were about seventy-five people present. Most peasants had had to go home earlier, but a representative from the Peasant Council did speak to the crowd. The march went down the main street of Lautaro and ended up at the governor's office.

A lot of work had already been done, and the first shipment of baskets was due in a few days. Five hundred were to be sent to Lautaro every two weeks. A problem had arisen because there were already seven hundred people signed up. Also the baskets were originally supposed to contain seventeen items, but that number had dropped down to only ten. The crowd wanted the number back up to seventeen and was asking for the governor's support. The demonstrators asked that the governor come outside to meet them, but he refused. Instead he asked for a seven-person delegation from the demonstrators, a proposal that was eventually accepted. The governor was less than enthusiastic about the baskets. The demonstrators were largely led by members of the Socialist Party and the MIR; the governor was a member of the Communist Party. The Communist Party's position was that the food baskets were a bad idea because they aroused the opposition of the small store owners. This was certainly a problem. The small store owners frequently had a small profit margin and were themselves ultimately dominated by the large private wholesalers. Both the MIR and the Socialist Party called for the expropriation by the government of the big private distributors. In the meantime, however, people were finding it difficult to buy enough food to live, and the immediate solution was some form of direct distribution.

In the end the governor met with seven demonstrators and was noncommittal. A few speeches were made and the crowd dispersed. A similar demonstration was held the same night in Temuco.

On April 15 two representatives from Lautaro went to Santiago as part of a delegation from the Peasant Councils of Cautín Province. The delegation met with the minister of agriculture and discussed the problems of production (inadequate machinery, seeds, fertilizer) and expropriation (too many delays, not enough farms). The peasants also reported on the political situation in Cautín where armed rightist groups were increasingly evident. The two representatives from Lautaro were also able to visit a textile factory in Santiago and talk to the workers about how in the south few textiles were sold at official prices. The textile factories that were visited formed part of an industrial belt, a group of factories in one area that got together to solve the problems of production, distribution, and self-defense. The workers at the textile plant urged the peasants to form some kind of organization which would unite the Peasant Council with urban workers in Lautaro.

On April 24 elections were held to restructure the Peasant Council. About half of the fifteen members of the Peasant Council who had been elected in 1972 had gradually become inactive, and there was a need to elect new members who would work hard. It remained very difficult for Peasant Council members to take time off to come in for meetings, especially when they received no pay for travel. Those who came from the cooperatives received their daily salary as usual when they went into meetings, but those small owners who came received no compensation for the time taken away from work. The elections took place from among those present at the meeting although in a few cases regional assemblies in the countryside had already made selections which were respected. There were about forty people at the meeting, and fifteen were selected to the Peasant Council. About half of the Peasant Council retained their posts. The new Council once again was composed half of peasants from the cooperatives and half of peasants who were small owners. Some of the small owners also worked on private farms seasonally. Only one woman was elected. As far as the age of the newly elected members, it ranged from the late twenties to the late fifties. Most members were in their thirties.

May:

May was late fall in Lautaro, the season for a late planting. Problems of production continued to plague the peasants. In late May a representative of CORA explained to the Peasant Council that only 270 metric tons of fertilizer had arrived, although 1,600 tons had been ordered. Transportation was the problem. The fertilizer was in Concepción, but there were insufficient trucks to transport it. The committees of small owners were most affected; many cooperatives had at least some small store of fertilizer in their warehouses, but small owners were entirely dependent on the government for their immediate needs.

Lack of transport had also delayed shipments of wheat seed. The transport problem was caused largely by the lack of spare parts, and was the direct result of the economic blockade engineered by Henry Kissinger. Most trucks in Chile depended on American spare parts, parts that were difficult to get without cash dollars. Short-term credits, normally offered for commercial transactions between Chile and the United States, had long before been cut off. The dramatic problems of transport in May seemed trivial when compared to the effects of the truck owners lockout of October 1972, which had caused a significant reduction in the area planted throughout Chile. The same lockout was to be repeated in late July of this year. (The CIA chose its targets well. Financial support of the truck owners lockout helped cripple an essential part of the Chilean economy since 75 percent of all Chilean shippped goods go by trucks.)

Also in May a member of the Peasant Council went to Concepción to find out what was causing the shortage of nails and wire. The lack of nails was hurting construction of housing on the cooperatives, and the lack of wire meant that it was impossible to repair the fences. The Peasant Council took advantage of a CORA vehicle which was going to Concepción to send one of its members to the Inchalan steel factory where both nails and wire were produced. The Council member discovered that production was normal; the problem was distribution. Much of the merchandise was being hoarded by merchants for sale on the black market. Once again the peasants found that it was the middleman who was getting the profits and intervening between the producers and the consumers to disrupt the market. The peasant representative who went to Concepción had a long talk with the workers at the steel plant. They in turn were wondering what had happened to the agricultural production, given that there were such food shortages in the city. The peasant responded that back in Lautaro they were producing sugar beets for sugar, rape for cooking oil, wheat for bread, barley for feed and beer, and cattle for meat. Yet all these products and others were lacking in the city. The negative role of the middleman was once again revealed. The workers at the steel plant laid plans to visit the Peasant Council in Lautaro to see the situation for themselves. All over Chile consumers were asking questions about the distribution of goods. The right wing claimed that the workers and peasants were not working, production had fallen off, and as a result there were shortages. The left claimed that it did not control distribution and that the private merchants were channeling products onto the black market and away from the average buyer. The peasants in Lautaro and the workers in Concepción, the direct producers, looked into the problem themselves and found that, despite real problems in production, the left was essentially correct.[2]

In late May food shortages caused a minor incident in Temuco, 25 miles south of Lautaro. A rumor had spread that the state distributing agency. DINAC, had received a large shipment of sugar and was going to sell some of it directly to consumers from its large central warehouse in Temuco. A crowd gathered in downtown Temuco early in the morning to wait for DINAC to begin to sell the sugar. After about four hours, members of Fatherland and Liberty (Patria y Libertad), the paramilitary right-wing group, began inciting the crowd to break into the warehouse and take the sugar. Eventually they succeeded. The crowd managed to break down the door and cart off quite a bit of sugar before the police finally acted, arresting thirty-five and shooting tear gas. All thirty-five were released on their own recognizance, and no one was ever brought to trial.

Fatherland and Liberty continually attacked the Allende government, accusing it of attempting to impose rationing against the will of the population while at the same time using the state distributing agency (DINAC) as a conduit to give food to left-wing government bureaucrats. The crowd at DINAC that May morning in Temuco was a natural place for Fatherland and Liberty to agitate.

They followed up their success by leading a crowd of about fifty or seventy-five people the next day to attack the headquarters of the Provincial Peasant Council in Temuco. The Peasant Council was a frequent target of verbal and written attacks by Fatherland and Liberty, which resented the failure of the Mapuches to act sufficiently subservient. This was the first time, however, that the Provincial Peasant Council had been physically attacked. The young crowd was composed mostly of middle- and upper-class youth, well-dressed, and having a good time. The confrontation had racial overtones. Many of the members of Fatherland and Liberty were blond and fair-skinned, reflecting the fact that much of the upper-class in southern Chile came from a German background. Inside the Peasant Council headquarters, a small number of peasants, mostly Mapuches, defended the building. The crowd threw rocks through the windows and tried to break down the door. When they were unable to do this they called the police, claiming that the peasants had been shooting at them. The police promptly gained entry to the building and searched it thoroughly for arms, finding none. Then they arrested several of the leaders of the Provincial Peasant Council and took them off to jail. Among those arrested were José Purrán, president of the Provincial Peasant Council, and Felix Huentelaf, vice-president. After a few hours in jail, all peasants were released on bail. Eventually the trumped-up charges were dropped. Another victim was less fortunate. The regional head of INDAP, a government agricultural agency that worked with small farmers, had arrived at the Provincial Peasant Council to protest the arbitrary arms search and the arrests. For his troubles he was arrested and then severely beaten, a fact he later denounced on the radio.

June:

On June 11 about fifty peasants from Lautaro joined groups of peasants from all over Cautín in a demonstration in Temuco called by the Central Labor Federation (the CUT, Central Única de Trabajadores). All leftist political parties participated, and all had their representatives on the podium. Each speaker denounced the attacks led by Fatherland and Liberty against DINAC and the Provincial Peasant Council, as well as the less serious incidents in which Fatherland and Liberty had led gangs of teenagers through Temuco breaking windows of stores owned by people who sympathized with the left. One of the main speakers was José Purrán, who described the recent attack on his headquarters. Most of the crowd was made up of workers from Temuco, but there was a good number of peasants and students. At the end of the demonstration a short march occurred. After the march most of the demonstrators disbanded; but one group, made up of the supporters of the MIR, the Socialist Party, MAPU-Garretón, and the youth of the Radical Party, split off to hold a small demonstration of their own. They were marching toward a square when they were blocked by police and by Sergio Fonseca, the governor of the province and a member of the Radical Party. No confrontation occurred because the marchers agreed to go down a different street. The slogans used reflected the differences within the left. "We want socialism, not reformism," "Move forward without compromise," "Create popular power," "Workers to power," and finally "The soldiers are also exploited." All these were chants which clearly identified the political sympathies of the marchers. The number of demonstrators in this second march was about 400. A speaker addressed the crowd and called for the expropriation of all farms over forty BIH, the strengthening of popular organizations like the Peasant Councils and Industrial Belts in order to confront the right, and unity between rank-and-file soldiers and the left.

The left was increasingly divided into two camps. One strategy, advocated generally by part of the Socialist Party, the MIR, MAPU-Garretón, the Christian Left, and the youth of the Radical Party, called for the formation of new organizations like the Industrial Belts which could begin to confront the continual right-wing offensives. The idea was that these new organizations would avoid the bureaucracy existing in the government and in some of the trade unions and would involve large numbers of people in the direct defense of their interests. The Communist Party and part of the Socialist Party continued to advocate the strategy of relying on the government, working through the existing trade union structure, seeking a political compromise with the Christian Democratic Party in order to relieve the continual crisis. A turnaround in the increasingly unfavorable situation would give the left a breathing space during which they could try to get the economy under control and once again begin the slow process of building momentum towards an eventual electoral majority for the left.

A meeting took place on June 27 in Lautaro that was the first step toward a new organization which would bypass existing political structures. The office of the Peasant Council was a dingy room with no heat and little furniture, but it served as a meeting place for representatives of the workers in Lautaro County. Representatives came from the two big agricultural machinery plants, the largest flour mill, the Peasant Council, and the agricultural bureaucracy. The idea was to form an Industrial Belt like the ones in Santiago, but one which would include the peasants as well. The new organization was to be called a County Comando.

The Imacor and Magrimsa agricultural machinery plants, which had been expropriated under the Popular Unity government, employed several hundred workers. These workers represented the largest concentration of industrial workers in Lautaro County. A representative from Imacor had recently gone to Santiago where he met with the workers in the Industrial Belt Vicuña Mackenna. There he learned what an Industrial Belt was and what had been done in Santiago the previous October in order to confront the economic crisis caused by the truck owners' lockout. He also learned how Industrial Belt Cerillos had worked together with the County Peasant Councils around Santiago to occupy thirty-seven farms between forty and eighty BIH. This event had taken place only a few weeks before.

The workers from Vicuña Mackenna encouraged the representative from Lautaro to go back home and try to form a County Comando. It was that representative who was in the office of the Lautaro Peasant Council on June 27 urging others in the room to form the Lautaro County Comando. Similar organizations had already been formed in the nearby towns of Temuco and Villarica. The representative from Imacor explained that the workers had to get together because the right wing was becoming more and more aggressive. He himself had almost been killed a few days before when a pickup truck tried to run him down while he was walking home from work. Small groups from Fatherland and Liberty had sneaked into the Imacor plant at night in order to carry out sabotage. The others in the room agreed to set up a meeting for early July to form the Lautaro County Comando.

Just two days after this meeting in the Peasant Council's office, an attempted coup dramatically confirmed the apprehensions of the workers and peasants in Lautaro. On June 29 six tanks from the 2nd Armored Regiment in Santiago surrounded the Presidential Palace and called for the overthrow of the government. Army Commander-in-Chief General Carlos Prats personally led loyal troops against the tanks, which eventually surrendered. It turned out that the coup attempt had been engineered by Fatherland and Liberty and a few officers from the 2nd Armored Regiment. They had hoped to gain the support of the top officers of the Armed Forces, but had failed. After the attempt, many top members of Fatherland and Liberty took political asylum in the Embassies of Ecuador, Paraguay, and Brazil. Twenty-two people, mostly civilians, were killed in the fighting on June 29.

The immediate response of the working class throughout Chile, especially in the big cities, was to occupy 350 factories and form more Industrial Belts to defend those factories. Although the government later attempted to return many of the occupied factories to their private owners, many stayed in the hands of the workers. The importance of the Industrial Belts as centers of opposition to a coup was increasingly clear.

The government, on the other hand, was unable to get the initiative it deserved after having caught the right in an unsuccessful coup attempt. Indeed, the military and right-wing parties, rather than be dismayed by the failure, quickly regrouped and began preparations for the next, more thorough attempt.

In southern Chile the right-wing commanding officers of the Armed Forces, including regimental commanders in Traiguén, Victoria, Lautaro, Valdivia, Osorno, and Puerto Montt, enthusiastically supported the attempted coup. Many wanted to continue the attempt in the south even though it had been crushed in Santiago. On June 30 soldiers from the Traiguén Regiment were sent out to occupy the small town of Galvarino as well as the town of Traiguén, itself. Soldiers from the regiment at Lautaro were then supposed to take over the town of Lautaro.

On the night of June 30 there was a dance at the social club of the National Party in Lautaro. There leading members of the Christian Democrats, the National Party, Fatherland and Liberty, and the military officers agreed to join with Traiguén and the other regiments to take over local government. After the dance, however, it turned out that some lower-ranking officers and troops in Lautaro's regiment, many of whom were Mapuches from the nearby countryside were openly expressing their disagreement with the plan.

This development meant that the planned rebellion did not take place in Lautaro. As a result the troops from Traiguén returned to their regiment on Sunday. On the night of July 1 a general from Santiago who was loyal to the government visited the Lautaro regiment to attempt to keep the situation under control.

Even though the insubordination in the south did not lead to military insurrection, it did have lasting consequences. Almost immediately after June 29, the military in Cautín began gradually to take de facto control of the province. This was begun with the setting up of roadblocks on the main highway through the province on both sides of Temuco, to check for arms. All vehicles were searched. The legal pretext for the roadblocks was the Arms Control Law, passed by Congress and signed by Allende in 1972. The Arms Control Law instructed the military to control the possession of arms. All arms had to be registered with the military. Previously the control of arms had been a function of the civilian government. After June 29 the military used the Arms Control Law to repress the left. Beside the roadblocks along the Panamerican Highway, the military also began to carry out numerous searches for arms at farms, party headquarters, houses of leftists, and government headquarters. The searches were always violent and were usually conducted more to frighten the left than to find arms.

In Lautaro County itself, on June 29, the peasants, when they heard the news of the attempted coup on their radios, cut down large trees across the roads which connected the town of Lautaro with the countryside. This was a prearranged plan to stop the military's immediate access to the countryside. As it turned out, no troops went out to the countryside. Instead the military set up a roadblock on the bridge over Cautín River. This bridge had to be crossed in order to get from the countryside to the town of Lautaro. The soldiers at the roadblock searched all vehicles for arms. This roadblock was put up, off and on, after June 29 until the coup on September 11.

On June 30, the same day the military in Lautaro was planning to take over the town, the police arrested eight members of the cooperative Che Guevara. They were charged with killing a cattle thief in October 1972 near the cooperative. Although there was no evidence linking any of the arrested with the murder, it was a convenient way to harass the members of the cooperatives in the area. Earlier arrests had been made at cooperatives Camilo Torres and Arnoldo Rios. Four peasants were still in jail from those earlier arrests. A team of three lawyers had been trying unsuccessfully to get the first four peasants out on bail, and they now began trying to get the eight new ones out.

July:

On July 2, at a meeting of the Lautaro Peasant Council, two members reported on their trip to Concepción to buy cloth. Borrowing 20,000 escudos from the Rural Supply Center (about $75), the two had gone directly to the Tomé wool factory. They had brought back the cloth and were preparing to sell it through the Rural Supply Center during the next week. Then they were planning to go to Santiago to look for cotton cloth. One of the two peasants who had gone to Concepción was a woman, and she outlined a plan for the formation of a cooperative of women in Lautaro County to sew the cloth together in order to make clothes for sale. Although this plan never materialized, it indicated the directions that the Peasant Council was going. Increased direct contact between producer and consumer and increased reliance on its own resources to handle economic problems were the goals of the Peasant Council. They were the natural result of the breakdown of traditional systems of distribution. The two peasants in Concepción had also talked to the JAP in the neighborhood of the Tomé factory, and a tentative plan was agreed on whereby the peasants in Lautaro would sell some of their future potato crop to the government agency that bought potatoes in Concepción (the local branch of ECA). The agency, in turn, would make sure that the workers of Concepción were able to buy potatoes at official prices in local stores. Also, in turn, the Tomé factory would sell more cloth to the Rural Supply Center in Lautaro.

On the same day, following the meeting at the Peasant Council, a meeting was held at the Magrimsa factory to form the County Comando. Thirty-three organizations were represented; and about seventy-five people attended. The most important organizations represented were Imacor, Magrimsa, the Peasant Council, CORA, and the flour mill. In addition many peasants came as representatives of their own cooperatives. An executive board was elected, and a demonstration was planned for July 12. A demonstration was also planned by the County Comando in Temuco for the same day.

The meeting in Lautaro and the plans for the demonstration had immediate repercussions within the left. The Communist and Socialist parties' provincial leadership moved to stop the participation of the workers from the town of Lautaro in the County Comando. Pressure was placed on those workers from Magrimsa, Imacor, and the flour mill who had attended the July 2 meeting and who were members of the Socialist Party.

The Socialist Party nationally was split on the issue of Industrial Belts and County Comandos.[3] In Lautaro County and in Cautín Province many leaders of the Socialist Party opposed the Industrial Belts and the County Comandos; many lower-level party militants favored them. In any case the Socialist Party leadership in the province gave its backing, initially, to the July 12 demonstrations. But a few days before the demonstrations they changed their mind. In Temuco on July 10 radio announcements called for all Socialist Party members to boycott the July 12 demonstrations.

The Socialist Party provincial leadership had previously agreed to work with the MIR, MAPU-Garretón, and the Radical Youth in other demonstrations in favor of what was known as "popular power." For example, on April 12 in Temuco a large meeting was held with all the abovementioned parties participating, favoring better food distribution through rationing, through Rural Supply Centers, and through food baskets. But now the situation was different. The Communist Party pressured the Socialist Party leadership strongly against such organizations, and at the last minute the Socialist Party withdrew its support.

The Socialist Party provincial leadership was able to convince most Socialist Party members in Lautaro and Temuco not to participate in the demonstrations on July 12. As a result on July 12 only peasants marched to announce the formation of the County Comando. This meant to all extents and purposes that the County Comando was a dead letter in Lautaro. A County Comando was supposed to be an effective organization that linked workers and peasants; when the workers withdrew, the County Comando was, at least temporarily, a failure. In Temuco the demonstration in the Municipal Theater did attract numerous workers but nowhere near the number that would have arrived had the Socialist Party not announced its boycott. The disunity on the left once again was painfully evident.

It should be pointed out here that the government did not take an official position in these disputes, either in Cautín or anywhere else in Chile. Since different leftist political parties in the government coalition were divided on the question of the Industrial Belts, the Popular Unity wanted to avoid taking a position. Even if the majority of the Popular Unity had favored the Industrial Belts, which was not the case, the government would not have said so because it was on the defensive. It was attempting to placate the right wing, not provoke it.

On July 14 the Lautaro Peasant Council met with the regional head of CORA to review the list of expropriations asked for in the county by the Peasant Council. Of the over 200 farms asked for, it was agreed that fifty-two would be visited by officials from CORA and checked in the notary for exact ownership. (Many little plots were owned by the same person.) An agreement was reached that all farms over forty BIH that could be proven to be poorly exploited would be expropriated. The regional head of CORA listed as problems the lack of adequate personnel to visit and evaluate all the farms as well as a lack of financing to pay for expropriations. He also pointed out that the Lautaro Peasant Council had asked for 200 farms while many other county peasant councils had asked for only twenty or twenty-five. Two hundred was excessive. The Peasant Council was neither surprised nor particularly indignant by the attitude taken by the regional head of CORA. It had been expected that the original list would be sharply reduced. Now it was the job of the Peasant Council to make sure all farms were visited and that a good number got expropriated. The peasants knew that the lack of personnel and money were real problems for CORA, but they also knew that to some extent it was up to them to see how well CORA performed.

In July the results of the wheat crop in the county were being calculated. A lot of interest centered on how well the state wheat monopoly had done, after the intense right-wing campaign against it. Although there were no results available for just Lautaro County, there were statistics for the three-county area that included Lautaro, Galvarino, and Perquenco. For these three counties the state had set a goal of 18,000 metric tons of wheat. But the state had been only able to buy 12,000 metric tons. There was an enforcement mechanism for preventing wheat sales to private merchants or directly to the flour mills, but it was woefully inadequate. It was estimated that the production of wheat by the reformed sector in the three-county area was 9,300 metric tons while private producers with more than 100 hectares produced 12,900 metric tons. It is likely that the 12,000 tons bought by the state came mostly from the 9,300 tons produced by the reformed sector. Most of the production of large private growers had found its way to the black market. And it was no wonder. At the beginning of the season (February, March) the state was paying 4,400 escudos for a metric ton; the black-market price was already 7,000 escudos per ton. By the end of the season (June, July) the black-market price was already up to 12,000 escudos per ton, almost three times the official price. Dry harvested wheat could be stored for two or three months without spoiling; many private owners stored their wheat, waited for the black-market price to go up, and then sold illegally to private owners.

Towards the end of July the political situation was once again heating up. The right wing had fully recovered from the monetary setbacks of June 29 and was carrying out sabotage and attacks throughout the country. An incident occurred in Temuco on July 25 when members of Fatherland and Liberty for the second time broke into the regional headquarters of CORA and stole documents. Their purpose was to collect information about the political stance of cooperatives and about which people in CORA itself were leftists. Such data would be useful in case of another coup attempt. On the same day the truck owners throughout the country announced a second lockout. Many people felt that this time a showdown would come. One way or the other the political and economic crisis would have to be resolved. There would be no truce like the one that solved the crisis of October 1972. The government declared a semistate of emergency, which formally meant that the Armed Forces shared the duty of maintaining law and order with the civilian authorities.

In the midst of mounting right-wing attacks, on July 26, the MIR organized an homage to the Cuban Revolution in Temuco. Workers and peasants from all over the country participated. About fifty peasants from Lautaro County attended. The rally filled the Municipal Theater, which held close to 1,000. Victor Toro, a MIR leader from Santiago, came to Temuco to speak.[4] His speech was broadcast on local radio stations, paid for by the MIR. In his speech he appealed for rank-and-file soldiers to resist any attempt at a coup. At the march after the rally the crowd shouted slogans appealing to the soldiers.

The Armed Forces reacted to the continual appeals to the rank-and-file soldiers. They objected to Toro's speech and also to the same message which the MIR presented on its weekly radio programs in Lautaro and Temuco. On July 29 the military brought court action against both radio programs and managed to have them taken off the air.

Finally, at the very end of July, peasants in Lautaro County attempted to take over the San Ramón farm but were dislodged by the military (see chapter 9).

August:

During August the right wing carried out daily acts of sabotage. During the first two weeks of August, for example, the *Diario Austral* of Temuco reported over thirty incidents in or near Temuco. Most involved shooting at trucks on the road or attacking the houses of the leftists. A bomb exploded at the house of a well-known journalist who worked with the agricultural agencies. Rocks were thrown through the windows of the house of a man who worked for DINAC, the state distributing agency which was trying to keep the population fed despite the truck owners' stoppage. Although no one was killed in these incidents, several truck drivers barely survived rifle shots which destroyed the windshields of their trucks. Trucks began to travel in convoys of seven or eight, and the truck drivers carried weapons.[5]

While the right wing was carrying out these terrorist attacks, neither the police nor the military was doing anything to prevent them. Using the Arms Control Law, the military could have searched the homes and hideouts of known right-wing terrorists. The left made numerous, detailed denunciations against those carrying out the terroism. Instead the military acted against the left. In August, the Arms Control Law was used almost daily to search the homes of leftists and party headquarters of leftist parties. Colonel Hernán Ramírez, the head of the Army regiment in the town of Lautaro, was especially diligent in carrying out searches. This was one of the reasons he was named to head the armed forces of Cautín Province on August 15. General Bravo, in charge of the Third Division which covered the provinces of Cautín, Valdivia, and Osorno, appointed Ramírez at the request of the government. The government was asking the armed forces to maintain law and order although theoretically the governor of the province was giving the orders to the military.

On August 15, the military searched the Socialist Party headquarters in Temuco and Lautaro at 8 P.M. No arms were found. On August 23, the Air Force searched the offices of public relations for the state agricultural agencies in Temuco at 6:30 P.M. The search took two hours and the offices were practically destroyed. The same evening the Air Force invaded the house of the head of public relations for the agricultural agencies, Gustavo Martín. Martín and his family were eating dinner when the Air Force troops approached the house firing into the air and then breaking down the door. No arms were found. On August 25, the military once again searched the headquarters of the Socialist Party in both Temuco and Lautaro, at 1:30 A.M. No arms were found. These are but a few examples of the activity of the armed forces in August. The right wing busily denounced arms caches here, there, and everywhere, and the armed forces diligently pursued all such denunciations.

A good example of the discriminatory use of the Arms Control Law occurred at a farm in the county of Galvarino, right at the edge of Lautaro County. The Santa Elena farm had been expropriated by CORA, and the official taking-of-possession of the farm was to occur on August 19. But when the peasants and the CORA officials arrived at the farm, they were chased off by twenty well-armed members of Fatherland and Liberty who were holed up in a house on the farm. The same thing occurred again on August 20. On August 22 the peasants and CORA officials returned, this time with the police as well; still the farm remained under rightist control. On August 19 the head of CORA in Lautaro had denounced the presence of armed men resisting the law at the Santa Elena. The denunciation was made to Colonel Ramírez, head of the Lautaro regiment. The good colonel did nothing.

In the midst of all the terrorism and military repression, less violent and more traditional political events continued. On August 14 the government named Major Aguayo, from the Army regiment in Lautaro, the government delegate in charge of getting the trucks back on the road in Temuco. Major Florencio Fuentealba was placed in charge of Cautín as a whole. The government hoped to use the authority of the armed forces to force the big truck owners to put their trucks into operation. This tactic was the same one employed by the government throughout the country.[6] Its results were poor. On August 19 Major Fuentealba reached an agreement with the truck owners to put a few trucks on the road in order to continue vital services. This agreement avoided the use of military force against the truck owners to requisition their trucks, which was what the government was threatening. In fact, throughout the country the military proved to be the faithful ally of the big truck owners. Few trucks were requisitioned with military force. Instead agreements were reached which, if they did put a few more trucks on the road, failed to end the economic paralysis of the country. Meanwhile the CIA provided funds to pay unemployed truck drivers and owners. A minority of small truck owners, grouped in an organization known as MOPARE, tried to keep merchandise moving. But they had few trucks compared to the owners of the big truck fleets, and they were subjected to constant terrorist attacks.

By mid August it was not only the truck owners who were sabotaging the economy. In a repeat of October 1973 the big store owners had led a movement to close down all private stores. Doctors were on strike, as were dentists, veterinarians, lawyers, and engineers. The professional classes and the big owners had organized another lockout and semiparalyzed the country.

Of course, there were splits in this united front of the right. Different economic interests sometimes caused conflict. For example, the store owners were organized into two groups, one made up of owners of large stores and one of small. The large store owners were more prepared to close down their stores for a long period of time without going bankrupt. They probably also were the chief beneficiaries of CIA aid. Small store owners, on the other hand, were more reluctant to close down. On August 17 the National Confederation of Retail Commerce (small store owners) asked its members to close their stores. But on August 23 the National Confederation told its members to go back to work. The provincial branch of the Confederation in Cautín rebelled and instructed its members to keep their stores shut down. Eventually other provincial branches in the south went along with Cautín. Once again the right in southern Chile was proving that it was more reactionary than its national leadership.

Meanwhile the left responded to the shutting down of commerce by demonstrations and public declarations. In Temuco the MIR organized a demonstration of several hundred people on August 18 to repudiate the closing of the stores. As the demonstrators passed various of the large supermarkets in Temuco, they were prevented from breaking into them by large contingents of Air Force and Navy guards. The Navy and Air Force troops were more reliable than soldiers from the Army since the last were conscripts and largely of worker or peasant origin. The first two were frequently volunteers from middle-class families.

At the national level political events became more and more chaotic. Perhaps the most important event was the resignation from all his posts of General Carlos Prats, Minister of Defense and Commander-in-Chief of the Army. Prats was a supporter of the constitution and a well-known opponent of a military coup. Shortly after his resignation the two other generals who opposed a coup, generals Sepúlveda and Pickering, also resigned. That cleared the way for General August Pinochet to take over the Army. There were no longer any top officers of the Army who were known to be opposed to a coup. Pinochet himself was thought to be a moderate who had remained silent during the confrontations between right and left among the Army generals.

Prats's resignation was just one event in the more or less permanent government shakeups. Allende was desperately trying to bring the military into the cabinet, as he had done in October 1972, in order to put them in the position of defending the government against the right. A merry-go-round of cabinets ensued as military men agreed to serve and then resigned after a few days. In the agitated weeks before the coup, there were at least a half dozen major cabinet changes. All in all, there were over twenty new cabinets installed during the three years of Popular Unity government.

As the month of August ended, the repression in Cautín Province escalated. The MIR was a favorite target of attack. On the night of August 26, around midnight, a small explosion destroyed a telephone pole in Temuco. An hour later police arrested two men who were driving a jeep one mile away from the site where the explosion took place. Ambrosio Badilla and Robinson Alarcón were the two men arrested. Ambrosio Badilla was a leader of the MIR.

The charges against the two men were based on hearsay evidence. The police said that the jeep had been seen leaving the area where the explosion took place at the exact time of the explosion. The witnesses were the Mora family who lived near the telephone pole. It turned out that the Mora family were well-known right-wingers. Several of their children were in Fatherland and Liberty, and the family owned a farm which had been taken over by peasants of the Revolutionary Peasant Movement.

The most likely explanation for these events is that the Mora's set the charge which knocked down the telephone pole and that a plan had been made with the police to arrest Ambrosio Badilla and charge him with the crime. The police reported to the Mora family, and told them the right moment to set off the explosion. The MIR was well-known, as were all leftist parties, for opposing the acts of sabotage carried out daily by the right. In any case the two men were sent to jail, despite the fact that no arms or explosives were found in their possession. Once in jail, they began conversing with the prisoners. After several days they had succeeded in creating a kind of continual uproar in the jail. For one thing, Badilla got up every morning and sang the *International;* more and more prisoners were joining in. Then he would sing songs from the Spanish

Civil War. The director of the prisons was getting upset. There were no solid charges against the prisoners. Finally, they were released on a high bail and had to report every day to police headquarters. The police passed on to the military a notebook with addresses and phone numbers found on Badilla. The military was excited because the numbers and names were in some kind of code. Actually the names and numbers were not a list of those in the MIR, but personal friends and acquaintances of Badilla. He had written their names and numbers in code only in order to practice using such precautions.

On August 30 Badilla's bail was revoked, and he went into hiding only a day after having been let out of jail. He did so because he and all MIR members were being sought by the military after the incidents at Nehuentue, incidents which reverberated throughout Chile.

On the morning of August 30, 150 select troops from the Tucapel Regiment in Temuco, under the command of Pablo Iturriaga, surrounded the cooperative Jorge Fernández near the town of Nehuentue on the coast of Cautín Province. At the same time six helicopters carrying eighty men flew low over the cooperative with machine guns pointing down. The helicopters were from the No. 3 Aviation Group of Temuco under the command of Andrés Pacheco. The idea was to occupy the cooperative militarily. The public was told by the military that the operation was an arms search, that the MIR had installed a guerilla training center at cooperative Jorge Fernández, and that large amounts of weapons were hidden there.

Cooperative Jorge Fernández had been taken over by peasants led by the Revolutionary Peasant Movement in May 1972. Its former owners were some of the most powerful men in the province. They not only owned several farms but also ran a series of supermarkets. Cooperative Jorge Fernández formed part of a large complex of farms in the area which had been taken over by the Revolutionary Peasant Movement. The zone was known as a stronghold of the MIR. That is why the military chose to attack it.

The soldiers on the ground joined the troops of the Air Force, which descended from the helicopters. All the peasants on the farm were rounded up and brought to the area around the big house (which was used as a clinic and meeting hall by the peasants). The men were separated and taken into the house where questioning began. At Nehuentue the military first showed their skills at torture. The peasants were beaten, dunked into water until they almost drowned, and tortured with electric shock. They were asked where the MIR had hidden the arms. Some peasants were hung by ropes and flown around in helicopters, dangling in the air. Others were taken down to the river and forced to remain nude in the freezing water for long periods of time. One man died of pneumonia as a result.

The troops stayed three days. They finally succeeded in finding what they were looking for. The military had originally decided to invade the area when three peasants at the cooperative went to the old owner with a story about how the MIR hid weapons at Jorge Fernández and trained guerrillas there. These three peasants had refused to support the original takeover. Nevertheless, they had been invited to become members of the cooperative. They did so, but they continued secretly to receive money on the side from the old owner in exchange for information about the cooperative.

The MIR had not hidden any arms on the farm, nor did they operate a guerrilla training school there. They had, however, hidden a small arms cache on an adjacent reservation, only a few hundred yards from the boundary with the cooperative. Taking advantage of close ties with the peasants on the reservation, some of whom had participated in the takeover and now worked at Jorge Fernández, the MIR had buried a supply of small arms and ammunition stored in boxes. In addition, in a shack on the reservation, a primitive workshop had been set up to manufacture crude grenades. Only a few of the peasants at Jorge Fernández or at the reservation had known about these things, for the protection of everyone involved.

Following the raid, a huge propaganda show was mounted. Commanders Iturriaga and Pacheco held a press conference where they assembled a large variety of weapons and literature, supposedly confiscated from the Jorge Fernández farm. Many of the weapons displayed, however, had been added by the military in order to impress the journalists. The military also arrested twenty-eight peasants, about half of the peasants at the cooperative. No members of the MIR were arrested, but the military published the names of seven MIR organizers who were being sought. Other Mirista leaders throughout the province, like Ambrosio Badilla in Temuco, took the hint and went into hiding. This wasn't much of a change for them. All MIR members had operated in semiclandestinity since June 29. Many leaders changed houses frequently and stayed out of public sight.

The military and the right wing made a national campaign out of the incidents at the Jorge Fernández farm. It was yet another excuse for the coming coup. A whole series of stories was invented to give the incident even more drama. The military said that shipments of arms were landing on the coast at night, probably from Cuba, and were being hidden at Jorge Fernández. Charges were levelled against doctors in the area who worked with the peasants, doctors like Arturo Hiller (who was murdered after the coup). Foreign doctors throughout the area were also denounced as extremists. The campaign against foreigners was a preliminary taste of what was to come after the coup when thousands of foreigners were persecuted by the junta. They were the culprits in the military's fantasies: only foreigners could have brought unpatriotic Marxism to Chile.

The Popular Unity gradually began to defend the peasants at Nehuentue. In Temuco provincial Governor Sergio Fonseca said that he did not believe the military had found any arms. In Santiago representatives of the government agreed to meet with the peasants and hear their side of the story.

September:

On a national level several events occurred which added fuel to the agitation for a coup. Socialist Party leader Carlos Altamirano had admitted that the Socialist Party had contact with the sixty patriotic sailors who had defended the government against the June 29 coup and for their efforts had been jailed and tortured by the Navy. Miguel Enríquez, the leader of the MIR, had gone underground to avoid capture by the Navy for his supposed involvement with the sailors. At the same time the MIR published details of meetings between U.S. Naval Intelligence officers and high officers of the Chilean Navy. Even more significant, when Air Force troops in Santiago tried to search the large Sumar textile factory for arms, they encountered serious problems. The workers would not let them into the factory, and a large crowd of civilians surrounded the troops and began to converse with them, urging them to stop the search. The troops began to mingle with the crowd, so the officers commanded them to withdraw.

The incidents at Nehuentue occurred against this background of increased confrontation between the military and the civilian population. Nehuentue was a carefully planned incident designed to be the southern military's contribution to the coming coup.

On September 4, a delegation of peasants from Nehuentue, representing the Peasant Council of the area, went to Santiago to tell the peasants' side of the Nehuentue story. They had interviews with Minister of Agriculture Jaime Toha, and then with President Allende. Both promised to investigate the incidents. The peasants were also interviewed by the newspaper *Clarín* and the weekly magazine *Chile Hoy*. One of the women peasants was interviewed on national television. The peasants outlined the brutal treatment dished out by the military. Commanders Iturriaga and Pacheco initiated a legal suit against *Chile Hoy* on September 8, claiming that the interview they published was libelous. Also on September 8, Minister of Agriculture Jaime Toha visited Temuco to inquire more into the Nehuentue incidents. Meanwhile, the military courts were beginning the trials of the peasants.

In Nehuentue itself on September 4 the left held a march to commemorate the third anniversary of the electoral victory of the Popular Unity. The traditional Chilean flags carried at such marches (both left and right claimed they were the patriots) were flown at half-mast in protest against the military invasion of the Jorge Fernández cooperative.

The right wing continued to carry out its sabotage. In early September the right started to block the roads throughout Cautín Province. Not content with shooting at truck drivers and spreading miguelitos around the roads to puncture tires, the right on September 6 cut trees down so that they fell across the Panamerican Highway around the town of Lautaro. The trees were set on fire along with hay and old tires. On the same day trees were cut to block the railroad tracks around the town of Vilcún, just outside of Lautaro County. Elsewhere in Cautín Province, on September 6 a group of eighty men blocked the road in and out of the small town of Gorbea. The crowd was made up of private farm owners from southwestern Cautín. The same day in Temuco a group of right wingers blocked the bridge leading into Temuco from the south. Again, on September 6, electrical lines were destroyed near Lautaro and also near Pitrufquen. All these actions were obviously coordinated.

Peasants from the countryside marched with workers on September 4 in the town of Lautaro without incident. But in Temuco the divisions within the left was dramatically revealed. Several thousand people marched to celebrate the third anniversary of the electoral victory of Allende. They crowded into a gymnasium in downtown Temuco to hear speeches. Once in the gym, different groups began to shout slogans which the crowd took up. Soon it became apparent that some of the crowd were being led in chants by the Communist Youth, while others were following the lead of the MIR. Slogans such as "We want socialism, not reformism," and "Move ahead without compromises" competed with more traditional slogans such as "Allende, Allende, the people will defend you." Physical attacks took place between students from the MIR and the Young Communists. A struggle took place over control of the microphone on the stage. The MIR wanted one of their representatives to speak. Finally order was restored, and the speeches took place. No one from the MIR spoke. As the demonstrators left the gym to go back to the street, the bitterness of the incident was still felt. The lack of unity was evident, yet unity was what was needed. The coup was only a week away.

The crowd struggled to get through the narrow door onto the street where a march was to be held. The bottleneck was not due to just the size of the doorway. Out on the street the marchers were penned in narrow space by army troops mounted on horses. As the march finally got started, the troops followed the marchers. At one point they charged a Socialist Party contingent and took the wooden sticks away from the Socialist youth group. At the same time army intelligence agents tried unsuccessfully to arrest several MIR leaders who were in the crowd. Many of the marchers were indignant. The Socialist youth marched shouting, "They're going to see, they're going to see, when the workers take power." The military wasn't going to see. Precisely to prevent it, the armed forces took over the government on September 11.

Chapter 11

The Coup

Ya los españoles
no saben que hacer.
En cuanto se mueven,
los van a detener.

Spaniards don't know what
to do anymore.
All they have to do is move,
and they get arrested.

"Que turu ru ru ru," song from the Spanish Civil War

September 11, 1973: Temuco

The town awoke to the sound of helicopters flying low over the houses. Machine guns were visible—pointing down from the helicopters, threatening the population. Soldiers in jeeps circulated continually through the streets. Those who thought it was just another arms search quickly found out differently. Most listened to the radio. They learned that the military had taken over Chile. Reports from Santiago were vague. All the radio stations in Cautín had been taken over by the military and were broadcasting communiques from local military commanders. Colonel Hernán Ramírez, formerly head of the army regiment in Lautaro, was now in charge of Cautín. With his authorization, the radio was broadcasting new laws. Communique No. 1 announced that the military had taken over the country and that the military in Santiago had appointed Colonel Ramírez the new governor of Cautín Province. A curfew was announced for 3 P.M. Anyone out after that hour was subject to arrest.

There was no armed resistance in Temuco. The overwhelming force of the military was uncontested. The left retreated, its leaders trying to hide in a town that was too small. The military arrested many on the day of the coup. All foreigners were ordered to report to the police the next day for registration. Most of the townspeople of Temuco went out and got as much shopping done as possible before 3 P.M. Those who supported the coup began to raise Chilean flags. Before long all of Temuco was covered in Chilean flags. The leftists obviously had flags up too. At the same time many were trying to use the few hours before the curfew to hide themselves, or their weapons, or their literature.

For many days news came only through the frequent official communiques and rumors. The military announced that all was orderly and peaceful; rumors mentioned the arrests, and sometimes executions, of local leftists. All too often the rumors started from fact.

Some of the communiques for Cautín Province are instructive:

Local Communique No. 1 was announced at noon on the eleventh. Beside the curfew and naming of Colonel Ramírez as governor, the communique asked everyone to stay home if possible. Extremists would be sanctioned with the full rigor of the law. Authorizations to have arms were cancelled. Sales of gasoline were suspended, and vehicles would need special authorization to travel. Cooperation with the armed forces was urged, and Colonel Ramírez announced that all rights of workers would be respected.

Subsequent communiques simply named new heads of various agencies, such as the electricity company, agricultural services, and so forth. In addition, the junta in Santiago began to broadcast communiques, always prefaced by the statement that they were national communiques. The national communiques were always more general than the local ones.

Local Communique No. 8, emitted at 11:40 P.M. on the eleventh announced that the next day stores would be open and trucks and buses would run. The owners agreed to end their lockout unconditionally. Their economic demands were simply dropped. The communique ended with the customary threat to extremists.

Local Communique No. 11, issued on September 12, demanded that eighty-eight persons present themselves the following day at the army regiment in Temuco for questioning. Twelve of these people, including this author, were foreigners.[1]

The eighty-eight were largely either people that the military wanted but had not yet arrested because they could not be found, or people who were suspects that the military wanted to locate and warn, but not arrest. Many of the eighty-eight were people who worked for the agricultural services.

(Most of these would soon lose their jobs.) As it turned out, those who showed up on the thirteenth were only those who felt that they wouldn't be arrested. Others refused to come in, preferring to go underground. The military did not arrest any who came in, but did order many to stay in their houses and not leave town. It was clear from the questioning that the military was relatively uninformed about the activities of many leftists. The military intelligence services were still very unsophisticated.

Most of the prominent figures of the local administration under Allende were not on the list of the eighty-eight. The military had already arrested them. For example, Governor Gastón Lobos, member of the Radical Party and head of the province of Cautín, had awakened on the eleventh to find his house surrounded by soldiers. He remained under house arrest until several days later when the military took him to the regiment and tortured him for information. He was eventually murdered.

Included on the list of the eighty-eight were Ambrosio Badilla and José Peraltra, leaders of the MIR; Alejandro Manque, peasant leader of the Revolutionary Peasant Movement; Arturo Hiller, a doctor who had worked in Puerto Saavedra and who was at the time of the coup head of the rural branch of the National Health Service for all of Cautín; Esteban Perle, a Socialist who worked for CORA in Lautaro; and Pedro Rios, a socialist who was head of a local development agency.

None of these came in. All were subsequently captured. Badilla was killed after having been tortured extensively. He was turned in by a neighbor of the person who was hiding him.[2] José Peraltra remained underground for many months and was captured in early 1974. He was then tortured and remains in jail. Alejandro Manque also remained underground until early 1974 when he was captured, tortured, and jailed indefinitely without charges. Arturo Hiller was captured and murdered shortly after the coup. (The military claimed he was shot while trying to escape.) Esteban Perle was caught and tortured extensively. He remains in jail. Pedro Rios was captured and murdered shortly after the coup. In many of these cases the military has denied ever arresting the person.

Local Communique No. 15, dated September 15, announced that all leftist literature was prohibited. The military ordered all existing stocks to be turned in to the regiment. This was an early measure. Later the military would be more thorough. They went to the public library, took all the books they considered subversive, and locked them in large trunks, which were then stored in the library's basement. The selection of the subversive books was frequently arbitrary. In one case the military confiscated a book entitled *The Industrial Revolution* because its title contained the word revolution. In another case, a book called *Cubism* was chosen because it was thought to be about Cuba.

Communique No. 15 also threatened anyone who caused industrial sabotage. The military warned peasants: "Don't listen to any extremists who claim that the military is going to throw you off the land and massacre you. Just the opposite, the military only wants to organize you so that you work better every day for the Fatherland."

Local Communique No. 18, also emitted on the fifteenth, dissolved all the Industrial Belts, JAPs, and County Peasant Councils in the province, as well as cooperatives formed in the latter part of the Allende period (the CERAs). The military considered all these organizations to be illegal because they were created during Allende's tenure.

Local Communique No. 30, issued on September 18, was directed at extremists. The military promised that any resistance would be answered with gunfire. Drastic sanctions would be taken against not only extremists but all those who hid them. Point No. 4 of the Communique read as follows: "For each innocent person who is killed, ten extremists will be killed immediately, following the procedures set out in the Code of Military Justice during war time."

These Local Communiques illustrate the atmosphere in the weeks following the coup. The province of Cautín was superficially calm. Many Communiques stressed the return to normalcy. Yet the repression was so extensive that almost everyone knew to some extent what was going on. The Communiques only occasionally became belligerent and threatening.

In the homes of leftists these weeks immediately following the coup were weeks of fear. Every night the military patrols passed down the street, and many families anticipated a dreaded knock on the door. People hid their emotions, masking their grief. It was necessary to pretend publicly that all was well so as not to attract suspicion from those who had welcomed the coup. To some extent all those who supported Allende had to learn to lead a partially clandestine life after the coup. Eventually this split personality, this divorce between public cheerfulness and private grief, became second nature.

As for the Communiques, they soon became less relevant. A few days after the coup, newspapers, the right-wing ones, were being published once again. They were censored. Transportation and telephone service were reestablished. The military clearly dominated the immediate situation in Cautín, but people were anxious for news from the north. They knew from the Communiques from Santiago that there was resistance in the large cities. (Valparaíso, for example, was completely cut off for four days.) Many people tuned in to Argentine radio stations to find out what was going on. The most discussed report was that Army General Carlos Prats, who had opposed the coup and had resigned only a few weeks before it, had gotten control of the town of Concepción (Chile's third largest city) and was marching on Santiago against the junta. This report came insistently from Argentina. Unfortunately for the poor and working-class people of Chile, the report was false. Prats had been arrested on September 10. In order to dispel the rumor, the military forced Prats to talk on television. He appeared pale and announced that he was not involved in politics and soon was leaving to go to Argentina. It was subsequently reported that he had been handcuffed for the interview; his hands were concealed below the table. These same reports said that guns were trained on him as he spoke.

Prats was in fact deported, right after his television appearance, to Argentina. There he had a low public profile and was writing a book about the coup. But the junta feared him as an important military leader opposed to the coup, even though he was in exile. Prats and his wife were blown to pieces by a bomb in their car in October 1974 in Buenos Aires. It is widely believed that the Chilean secret police (the DINA) were responsible for the crime.

Within a week after the coup it became clear that the immediate resistance in the big cities had been overcome. The population in Cautín knew that the coup had been successful. The official news from time to time carried reports about the repression, even if you had to read between the lines. On September 24, two Canadian Catholic priests from Temuco were expelled from Chile for extremist activities. They had helped hide people. Some soldiers from the regiment had rebelled and fled to a park in the center of Temuco for hiding. They wanted to link up with a civilian resistance but did not know where to go. The military surrounded the park and let them stay there for weeks, but on October 12 troops moved in and cleared the park out.

In late October the papers announced that six extremists had been killed when they attacked the army regiment in Temuco. This story was so ridiculous that one wondered why the military had even bothered to publish it. In fact, the military had murdered the six who were leaders of the Popular Unity parties in Temuco. All had been captured weeks before. They included the Regional Secretary of the Communist Party of Cautín, Alberto Molina, and the head of the Young Communists for the province, Antonio Chávez.

Most atrocities, of course, went unreported. The military massacred many Mapuche peasants who were suspected of cooperating with extremists. Eyewitnesses from the small town of Pitrufquen told this author of seeing Mapuche bodies being brought into town in trucks. They were from the Puraquina Reservation. A right-wing informer had said there were weapons hidden on the Puraquina Reservation; and the military had, after torturing several peasants, found the arms. Then many peasants were murdered by the military. Some were thrown into the Toltén River, others loaded onto trucks and taken into Pitrufquen.

The incident at Puraquina was not an isolated one. Doctors at the hospital in Temuco reported that large numbers of bodies of peasants arrived at the hospital morgue in the weeks following the coup. They had died from bullet wounds.

The reign of terror continued throughout the province. The people of Cautín learned to live in fear. They talked quietly only with trusted friends about what was really going on.

September 11, 1973: Lautaro County

At Elicura farm the peasants took precautions as soon as they heard news of the coup on the radio. As they had on June 29, they quickly went out and cut down trees across the roads. They concealed any compromising material on the farms, including weapons and literature. A few of the peasants who were most closely associated with the MIR went into hiding, leaving the farm for houses on the reservations. These few carried weapons. They had prepared hiding places, and they kept in touch with the MIR militants who were also hiding in the countryside. Communications were extremely difficult in the first days since the roads were cut and messages were passed by people walking long distances. The MIR militants who were in the town of Lautaro at the time of the coup got out to the countryside as best they could, taking as much material as they could with them. When possible, they stole vehicles from the agricultural services and then hid them in the countryside. These were later found by the military.

The Army regiment in Lautaro had a prearranged plan for the coup. First the town of Lautaro was secured and as many important figures as possible were arrested. In some cases Fatherland and Liberty (Patria y Libertad) was able to carry out its own terror with the permission of authorities. The most outstanding example of this was in the case of the governor of the county, Fernando Teillier. Fatherland and Liberty members caught him fleeing in an automobile on the outskirts of town and murdered him on the spot. They had been out to eliminate him for a long time.

As soon as the town was secured in the early afternoon, groups of soldiers were sent out to major farms. These were the farms that had been taken over, that were known to oppose the coup strongly or to have worked closely with the leftist parties. Elicura was one such farm. A group of thirty soldiers was assigned to occupy Elicura.

The soldiers never made it to Elicura that afternoon. They spent their time clearing the trees from the road, cautiously, in case of ambush. Several times crude booby traps exploded. Two soldiers were wounded. After that, ropes and chains were thrown around the trees, and they were dragged away with jeeps. At sunset the soldiers retreated into town. During the night the peasants cut down more trees.[3]

The troops started out again early the next morning. This time they had chain saws, and they were able to open the road as far as Elicura by late morning. No more booby traps exploded.

When the troops arrived at Elicura, the lieutenant in charge ordered them to approach the first house, near the road, while firing their weapons. The flimsy houses were penetrated by bullets, and the peasants inside of them took shelter by lying on the floor. The soldiers broke down the door of the first house they came to and grabbed Pancho, the treasurer of the cooperative, who was prone on the floor. A couple of soldiers beat him for a minute or two. He was then told that all the peasants on the farm had to be present for a meeting in thirty minutes. The military knew how many men, approximately, worked at the cooperative, but they did not know their names. Pancho was sent running to the more distant houses. The lieutenant told him that if he did not come back, his wife and children would be shot. Meanwhile, the troops continued to drag other peasants from their homes.

In thirty minutes all the men on the farm were assembled, except those who had fled. The lieutenant announced that the junta had taken over the country, that the land reform was over, and that the peasants had better cooperate or they would be killed. He said that he knew some of the peasants knew where MIR militants were hiding and that he was going to find out who cut those trees down and who set the booby traps which had exploded. He demanded to know who the officers of the cooperative were. Pancho and Pedro finally stepped forward. They were both hauled off while the rest of the peasants were herded into the house they used as a meeting hall.

The lieutenant recognized Pedro from some of the demonstrations in town. He took Pedro to Pedro's own house, and there proceeded to have him beaten until he could not stand up. Pedro's wife Amalia was also beaten severely. Pedro answered all the lieutenant's questions by saying he did not know. He said that he had not seen anyone from the MIR for over a year and that he did not know who had cut down the trees.

Meanwhile another officer took Pancho to his own home, where he was put through the same treatment. Other peasants were taken singly out of the assembly hall and beaten. The soldiers asked everyone about the MIR and the trees and booby traps.

This process went on for about four hours. The lieutenant was not getting any information. When it began to grow dark, he took his troops and left. He took with him Pedro and Pancho, as well as a list of names of all the peasants who had assembled. He told those who remained that he would be back the next morning and that he expected them all to be assembled at 8 A.M.

Pedro and Pancho were tortured all night with electric shocks, beating, and extensive submersion in water and excrement. Pedro almost drowned during this last torture. Pancho blacked out twice during the electric shocks. Neither gave very much information. They gave the names of MIR militants who had been involved in the takeovers in 1970 and 1971, and who had long since moved out. (Even these names were false. Pancho and Pedro had never known the real names of any MIR militants.) Finally, in the early morning hours, they were thrown into a cell and left alone. Both were in very bad shape.

The lieutenant went back out to the farm. The peasants were assembled and waiting for him. The lieutenant threatened to kill all of them if they did not talk that day. He again took them one by one and beat them. Still he received little information. The peasants had all agreed only to give information about those MIR organizers who had long since left the area. In any case, no one at the farm knew where the MIR militants, who *were* in the area, were hidden. Finally the lieutenant gave up. He took his troops back to Lautaro in the afternoon and told the peasants he would be back the next day to organize work on the cooperative. This he did. For the next two months the lieutenant went every day to the cooperative to make sure the peasants were working.

Pedro and Pancho were kept in the army regiment in Lautaro for the entire week. They were accompanied by peasant leaders from cooperatives all over the county, except for those who had gone into hiding. All were tortured. The military did obtain some information. One peasant confessed that a man and a woman had driven a jeep out from town on September 11 and had then hidden the jeep underneath some tree branches in a ditch. The military went out and found the jeep. Further beating elicited the information that the woman was blond and the man was small and dark. Their nicknames were given as well as the fact that they had been involved in organizing demonstrations. The peasants who lived near where the jeep was found said that the man and woman had left the area on foot.

The military learned what they had already suspected—that some leftists had hidden in the countryside where surely they were planning to cause whatever trouble they could. The military believed the two who had abandoned the jeep were members of the MIR. Efforts were redoubled to find them. This was a difficult task. There were probably ten or fifteen members of the MIR who were hidden in the rolling hills of Lautaro County. Trying to find them was like trying to find the proverbial needle in a haystack. The only hope for the military was that someone would betray the miristas.

Pedro and Pancho were finally sent back to Elicura, more dead than alive. After they got home, they stayed in bed for another two weeks in order to recover.

Meanwhile the peasants became resigned to the fact that, at least for the moment, the military had won. The coup was a success. The lieutenant was running the farm. He frequently brought a ring-wing agronomist from the state agricultural services along with him. Together they decided what work had to be done on the farm. The peasants certainly did not like it, but they were concerned about keeping their cooperative. They did not want to be forced to leave Elicura. They worked as they were told. They feared and hated the lieutenant at the same time. They received their pay on time, but it was at the old rate. Inflation shot up drastically after the coup due to the decontrol of prices.

Two months later Fernando Schultz arrived with the lieutenant. They carried a piece of paper which they showed to the peasants. Guillermo, who knew how to read, looked at it. He could see that what the lieutenant and Schultz were saying was correct. The farm had been returned to Schultz. The cooperative was dissolved. The paper was signed by Colonel Hernán Mardones, head of the regiment in Lautaro. Schultz said the peasants had two days to clear off the property. Three peasants, who were considered by the lieutenant to have been the most cooperative, were allowed to stay. They would work, at least temporarily, for Schultz.

The agrarian reform at the Elicura farm was over.

Somehow the lieutenant suspected that Pedro knew more than he was telling, so Pedro was harassed periodically. A list of all the people who worked at Elicura had been discovered at the state bank, and it was known that two of the men were missing. Pedro said that they had gone north to work as summer laborers in the harvests, but the lieutenant did not believe this story. He thought that Pedro knew where the two men were. From time to time Pedro was dragged from his family's house on the reservation and taken into the regiment for another session of beatings and torture. It seemed endless. After months and months of this treatment, Pedro cracked. He didn't tell the lieutenant anything. He didn't tell anyone anything. He borrowed an old shotgun which a friend of his had hidden, saying he wanted it to hunt rabbits. He went out to the woods and killed himself.

Pedro was the only death at Elicura. At other cooperatives the peasants were not so lucky. The military managed to capture some of the members of the Peasant Council. One was taken to the regiment at Lautaro and shot. The others were beaten and jailed. One, Rafael Railaf, remains in jail in Temuco.

Luis Mora was a peasant leader at another cooperative; he refused to talk when the farm was initially occupied by troops, and an enraged sergeant shot him. Two other peasants who had been singled out as ringleaders at other cooperatives eventually committed suicide, driven to it by the continual beatings and torture. Undoubtedly many other peasants, whose names we do not yet know, were murdered in Lautaro County.

Meanwhile, the old landowners were coming back to regain their farms. Many of the farms in Lautaro County which had been expropriated by Allende were returned. Almost all those that had been taken over by force were returned.[4]

The handful of MIR militants who were hiding in the countryside of Lautaro County kept in touch with each other and with the peasants who had been recruited to the Party during the Allende period. They organized diversionary tactics to confuse the military. The most common was to light fires on the hillsides at night. The military who were patrolling the roads would go to investigate and find no one. At the same time another fire would light on a distant hillside, and the patrol would have to go to investigate that one.

It was difficult to hide in Lautaro County, however, because of informers. There were always a small number of peasants who were willing to give information to the military, either from fear or for money. This meant that the MIR militants had to move frequently during the daytime. It was necessary to move often from reservation to reservation, to change hiding places. Through torture, the military was gradually beginning to have some idea of the structure of the MIR in Cautín Province. Troops began to ask for the MIR militants by name.[5]

By early 1974 the MIR decided to transfer its organizers out of Lautaro County and send them to the cities in the north where they would be safe. Several from Lautaro left, but a few stayed. By mid 1974 two had been caught.

Alejandro Manque, the leader of the Revolutionary Peasant Movement, was also hiding from time to time in Lautaro County. He was eventually caught as well, during a trip he made to town. He was recognized by someone who informed the military. Manque was tortured severely and remains in jail as of early 1977. Felix Huentelaf, vice-president of the Revolutionary Peasant Movement, was arrested in early 1974 and remains in jail in Temuco.

One of the two MIR organizers who were caught was able to get out of jail after about a year. The military never really determined who he was. He was tortured, but he was finally released. The other MIR organizer was well-identified. He was tortured and finally executed. His name appeared on the list of 119 prisoners which the junta published in August 1975. The junta claimed these prisoners had been killed abroad in quarrels with the Chilean left or in confrontations with the police of foreign countries. This lie was quickly exposed by the international press. The junta was trying to escape the blame for the murders of some of the thousands of prisoners who have been killed. (There is ample documentation of the arrests within Chile of almost all of the 119 prisoners. They had never gone abroad. They died in Chilean jails.)

The peasants who had been recruited by the MIR during the Allende period remained in the countryside and maintained contact with the MIR. This was the case for the two peasants who left the Elicura cooperative the day of the coup in order to go into hiding.

The other leftist political parties did not have as extensive a structure in the countryside of Lautaro County, and they had a much harder time keeping in contact with their peasant party members.[6]

Thus ended the agrarian reform in Lautaro County. The peasants of Lautaro have been forced to suffer extreme poverty as well as political repression since the coup. The economic policies of the junta have meant a severe reduction in the already low standard of living of the peasantry. Few peasants in Lautaro have been hired to work on the farms, which, once again, are largely in private hands. The reservations are now overcrowded, after the return of those peasants who were expelled from the cooperatives. Many have been forced to migrate to the cities where there are no jobs to be found.

But the seeds sown in Lautaro County during the Allende years have not died. In Lautaro County, and throughout Chile, the lessons learned under Allende are well-remembered. The junta has lost almost all of its initial support, and its rule by terror will not last indefinitely. Agrarian reform will probably come once again to Lautaro County. When it does, the peasants will be likely to take measures to ensure that it is more permanent.

12

Three Years of Agrarian Reform in Lautaro County

Statistics and Maps

Three years of Allende's agrarian reform in Lautaro County produced impressive results. The peasants were able to pressure the government to carry out large-scale expropriations. They organized themselves into a County Peasant Council which was one of the strongest and most democratic in the country.

The strength of the peasantry in Lautaro County can be measured by comparing the amount of land expropriated there to the amount expropriated in other areas. Since the passage of the Agrarian Reform Law in 1967, a total of 42,768 hectares were brought into the reformed sector in Lautaro. Seventy percent of this land was expropriated under Allende. The breakdown is as follows (see Map 2):

Expropriated land in Lautaro County (1967–73)

1967–70 (under Frei)	13,055 hectares	30%
1971 (under Allende)	16,976 hectares	40%
1972 (under Allende)	12,737 hectares	30%
Total	42,768 hectares	100%

What part of Lautaro County did this represent? One useful way to consider this question is to compare the amount of hectares expropriated with the amount of hectares left for the big landowner. Any farm over twenty BIH used permanent hired laborers and totalled several hundred hectares. In September 1973 in Lautaro County there were 21,978 hectares of farms greater than twenty BIH in private hands.

Private large farms in Lautaro County in 1973

Private farms 20–40 BIH	10,688 hectares
Private farms 40–80 BIH	7,645 hectares
Reserves granted to owners of expropriated farms	3,645 hectares
Total area of large private farms	21,978 hectares

An overall view of the agrarian reform in Lautaro is possible by taking into account the above figures. Combining the reformed area of large private farms, there were 64,746 hectares of farms over twenty BIH in Lautaro County as of September 1973. Of these 64,746 hectares, 42,768 hectares, or *66 percent*, had been expropriated (see Map 3.)[1]

In Cautín Province as a whole about 277,000 hectares had been expropriated by September 1973, while 461,000 hectares of farms over twenty BIH remained in private hands. Only *38 percent* of the landowners' holdings had been expropriated.[2] In Chile as a whole about 35 percent of the land over twenty BIH had been expropriated.[3]

These figures show clearly that the peasant movement in Lautaro County was a strong one in relation to the rest of the country.

The larger amount of land expropriated in Lautaro was the result of peasant pressure, not because of unusually active government agencies. Only seven out of forty-two cooperatives formed in Lautaro County were the result of expropriations due to size. These seven had originally been farms greater than eighty BIH. Six had been expropriated under Frei. These six farms were all in the eastern part of the county near the Andes. Here the land was poorer, and the population was sparse (see Map 4).

Most of the farms expropriated under Allende were between forty and eighty BIH and were expropriated because of poor exploitation. The government was pressured to expropriate these farms because the peasants had occupied many of them. Sixteen farms were taken over by the peasants of Lautaro during the Allende period, out of a total of thirty-six expropriated. In terms of hectares, 39 percent of the land expropriated in Lautaro under Allende had been occupied illegally (see Map 5).

There are no comparable statistics for Cautín Province or for Chile as a whole. The percentage of land in the reformed sector that was occupied before expropriation is not reliably known. Rough estimates indicate that, here again, Lautaro County was exceptional. Illegal occupations were much more common in Lautaro than in most of Chile.[4]

The larger size of the reformed area in Lautaro County in comparison with other parts of the country was also reflected in the figures for production and labor force. The reformed sector accounted for about 33 percent of agricultural production. In Chile as a whole the reformed sector accounted for between twenty-five and thirty percent, slightly less.[5]

As for the labor force, statistics are very unreliable. Nationally the reformed sector was estimated to employ 18 percent of the rural labor force. In Lautaro County the reformed sector employed about 26 percent of the labor force (about 1,200 cooperative members out of a rural work force of about 4,600).[6]

One of the reasons for the larger size of the reformed sector in Lautaro County was the land hunger of the Mapuche Indians. Map 6 shows the structure of landholdings in the county in the mid 1960s before the land reform. Map 7 shows the areas occupied by reservations in the mid 1960s. It can be seen, by comparing these two maps, that the landholdings under fifty hectares largely corresponded to the Mapuches. The situation was in fact worse than is indicated by these maps. Most Mapuches not only had less than fifty hectares; they had a lot less. An average Mapuche landholding was under five hectares. Over an eighty-year period the Mapuches had been pushed onto smaller and smaller plots of land. By 1970 they were desperate. The Mapuches were quick to take advantage of the opportunity provided by Allende's election to regain land.

Map 8 shows where the Mapuche reservations were located in relation to the reformed sector in 1973. This map shows that the Mapuches moved from their reservations to take over adjacent farms. The Mapuches considered that these farms had at one time belonged to them.

In many cases some of the oldest members of the reservations remembered that the big farms had once been unfenced and had been part of Mapuche territory. The landowners had stolen them by force. Most could not remember that, but many did remember how the landowners had gradually swindled parcels of reservation land from the Mapuches over the years, incorporating these parcels into the big farms. These long-standing and bitter grievances led the Mapuches to take over the farms illegally, going ahead of the government's expropriations.

If the peasants in Lautaro County were able to take over so much of the land, then can we presume that the landlords were left destitute in many cases? The answer is no.

In Lautaro County over the six-year period of agrarian reform, seventy-one landowners lost their land due to government expropriations. Many of these landowners were brothers, sisters, husbands, and wives. Only about thirty *families* lost land.

Of the seventy-one landowners, this author was able to trace thirty-two. None were destitute. Three had died or retired on a pension. The rest were relatively prosperous. Eleven had received reserves when their farms were expropriated, and these reserves were large enough to provide a good income. Although precise statistics are not available, reserves in Lautaro County averaged between thirty and forty BIH. Some of these eleven, in addition to receiving reserves, had other farms outside the county. Many also had relatives with land. For example, Manuel García Miranda lost part of his El Cipres farm. He was granted a reserve of twenty-one BIH (314 hectares). If this reserve proved too small and Manuel García got into a tight spot, he could always rely on his brothers. José García, Francisco García, and Martín García had four farms in Lautaro County. Their farms Santa Eduvigis, San Lorenzo, Tres Esquinas, and Chimbarango totalled 120 BIH (907 hectares).

Eight of the landowners did not receive reserves but did have other farms either in the county or outside of it. These farms provided them with a good living. For example, Pablo Paslack Weber found that his Santa Ana farm had been taken over by angry peasants. Eventually the farm was expropriated and became the cooperative Arnoldo Rios. But Pablo Paslack Weber, although unhappy, was not desperate. He owned three other farms in Lautaro County, totalling fifty-one BIH (457 hectares). Primitiva Fernández Diez lost her Verdún farm to the government but retained El Capriche, which had twenty-five BIH (171 hectares). And her brother René Fernández Diez had the El Pedregal farm in Lautaro County. It totalled twenty-seven BIH (196 hectares).

Another eight had other businesses. In many cases they had had these businesses even before their farms were expropriated, but they expanded them during the Allende period. Two had grocery stores, and two had trucking businesses. One owned an apartment building, one had a sawmill, and one was a long-time diplomat for the government. Another was a congressman for the National Party. There is no reason to believe that any of them lost money during the Allende period. Three landowners felt so distressed by Allende's election and the expropriation of their farms that they left the country. Andrés Truán went to Australia, Pablo Goebel went to Argentina, and Héctor Rodríguez went to Spain. They were the exception. Most landlords were sure that they could continue to make a good living under Allende, and believed that with any luck at all, the military would overthrow the government.

Thus, even in Lautaro County, where the agrarian reform was more thorough than in the rest of Chile, the landlords who lost their farms were not economically crippled. They continued to control most of the wealth of the area.

Analysis

The long history of injustice towards the Mapuches in Lautaro County led to an explosion in 1970. The Mapuches in Lautaro sought to redress long-held grievances. Their desire for land led to massive takeovers of farms. There was no hesitation on their part once they realized that the police would not use force of arms to throw them off the occupied farms. The Mapuches knew that all the land had once belonged to them, and they felt they had a right to take it back. The Mapuches had an even greater incentive than most peasants.[7] This is reflected by the great number of takeovers in southern Chile right after Allende's election.

Once the Mapuches were able to regain the land, they sometimes wanted to divide it into individual plots. They were accustomed to individual holdings on the reservations. Few Mapuches had been rural proletarians or farm laborers who worked for wages but held no land. Most Mapuches who had worked on the big farms for the landlord either had a few hectares back on the reservation or were hoping to get them. There was a tradition of individual, not collective production. The Mapuches carried their habits from the reservations over to the new cooperatives, and they found it difficult to work collectively on the expropriated land.

Yet any rational scheme to increase production had to rely on cooperatives. It made no sense to allow the expropriated farms to be divided into small plots. The result of that would only be continued subsistence production and a gradual reconstitution of the large landholdings as the landlords were able to buy out the small owners.

Recognizing this, Frei's Agrarian Reform Law called for cooperatives on the expropriated land. Under Allende, CORA continued to set up cooperatives. It was the job of CORA and the leftist political parties to convince the peasants of the advantages of the cooperatives.

There were political as well as economic reasons for the government to stress collective production. The reformed sector was to be a political base for the government. The peasants would collectively fight for the land reform and the government rather than concern themselves only with their own problems on their own little piece of land. Eventually, when the Chilean economy as a whole moved closer to socialism, the countryside would move in that direction more easily. The individualistic traditions of the Mapuches made it more difficult for the government and the left to persuade them to set up working cooperatives. Previous chapters have documented the problems involved, such as the tendency for the Mapuches to spend more time on their individual plots than on the production of the cooperative and the refusal of many Mapuches to give up their small plots on the reservations. These were problems that were true of all peasants throughout Chile. They were built into the system of the agrarian reform. The fact that the government guaranteed the salary of the peasants in the reformed sector, regardless of their work record, tended naturally to encourage the peasants to work less on the cooperative and more for themselves.

In Lautaro County, however, these problems were more serious because of the special history of the Mapuches. A counter-balancing factor was that the peasants in Lautaro County were more politically aware and better organized than peasants in many other areas. One reason for this, of course, was the lesson learned by thousands of peasants when they acted to take over the farms themselves. This direct experience taught many peasants an important political lesson, one that could not have been learned by years of talk and explanations. Many peasants involved in the takeovers learned that it was possible to take history into their own hands rather than passively reacting to events. A self-confidence developed and overcame years of quiet resignation. Many realized that only by fighting together could gains be won.

There was another factor peculiar to Lautaro County, the influence of the MIR. The numerous takeovers resulted from a combination of the Mapuches' desire for land and the leadership of the MIR. The development of the Lautaro County Peasant Council was also affected by the policies of the MIR. The MIR had encouraged a strong Peasant Council independent of the government agricultural agencies and elected by the rank and file.

The MIR encouraged illegal occupations while the larger leftist parties in the Popular Unity coalition generally discouraged them, urging the peasants to wait for the orderly process of expropriation. The MIR had several reasons to encourage the takeovers. The MIR was worried that an extensive agrarian reform would not be carried out by the government bureaucracy. For example, many farms between forty and eighty BIH might not have been expropriated for reason of poor exploitation had they not first been occupied by the peasants. The priority for the government was all farms over eighty BIH. The MIR believed that the agrarian reform law should be stretched to its limit and that the poor exploitation criteria for expropriating farms between forty and eighty BIH should be used as much as possible.

The MIR was also concerned with the development of the peasantry's own political consciousness. The MIR wanted the peasants to be able to rely on themselves, not just on the government. The MIR believed that the right wing would not allow the government to fulfill its program, including the agrarian reform, without attempting to organize a military coup. A coup could be avoided or defeated only if the rank-and-file workers and peasants were deeply committed to the reforms proposed by the Allende government, committed enough to fight for them. The MIR believed that in order to develop this committment it was necessary that the rank-and-file workers and peasants themselves be the main force in carrying out the reforms. For this reason, the MIR encouraged the peasants to take over farms and then to form a Peasant Council to represent all poor peasants.

This view was opposed by most parties in the Popular Unity coalition although the Popular Unity was divided. The predominant view was that the reforms proposed by the Popular Unity could be carried out with strict adhesion to the law. Then the right wing would try to persuade the Armed Forces to carry out a coup, but would fail. The reforms would gain the support of an increasing number of Chileans, so that by the 1976 elections the left would be able to win a majority of the voters. This view relied upon the military's support of the constitution. No preparations were made to resist a coup seriously if one were carried out. According to this view, any actions by the left that were outside the law, or even that stretched the law too much (without actually breaking it), were dangerous because they would give the right wing the opportunity to persuade the military that the Popular Unity government was no longer abiding by the constitution. The Popular Unity coalition opposed peasant takeovers. The Popular Unity also originally called for Peasant Councils, appointed from the leadership of existing organizations rather than elected. The Peasant Councils were seen as a means to carry out government policy rather than as bodies to formulate policy.

In Lautaro County the MIR worked hard to carry out its strategy. It succeeded in mobilizing large numbers of peasants, who were able to take over many farms. This led to more government expropriations and to a larger reformed sector than was the case for the rest of the country. The MIR was also able to help organize a strong Peasant Council, which in turn represented many of the most serious grievances of the peasantry.

The leadership of the Popular Unity in Lautaro County generally opposed both the massive takeovers and the Peasant Council. In many cases this opposition was not public. It took the form of passive instead of active cooperation. Sometimes the divisions became public, as in the May 1972 incident at the hospital.

As pointed out earlier, despite the expropriation of many farms between forty and eighty BIH in Lautaro County, private absentee landowners (largely members of the National Party) continued to control most of the wealth of the county. This was true despite the fact that the landowners had been hurt more in Lautaro County than in most parts of Chile.

Surprisingly enough, the differences in strategy in the left were not resolved with the coup. The MIR claimed that its predictions had come true. The armed forces had been used by the ruling class to overthrow the Allende government. The Popular Unity had not been prepared to resist a coup. No systematic effort was made to win the rank-and-file soldiers over to a position of refusing to participate in a right-wing coup. Instead a vain effort to work with the top officers had been made, only to end with the discovery that the top officers were traitors to their own oaths to uphold the constitution. This position was also that of part of the Socialist Party and of MAPU.

On the other hand, the Communist Party and part of the Socialist Party blamed the coup partly on the adventurous strategy of the ultraleft. Their interpretation was that by pushing too hard and too fast, the MIR, part of the Socialist Party, and MAPU had helped create a climate of anarchy and lawlessness. This climate was used by the right to justify a military intervention. The basic strategy of gradual political gains leading to a majority in the 1976 elections was seen to have been correct. It was the divisions created by the far left that caused this strategy to fail. Coup attempts would have failed were it not for the actions of undisciplined hotheads on the left.

Both sides in the debate put the blame for the coup primarily on the United States and the Chilean right wing. The U.S. economic blockade had proved effective in disrupting the Chilean economy and had provided fertile ground for right-wing plotters. Top officers in the military had allowed themselves to be persuaded to intervene in favor of the Chilean wealthy. The CIA secretly spent millions of dollars funding the right wing and promoting the coup. And the Chilean wealthy preferred the murder and torture of tens of thousands of Chileans to the loss of its privileges.

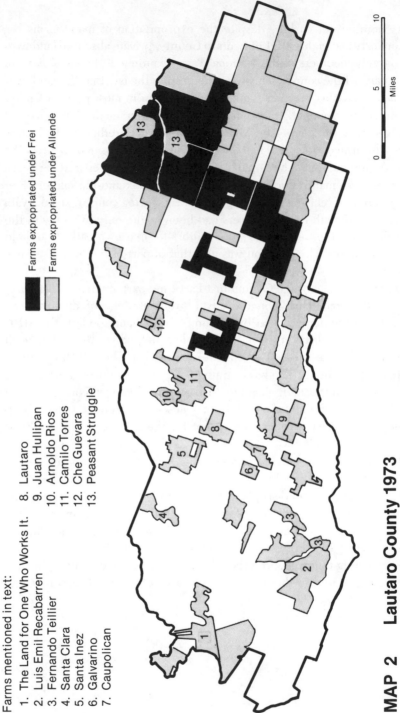

Farms mentioned in text:

1. The Land for One Who Works It.
2. Luis Emil Recabarren
3. Fernando Teillier
4. Santa Clara
5. Santa Inez
6. Galvarino
7. Caupolican
8. Lautaro
9. Juan Hullipan
10. Arnoldo Rios
11. Camilo Torres
12. Che Guevara
13. Peasant Struggle

■ Farms expropriated under Frei

▨ Farms expropriated under Allende

0   5   10
|--------|--------|
         Miles

MAP 2   Lautaro County 1973
Area Expropriated under Frei and Allende

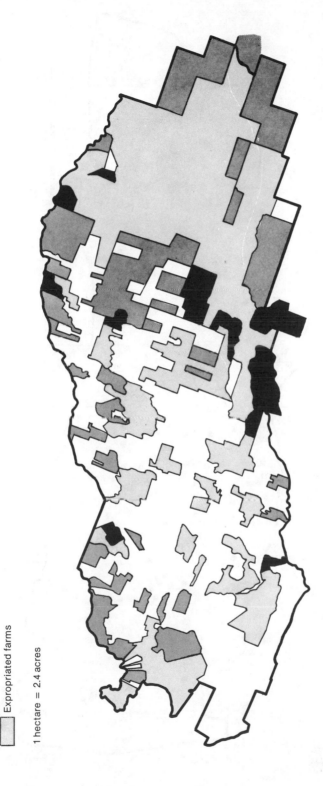

Reserves left to landlords

Private farms between 20 and 80 BIH

Expropriated farms

1 hectare = 2.4 acres

0   5   10

Miles

MAP 3   Lautaro County 1973
Private and Expropriated Farms

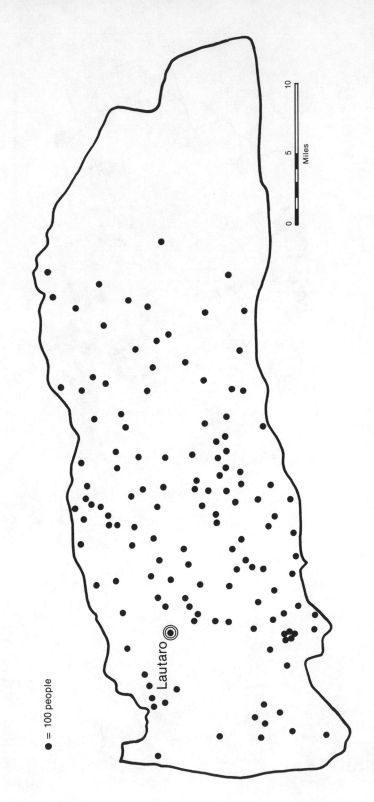

● = 100 people

Lautaro ◉

MAP 4　Lautaro County 1973
Population

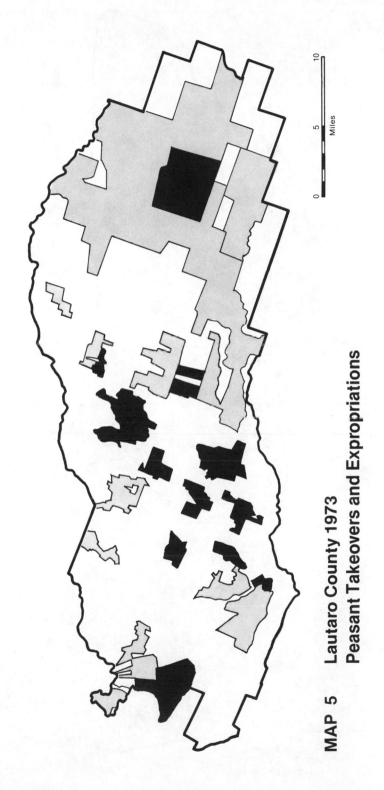

■ Farms expropriated after peasant takeover

▨ Farms expropriated without peasant takeover

0   5   10
├────────┼────────┤
         Miles

**MAP 5   Lautaro County 1973
Peasant Takeovers and Expropriations**

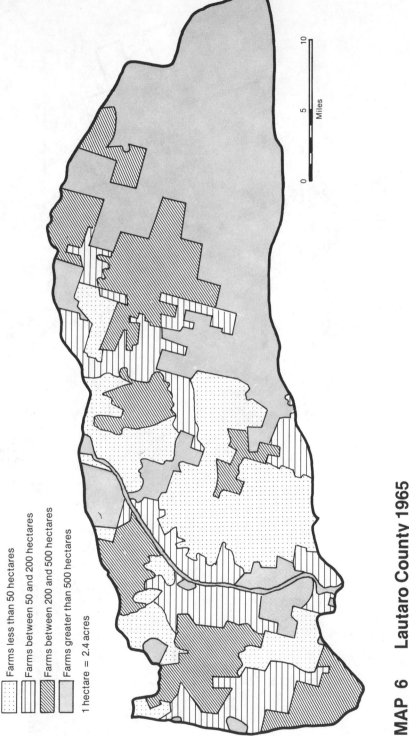

Farms less than 50 hectares

Farms between 50 and 200 hectares

Farms between 200 and 500 hectares

Farms greater than 500 hectares

1 hectare = 2.4 acres

MAP 6 Lautaro County 1965
Land Ownership Before Agrarian Reform

0   5   10
        Miles

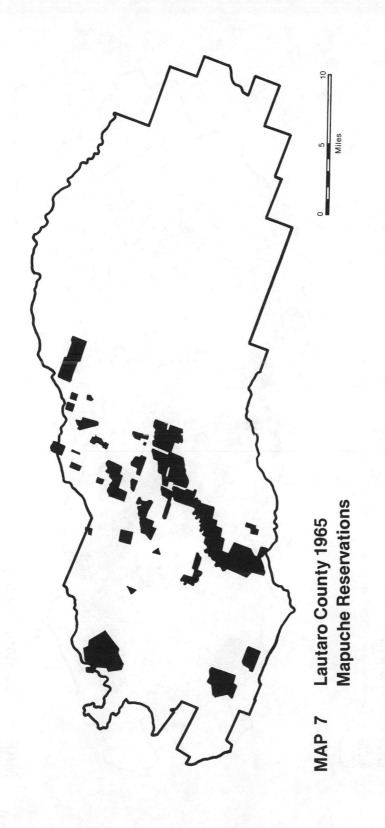

MAP 7   Lautaro County 1965
Mapuche Reservations

0   5   10
Miles

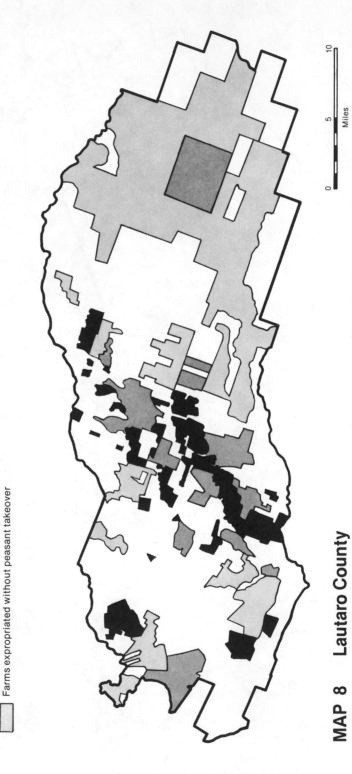

■ Mapuche Reservations

▨ Farms expropriated with peasant takeover

☐ Farms expropriated without peasant takeover

MAP 8   Lautaro County
Reservations, Takeovers, and Expropriated Farms

0   5   10
                    Miles

Glossary

afuerino: a wage laborer in the countryside, frequently a migrant laborer, employed seasonally. Does not live on the farm.

Araucanians: the main indigenous people of Chile, divided into three groups, the most southern of which are the Mapuche. The two northern groups no longer exist.

asentado: a member of an asentamiento, a cooperative set up as a result of Chile's agrarian reform, begun in 1967.

BIH (Basic Irrigated Hectare): the amount of land necessary to produce as much as one hectare of good irrigated land in Chile's central valley. A term which originated with the 1967 Agrarian Reform Law.

Christian Left: also known as the Izquierda Cristiana, or IC, a small political party which was created in 1971. Part of the Popular Unity coalition.

Communist Party: one of two main parties in the Popular Unity coalition, founded in 1922. Received about 20 percent of the vote in the 1973 elections.

CORA: Corporation of the Agrarian Reform, the basic state agricultural agency in charge of the agrarian reform.

encomendero: a Spaniard who received an encomienda from the Crown during the time when Chile was a colony. An encomienda was a grant of Indian labor.

huinca: Mapuche for white man or person of Spanish descent.

INDAP: a state agricultural agency that lent support to the small private farmer or minifundista.

inquilino: a rural laborer who lives on the farm and has his own plot of land as well as pasture rights. He receives a salary.

intervention: in the countryside, a government takeover of a farm where there was a labor dispute, a temporary measure used frequently during the Allende government.

latifundista: a large landowner who employs many laborers.

MAPU: one of the smaller parties which was a member of the Popular Unity coalition, founded as a split from the Christian Democrats in 1969.

Mapuche: the southern Araucanian Indian. There are about 600,000 Mapuches in Chile (the figure is not really known) most of whom live in the countryside in southern Chile.

221

mediero: a sharecropper.

merced: a grant of land in colonial Chile.

minifundista: a small private farmer with only a few hectares, who does not hire outside labor (or only very rarely).

MIR: Movimiento de Izquierda Revolucionaria, or Movement of the Revolutionary Left, a small leftist party not in the Popular Unity coalition. Founded in 1965, its influence and numbers grew before and during the Allende government.

Patria y Libertad: Fatherland and Liberty, a small paramilitary fascist group begun after Allende's election. Carried out terrorism and sabotage.

Peasant Council: committees of poor peasants set up in early 1971 by county, uniting rural wage earners, minifundistas, and asentados, initiated by the government (Consejo Comunal Campesino).

Popular Unity: the coalition of left political parties which was elected with Allende or its candidate in the presidential elections of 1970 and overthrown by the military in September 1973. The Communist Party and Socialist Party were the most important members of the coalition.

reservation: a small area of land inhabited by Mapuche Indians in southern Chile. Set up in the late 1800s to restrict the Mapuches, there are more than a thousand reservations.

reserve: an area of land given by the government to a landlord whose farm was expropriated under the Agrarian Reform Law. It varied in size but always was less than eighty BIH and usually was the best land on the expropriated farm.

Socialist Party: one of the two main parties in the Popular Unity coalition, founded in 1932, which received about 20 percent of the vote in the 1973 elections. Allende was a member.

Notes

Chapter 1

(Many references are made to material now difficult to obtain due to its suppression by the present military regime. Some of this material has been saved by exiled Chilean leftists and has been collected in a special library in Mexico City.)

1. See p. 204 of *Land Holding and Socio-Economic Development in Agricultural Sector*, published in Santiago in 1966, prepared by CIDA, the Inter-American Committee of Agricultural Development. This book will be hereafter referred to as the CIDA study. Also see p. 135 of *Chile Hoy*, (Mexico City: Siglo XXI, 1970). This book contains an excellent essay by Aranda and Martínez about agriculture.

2. Proportion of dollar income from exportations committed to the importations of agricultural products.

	Food Imports	Imports of Agric. Prod. for industrial use	Fertilizers and Machinery	Total Imports for Agriculture
1965/70	11.7	5.6	3.1	20.4
1970	8.8	4.2	3.1	16.1
1971	15.7	7.3	2.7	25.7
1972	33.1	15.5	4.8	53.4

These figures come from the ICIRA diagnosis. ICIRA was a state organization under the control of the Ministry of Agriculture. The ICIRA diagnosis is an analysis of the agrarian reform under Allende through June 1972. It was presented to the Minister of Agriculture in November 1972. It is the fundamental document for an analysis of the Allende agrarian reform. It is available in Spanish through Siglo XXI.

Chile did export some agricultural products during the Allende government. Total exportations of agricultural products were only about $20 million a year. The military junta has greatly increased exports of agricultural products in order to improve its poor balance of payments despite drastically reduced agricultural production and reduced food imports.

3. For data on food consumption and importations, see ICIRA diagnosis. It should be remembered that all the statistics for 1972 and from the ICIRA diagnosis are estimates.

A note on statistics. In Chile there were lots of them. Both the right and the left had their own statistics, which, naturally, were very different. In general, the ICIRA statistics are the most reliable. Nevertheless, they too are subject to large margins of error. Despite the many studies on the agrarian reform and the tremendous quantities of statistics, the Popular Unity government at times had only the remotest idea of exactly how many hectares of a given crop had been sown or how many farms had been expropriated in a given area.

4. For an analysis of peasant voting patterns in the March 1973 elections see the April 1973 *Revista Agraria*, a separate section of the magazine, *Chile Hoy*.

5. For a discussion of these two strategies see the article by Sergio Gomez in April 1973

Revista Agraria, in the magazine, *Chile Hoy.* For the view of MIR see its insert in the newspaper *Clarín* of February 6, 1972.

6. For a discussion of the debate in Russia see Chapter 4 of *Soviet Agriculture in Perspective* by Erich Strauss (New York: George Allen and Unwin, 1969), and *Socialism in One Country, 1924–26* by E. H. Carr (New York: Macmillan, 1962). For China, among others, see *Fanshen* by William Hinton (New York: Monthly Review Press).

7. These figures come from a detailed discussion of the stagnation of Chilean agriculture in the article by Aranda and Martínez in *Chile Hoy* (Mexico City: Siglo XXI, 1970).

8. See the CIDA study, page 296.

9. For a study of agrarian reforms as a task of the bourgeoisie, based on Marx's concept of surplus value and the role of rent in agriculture, see Michel Gutelman's article in *Transición al Socialismo y la Experiencia Chilena* (Santiago: PLA, 1972).

10. These data come from the ICIRA diagnosis. The costs per peasant come from an article by Solón Barraclough in the magazine CEREN, No. 7, March 1971.

11. Data from ICIRA diagnosis. For a good study of the farm occupations under Allende, see "Las Tomas" by Juan Carlos Marín, in the magazine *Marxismo y Revolución,* August 1973.

12. Data from ICIRA diagnosis.

13. Data from ICIRA diagnosis.

14. See page 128 of *El Inquilino de Chile Central,* by Alexander Schectman (Santiago: ICIRA, 1971).

15. In the province of Valparaíso the Popular Unity was experimenting with material incentives in order to induce the asentado to work on the collective part of the asentamiento. See article by Sergio Gómez in the *Revista Agraria,* a separate section of the magazine *Chile Hoy,* February 16, 1973.

16. Data from ICIRA diagnosis.

17. For data on CEPROs see Maffei's article in the *Revista Agraria,* a separate section of *Chile Hoy,* June 5, 1973.

18. For a discussion of the privileges of the asentados see "La Nueva Estructura de Clases en el Campo," by Dagoberto Perez, a special document published in *Punto Final,* September 26, 1972.

19. The toleration of parallel markets in the reformed sector also took place in Russia in the 1930s after the first great wave of expropriations. See chapter 5 of *Soviet Agriculture in Perspective* by Erich Strauss (New York: George Allen and Unwin, 1969).

20. For an example of the polemic see the articles in the magazine *Punto Final* in its issues of February 13, February 17, March 13, 1973, concerning the congress of Peasant Councils in January 1973.

21. On this point see the article by Marchetti and Maffei in CEREN, the October 1972 issue. This is one of the very few studies of Peasant Councils.

22. These data come from INDAP as published in *Chile Hoy,* August 25, 1972.

23. For a view of the legal proficiency of the right wing, see the magazine of the NAS, *El Campesino,* of June 1973.

24. For details of right-wing violence in the countryside see *Punto Final* of July 3, 1973, and *Chile Hoy* of September 8, 1972.

25. Sometimes the approval of the military authorities was paid for. Minister of Agriculture General Sergio Crespa was forced to resign in September 1974 after it became known that he had accepted money in exchange for this permission for former landowners to take back their land.

26. See the magazine *Mensaje,* published in Santiago in March–April 1976.

27. See *Chile Monitor,* No. 13, June 1975.

28. See *Latin America Ecnomic Report,* December 5, 1975.

29. *Chile Monitor,* No. 13, June 1975.

30. Ibid.; *Latin American Economic Report*, Dec. 5, 1975.
31. See the *New York Times*, January 25, 1976.
32. See *Latin America Economic Report*, March 15, 1974, *Chile Monitor*, No. 13, June 1975, and *NACLA*, October 1975.
33. See *Chile Monitor*, No. 21, September–October 1976.
34. See *El Mercurio*, April 30, 1976.
35. *El Campesino Chileno Escribe a Su Excelencia*, edited by Brian Loveman, published in Santiago in 1972 by ICIRA.

Chapter 2

1. See *Capitalism and Underdevelopment in Latin America*, pp. 1–121, for Frank's essay on Chile.
2. See Lenin, *The Development of Capitalism in Russia*.
3. See Laclau's article "Feudalism and Capitalism in Latin America." The value of Laclau's article, as has been pointed out by Frank himself (*Latin American Perspectives*, 1:98), is due not only to this emphasis on precapitalist internal relations of production, but to his tentative sketch of how these relations of production might have been necessary to capitalist development in the imperialist metropolis. Laclau speculates that investment in the colonies might have slowed the falling rate of profit in the metropolis because the rate of profit to be obtained in the colonies was higher than that of the metropolis. Here he quotes the tantalizing but tentative lines of Marx concerning the effect of foreign trade upon the rate of profit (Vol. 3, *Capital*, pp. 238–39). Ruy Mauro Marini takes this idea further still in an important article about dependency, where he describes the role of raw material-exporting countries in the world division of labor (see bibliography). The industrial countries can buy new materials abroad more cheaply than at home, thereby both decreasing the cost of maintaining their workers and the cost of raw materials for production. This means simultaneously increasing the rate of surplus value and decreasing the amount of constant capital a combination which means a higher rate of profit. At the same time, the industrialized countries can sell manufactured goods in underdeveloped countries not at competitive prices, but at monopoly ones.
The industrialized countries can conduct both these operations because of a higher development of labor productivity at home and a higher rate of surplus value (cheaper labor) abroad. The maintenance of precapitalist labor relations abroad becomes a necessity in order to perpetuate these conditions.
Of course, this scheme is applicable less and less today. Two factors have changed it. First, the development of capitalist relations of production in industry in Latin America, followed by the development of a national bourgeoisie and manufacturing production in the 1930s. These capitalist relations of production spread to agriculture. Second, recently we have seen that raw materials are now able to command their own monopoly prices, thereby changing drastically the relation of the underdeveloped world to the metropolis (e.g., oil, coffee, bauxite, and so forth).
4. See Marx, Chapters 26–32 of Vol. 1, and Chapter 47 of Vol. 3, *Capital*. "The mere appearance of the cirulation of commodities and the currency of money does not suffice to supply the historical conditions necessary for the existence of capital. It arises only where the owner of the means of production and the means of subsistence finds in the market a free worker who offers his labor for sale." (*Capital* 1:170).
5. On the rebellions, see *Bond Men Made Free* by Rodney Hilton.
6. This process began earlier in France than in England. See Bloch, *French Rural History*, pp. 94–101 and Tawney, p. 91.
7. Tawney, pp. 43, 53.

8. See Marx on rents, *Capital* 3:797.

9. The potential conflict between landlord and merchant did not develop in Chile. Unlike in Europe, where landlord and merchant frequently had distant sources of wealth (e.g., Italy), in Chile both depended on agricultural production until the mid nineteenth century.

10. See Marx, *Capital* 3:327–28.

11. Marx, *Capital* 3:333.

12. Dobb, p. 39; Hilton, p. 156; See Sweezy's comments in *The Transition from Feudalism to Capitalism*, p. 34. If the exports are to a far-away market, the increase in commodity exchange and circulation of money may not affect the peasantry at all. If the trade is carried on nearby, the participation of the peasantry would at least be partially related to whether they were tenants on a divided demesne or still subject to labor services.

In general, it can be said that in the history of all Latin American economics the export of raw materials has often prolonged the slave or feudal oppression of the peasantry. A contemporary observer, Ruy Mauro Marini described the Latin American export economy in an article written in 1972:

> [In the industrial countries] the individual consumption of the workers represents, then, a decisive element in the creation of demand for the commodities produced, being one of the conditions which enables the flow of production to be adequately transformed into the flow of circulation. . . . In the Latin American export economy, things are different. Since circulation is separated from production and takes place basically through the foreign market, the individual consumption of the worker does not interfere in the realization of the product although it does determine the amount of surplus-value. As a consequence the natural tendency of the system will be to exploit to the maximum the labor power of the worker, without worrying about under what conditions that labor power can be reconstituted, as long as that labor power can be replaced by the incorporation of new workers in production.
>
> Thus the sacrifice of the individual consumption of the workers, in order to increase exports to the world market, depresses the level of internal demand and makes the world market the only way out for production. Parallelly, the increase in profits which the capitalist derives from this puts him in the condition of wanting to increase his own consumption without doing so through internal production, which is oriented towards the world market, but by increasing imports. . . .
>
> The harmony which is established at the level of the world market between the exportation of raw materials and food by Latin America and the importation of manufactured goods from Europe covers up the tearing apart of the Latin American economy, manifested by the split of total individual consumption into two opposing spheres. When, after the world capitalist system has reached a certain grade of development, Latin America enters the stage of industrialization, it will have to do it starting from the bases created by the exportation economy.

Consistent with the argument made here, this author would have substituted "merchant capitalist" for "capitalist" in the above quote.

13. On the other hand, Frank has stated that he never claimed to be a Marxist in *Latin American Perspectives* 1:98.

14. Another possible term would be semicapitalist. For a thorough discussion of Marx's thought on precapitalist formations see Hobsbawm's introduction to *Pre-Capitalist Economic Formations* and Mandel, Chapter 8. For a good discussion of the plantation economies of Latin America and their classification according to Marxist categories, see Jay Mandle's article in *Science and Society* 26:49–62.

15. See Larraz's excellent book.

16. See Vicens V., pp. 429–31.

17. Elliott, p. 100.

18. Elliott, p. 102, and Vicens V., p. 293.

19. See Elliott, p. 290, on imports, and Vicens V., p. 299, on serfs.

20. Vicens V., p. 259 and pp. 302–4.

21. Vicens V., p. 433.

22. This is a much debated question. In any case, it is agreed that prices were higher in Spain than in the rest of Europe. See Elliott, pp. 183–88.

23. Elliott, p. 198.

24. Borde and Góngora, p. 48.

25. Amunátegui, *Encomiendas*, vol. 1, p. 69.

26. Jara, p. 30.

27. Amunátegui, *Encomiendas*, vol. 1, p. 226. For population, see Ramírez, p. 34.

28. McBride, p. 68.

29. Amunátegui, *Encomiendas*, vol. 1, p. 174.

30. Amunátegui, *Encomiendas*, vol. 1, p. 307. This was a general problem throughout Latin America. See Rafael Altamira y Crevea, *Manual de investigación de la historia del derecho indiano* (Mexico: Instituto Panamericano de Geografía e Historia, 1948); Mario Góngora, *El estado en el derecho indiano. Epoca de fundación (1492–1570)* (Santiago: Instituto de Investigaciones Histórico-Culturales, 1951); José María Ots Capdequí, *España en América. El régimen de tierras en la época colonial* (Mexico City: Fondo de Cultura Económica, 1959), and the same author's *Historia del derecho español en América y del derecho indiano* (Madrid: Aguilar, 1969). General works in English that discuss the problem include Francois Chevalier, *Land and Society in Colonial Mexico. The Great Hacienda*, trans. by Alvin Eustis, ed. by Lesley Byrd Simpson (Berkeley and Los Angeles: University of California Press, 1963) and Lesley Byrd Simpson, *The Encomienda in New Spain. The Beginning of Spanish Mexico* (Berkeley and Los Angeles: University of California Press, 1950).

31. Amunátegui, *Encomiendas*, vol. 1, p. 238. Royal regulations ordering an end to forced labor included the Regulations of Santillan (1559), the Regulations of Governor Gamboa (1580), and the Regulations of Viceroy Esquilache (1622).

32. Amunátegui, *Encomiendas*, vol. 1, p. 363, and Góngora, p. 30.

33. Jara, p. 37.

34. Amunátegui, *Encomiendas*, vol. 2, p. 42.

35. Bagu, p. 87.

36. Amunátegui, *Encomiendas*, vol. 1, p. 188.

37. Jara, p. 41. In 1654 a captured male Araucanian was worth 100 pesos.

38. Amunátegui, *Encomiendas*, vol. 1, pp. 362–3.

39. Amunátegui, *Encomiendas*, vol. 1, p. 421.

40. Amunátegui, *Encomiendas*, vol. 2, p. 207.

41. Borde and Góngora, p. 58.

42. Sepúlveda, p. 14.

43. Sepúlveda, p. 23.

44. McBride, p. 87, and Amunátegui, *Encomiendas*, vol. 2, p. 253.

45. Góngora, pp. 41–42, 72–73, 89.

46. Kautsky, p. 20.

47. Ramírez N., pp. 47–53, 68–69.

48. Ramírez N., p. 79.

49. Ramírez N., pp. 77–78.

50. Amunátegui, *Encomiendas*, vol. 1, p. 422.

51. Ramírez N., p. 76.

52. Trade with England increased ten to twenty times in the 1820s. Vitale, vol. 3, p. 55.

53. Vitale, vol. 3, pp. 115–25.

54. See the book by Feliu Cruz.

55. Pinto, pp. 36–37.

56. Vitale, vol. 3, pp. 158–59.

57. Jobet, p. 47.

58. By 1969, for example, 75 percent of the investment in fixed capital in Chile was made by the state, but it was the private sector which benefitted from this investment.

59. Vitale, vol. 3, p. 146.

60. Pinto, pp. 26, 90.

61. From Vicuña Mackenna, cited in Vitale, vol. 3, p. 183.

62. Jobet, p. 55, and Pinto, p. 26.

63. Schejtman, pp. 193–94, and Sepúlveda, p. 44.

64. Vitale, vol. 3, pp. 196–97.

65. Bauer, cited in Vitale, vol. 3, p. 144.

66. Vitale, vol. 3, p. 182.

67. Jobet, pp. 67–68.

68. Jobet, p. 54.

69. Jobet, p. 174, and Borde and Góngora, p. 133.

70. Sepúlveda, pp. 54, 82, 97.

71. Sepúlveda, p. 92.

72. Pinto, p. 110, and Jobet, pp. 50, 133.

73. Schejtman, p. 204.

74. Jobet, p. 84.

75. McBride, p. 164, and Schejtman, p. 201. McBride's and Schejtman's figures are very different. Adolfo Mattei in his book *La Agricultura en Chile* (1939), lists 108,000 inquilinos, 95,000 afuerinos, and 106,000 peones. Probably about 50 percent of the peones should be considered members of inquilino families, and the rest considered afuerinos.

76. Gay, cited by Schejtman, p. 195.

77. All three passages are from McBride, pp. 161, 149, and 156, respectively.

78. Jobet, p. 51, and Schejtman, p. 192.

79. Almost all Latin American agricultural economies exhibit vestiges of feudal relations of production. Perhaps those areas which most clearly are predominately capitalist are Venezuela, the coast of Peru, and parts of Mexico and Brasil, wherever subsistence agriculture is weakest, and wage labor most common.

80. Sepúlveda, pp. 89, 91.

Chapter 4

1. The judiciary was rewarded after the military coup by being the only branch of government which was allowed to continue to exist although all political cases have been decided by the military's own courts. The Supreme Court outdid itself shortly after the coup by solemnly declaring that the military takeover was "constitutional."

Chapter 5

1. The future was to show how slowly the agricultural bureaucracy could work. Sometimes more than a year would pass between expropriation of a farm and the constitution of a cooperative. During that time the farm remained unproductive and the peasants unemployed.

CORA was the most important government agency involved with the land reform, but there were twenty-four others. Many had overlapping functions. Altogether twenty-four thousand people worked for these agencies. Seventy-five thousand families of peasants eventually received land during the Frei and Allende governments, so there was a bureaucrat for every three peasants in the reformed sector. The yearly budget of the twenty-four agencies was about equal to the total value of one year's agricultural production. See *Punto Final*, August 28, 1973, p. 18.

2. The MIR was not alone in these fears. Many members of the Popular Unity coalition felt the same way. Some of them had brought up the same criticisms of the Agrarian Reform Law when it was passed in 1967.

3. Some of the younger peasant women in Lautaro County, a very few, were recruited for party work by the MIR organizers. They, of course, participated fully in all party work with their male counterparts. They also helped show other peasant women how women could and should take on responsibility.

4. The state bureaucracy was itself divided. Many technicians in the local CORA office in Lautaro County frequently sided with the peasants against the state bank or against their own CORA superiors at the provincial level.

5. Although there are no statistics for Lautaro County about tractors, in the province of Cautín there were 100 tractors in September 1970 in the reformed sector. At the end of 1972 there were 650, according to CORA in Temuco. Expropriated land area tripled in Cautín Province under Allende, but the number of tractors increased six times.

Chapter 6

1. That same day Allende pardoned nineteen members of the MIR who had been imprisoned during the Frei government.

2. Lautaro County produces more wheat than any other county in Chile.

3. Under Allende there were thirty-eight interventions in the province of Cautín. All took place in 1971. They were a sore point with the right wing. At the Ruculán farm in western Cautín the owner, Landaretche, initiated court action to prevent the government intervenor from hiring new workers. A similar conflict arose in Lautaro at the Three Pastures farm. Chonchol publicly backed the intervenors. Both court suits became irrelevant shortly thereafter when both farms were expropriated. Nationally, as of June 1972, there had been interventions in 400 farms. One hundred fifty of those had been expropriated, and 250 were still intervened. These statistics, the best available, are still only approximations. The government never knew *exactly* how many farms were intervened. See the report by Maffei and Marchetti presented to ICIRA in June 1972, mimeograph.

4. The provincial Communist labor union federation, the Recabarren Federation, condemned both Carmine and the "ultraleft" in a declaration on February 18. At times the policy of the Communist Party was to view both the extreme right and the MIR as similarly dangerous.

5. Many of the landowners in Cautín had German names, because German immigrants had colonized southern Chile in the mid 1800s. Most of this colonization took place in the provinces of Osorno and Llanquihue, south of Cautín. Even so, the German influence spread throughout the south.

6. There were 126 farm takeovers in Cautín in 1971, more than in any other province except Valdivia, which had 156. See *El Mercurio* of June 5-6, 1972, for a study done by the Centro de Estudios Agrarios of the Universidad Católica.

7. Luciano referred to Luciano Cruz, a leader of the MIR until his accidental death in 1971.

8. See *Punto Final*, February 16, 1971, passim. The same article contains a comment from a regional leader of the MIR, discussing the future of the Peasant Councils. He said:

> It is not just a question of organizing the peasantry. It's a question of mobilizing the peasantry, creating a consciousness, and winning the peasantry to a revolutionary political attitude. There are two possibilities here: the Councils become a bureaucracy and thereby lose real control of the masses, or they offer a leadership which is really linked with the rank and file so that the rank and file takes control of production.

The MIR obviously hoped for the latter alternative. For a variety of reasons, to be discussed in future chapters, the councils were unable to fulfill the hopes that many placed in them when they were founded.

Chapter 7

1. The statistics for land held on the reservation by those at Elicura refers to land held by the male members of the cooperative. Some women had land back on the reservations as well. Because of the severe land shortage on the reservations, often some children did not inherit any land. Since it was felt that women would be provided for by their future husbands, it was relatively common for female children to be excluded. This was a departure from Mapuche tradition. Traditionally women had the same rights to inherit and own land as did men.

2. As for the long-term debt, not only was it something incomprehensible which concerned only a few government accountants, but there was another reason why the peasants were not too concerned about paying it off. The MIR had taught them that they should not have to pay for the land or the buildings which had been stolen from them in the first place. The MIR argued that neither the government nor the peasants should have to spend valuable resources to compensate the old landowner.

3. Polygamy used to be common among the Mapuche, now it is rare. There was only one case at Elicura.

4. The Chilean Medical College was more interested in profits than health care for the public, and it opposed Allende's health programs at every step. After the coup the "leaders" of the Medical College actively collaborated with the junta in denouncing leftist doctors, leading in many cases to their imprisonment, torture, and death. Some doctors, now notorious among Chile's political prisoners, became technical advisors to the military in order to help refine torture techniques.

5. The witranalhue is a malevolent spirit that appears late at night, frequently confronting travelers on the roads. Originally the size of a man, the witranalhue instantaneously grows very large and can cause severe injury. Anchimallen, on the other hand, is a young girl or a female child. She also appears at night, and often her eyes glow. As a young woman she can sneak into bed with a young man. As a young girl she simply wanders about whining softly. Her appearance often leads to illness in the victim's (the observer's) family, illness that may result in death. She can be warded off by burning a fire with a variety of rare ingredients. One night a tractor driver saw anchimallen, appearing as a young child. Immediately Pedro and his wife went outside and built a fire on top of which they threw salt, hot peppers, and string.

The trutruca is a long hollow reed with a cow's horn on the end. The nillatun is a dance led by the machi that was traditionally danced to ensure good crops.

6. The Peasant Council in Lautaro County kept a list of the unemployed from which were chosen members of any cooperatives to be formed on any newly expropriated land. The Peasant Council presented candidates to CORA which in theory was simply supposed to

approve them without argument. In fact, often there was a process of negotiation. Of course, on land which was occupied illegally, the occupiers became the new cooperative members if the takeover was successful.

Chapter 8

1. For information on CIA aid to Allende's opposition see the report on Chile by the Senate Intelligence Committee, that came out in December 1975. The information contained in the report undoubtedly is only a small part of the story. The full disclosure of the CIA complicity in the Chilean coup will probably come out only after a long period of time has passed. For example, consider a similar case, that of the 1964 military coup in Brasil. It took twelve years before it became known that the United States had a naval task force poised to intervene in favor of the Brasilian generals in case they needed help in overthrowing the democratic and left-leaning government of Goulart.

2. The takeovers in Nuble caused a strong right-wing reaction in much the same way as did those in Cautín in 1970–71. *La Tribuna,* for example, ran a headline on March 20 which read "More than 300 farms invaded by Mirista hordes. *El Mercurio* of March 18 was only slightly more subdued. "Explosive situation in the countryside. Kidnappings and takeovers in Nuble."

3. Other ads were equally harsh. For example, in *Clarín* on April 10 a large ad read "They talk about revolution. The CIA knows that they are useful." This was followed by quotes from the ITT papers, recently released by Jack Anderson. The quotes refer to potential violence from the left which might provoke the military to intervene and overthrow the government. The ad concludes "The ultraleft acts against the revolution." For a MIR analysis of the Communist Party campaign, see *Punto Final* of June 6, 1972, pp. 16–17. The Socialist Party was divided on the issue. One sector of it clearly backed the Communists. For example, see *Posición,* the Socialist Party weekly magazine, of May 23. Another sector, however, supported the MIR in the pages of *Ultima Hora,* the Socialist Party daily newspaper.

4. See the interview with Miguel Enriquez in *Chile Hoy,* August 25, for an account of these conversations. Some degree of unity had been agreed upon concerning the agrarian reform, probably along the lines of the Linares program which had been worked out in January 1972 for the election in that province for senator. The Linares program was agreed on by the MIR and the Popular Unity in Linares.

5. The Provincial Congress published its conclusions in a pamphlet printed in Temuco in August 1972.

6. The Constitutional Reform bill referred to in Point 1 was the Christian Democratic bill to limit the state's expropriations of industry. This bill was eventually passed by Congress but then vetoed by Allende. The arms control law was passed by Congress and signed by Allende. It gave the military the authority to control arms. In 1973 this authority was used extensively by the military to intimidate workers and to provide "practice" for the coup. The workers' councils referred to in Point 2 became a reality in October 1972 with the creation of the industrial belts (cordones industriales). The political resolution of the Congress can be found in *Punto Final,* August 1, 1972, pp. 10–11.

7. A resolution was passed by the Congress calling for a national meeting of Peasant Councils to strengthen further the Councils. This meeting was eventually held in January 1973 in Nuble.

8. One version says miguelitos were named after Miguel Enríquez, head of the MIR until his death in a shoot-out in October 1974. The MIR used miguelitos in 1969 and 1970 when they were underground and carrying out several bank robberies. The miguelitos snarled traffic and prevented the police from pursuing the Miristas.

9. Evidence of CIA aid to the truck owners is circumstantial but abundant. A *Time* magazine reporter was told by truck owners in October 1972 that they were being paid by the CIA to keep the trucks off the road. The *New York Times* in September 1974 cited inside sources as confirming that the CIA gave money to the truck owners in October 1972. The black-market rate for the dollar dropped sharply in October because of the large influx of dollars into the country.

Chapter 10

1. These statistics come from an internal CORA document of 1973, entitled "Antecedentes Agropecuarios de la Provincia de Cautín."

2. The fact that the middlemen were responsible for the shortages was made clear by statistics put out in late 1972 by the National Institute of Statistics. The figures are published in *Chile Hoy*, January 5–11, 1973. They show that production of popular consumer items such as condensed milk, flour, margarine, oil, and sugar had increased an average of about 25 percent between 1970 and 1972.

3. See the *Diario Austral* of Temuco, June 12, 1973.

4. See the speech by Carlos Altamirano on July 12 in Santiago. Altamirano, head of the Socialist Party, endorsed both Industrial Belts and County Comandos in this speech, which was carried in several left-wing dailies the next day.

5. Victor Toro was captured by the military in early 1974. He was extensively tortured. He was put on trial with thirteen other members of the MIR in April 1975. Toro and other defendants read statements at their trials which denounced the military dictatorship and defended the MIR. He received a heavy sentence. International support for the defendants prevented the military from conducting the trials in secrecy. Toro was released and deported in November 1976.

6. See the *Diario Austral* of Temuco on August 12, 1973.

7. The decision to use the military to try to bring the truck owners in line was made on August 12 (see *Chile Hoy*, August 17–23, 1973). Undersecretary of Transport Jaime Faivovich, a left-wing civilian, remained in charge of overall policy towards the truck owners, but his orders were sabotaged by the military appointees on the local level. The MIR's position on the use of the military can be found in a full page ad in *La Tercera* of August 22, 1973.

Chapter 11

1. The junta unleashed a publicity campaign against foreigners after the coup. It was convenient to blame Chile's social unrest on "outside agitators." Despite the fact that Chile's Marxist parties had forty or fifty years of history behind them, the junta claimed that Marxism was a foreign creed, that Chileans who considered themselves Marxists had been fooled and tricked by devious foreigners, and that ten thousand foreigners had infiltrated Chile under Allende and had succeeded in exacerbating social unrest.

It is well known that the junta brought in Brasilian police to interrogate (torture) Brasilians who were arrested after the coup. It is likely that similar arrangements were made with Bolivian, Uruguayan, and perhaps Argentinian police.

2. Informers have been responsible for most of the arrests of leftists since the coup. The

junta has paid thousands of civilian sympathizers to act as informers. The military also often agrees to free a prisoner from the horror of jail and torture upon the condition that he or she act as an informer. In reprisal the Chilean Resistance has executed numerous informers as has been admitted by General Baeza, head of the Chilean police. See for example, the interview with Baeza published in the Buenos Aires paper *La Opinión* on October 27, 1973.

Of course, many informers have acted voluntarily because they supported the junta and feared the left. This was more often the case right after the coup. As the Chilean people have come to recognize the brutality of the military, however, fewer people support the junta and fewer voluntarily provide the junta with information.

3. The resistance of the peasants in Lautaro was similar to the resistance of peasants throughout Chile. Harassment of the troops, light sabotage, and noncooperation have been the tactics used by peasants who are overwhelmingly outnumbered and outgunned. In a few areas, however, there was armed resistance. For example, in Panguipulli in the province of Valdivia, small guerilla bands operated after the coup. They were eventually crushed by a large-scale military operation. In other provinces some military personnel have been ambushed by snipers in the countryside. By and large, however, such armed resistance is and has been unusual.

4. There are no reliable statistics for the return of land in Chile since the coup. However this author has been able to learn something of the general situation in Lautaro County through personal correspondence. For an overview of the agrarian reform throughout Chile since the coup, see the end of Chapter 11

It should also be emphasized that this account of the repression in Lautaro County and in Cautín as a whole is necessarily a limited one. A complete account is not possible until the present military junta no longer rules Chile. The details of the extensive repression, the names of the thousands killed will only be revealed when the Chilean people can rid themselves of the junta and systematically document the brutalities.

The only thing that can be certain is that the dead mentioned here are only a small percentage of those actually killed by the military in Cautín and in Lautaro County. This account is based on newspaper articles, personal observations by the author, or descriptions by reliable eyewitnesses who spoke with the author.

5. In late March 1974 the newspaper *El Mercurio* published a fairly accurate list of MIR militants in Cautín Province. Also included was a description of the party's structure. However this information was not very useful to the military. Shortly after the coup many members of the MIR were transferred to different cities and replaced. This was a standard policy for smaller cities and towns. Sometimes, depending on the extent of the repression, this policy was also used in the countryside.

On March 28 in Temuco the military held a "trial" for members of the MIR. Fifty people were tried and sentenced. No lawyer in Temuco, where the trial was held, was willing to take the case. The military assigned an officer to act as the defense lawyer. Five of the defendants were acquitted, and the rest were sentenced to jail for periods ranging from one month to twenty years. Most of the defendants were peasants. Only a few were MIR organizers.

Most of the members of the MIR who were listed in the *El Mercurio* article remained at large in March 1974. Cautín's military prosecutor published a list of MIR members who were wanted by the military. This list was published on March 24, 1974, also in *El Mercurio*. It contained sixty-one names. All were at large.

The trial of March 28, 1974, in Temuco was declared null on June 22, 1974, by the military because of the complete irregularity of the proceedings. However, the same defendants were simply retried and sentenced.

6. Of course, Lautaro County is unusual in this respect, and throughout much of Chile it was the parties of the Popular Unity which had strong organizations in the countryside, not the MIR.

Chapter 12

1. All statistics on landholdings in Lautaro County are based partially on data provided by the local CORA offices and largely on this author's own research. The same is true for the maps used in this chapter, except for the maps about population and the size of landholdings before the agrarian reform (maps 4 and 6). These two maps come from the Instituto de Investigaciones de Recursos Naturales, a branch of CORFO.

2. The statistics on Cautín come from a mimeographic document produced by the CORA headquarters in Cautín in 1973.

3. The statistics on Chile as a whole come from the well-known *Diagnóstica* produced by ICIRA in November 1972. It covers Chilean agriculture between November 1970 and June 1972. It was largely put together by Solón Barraclough and Almino Affonso. A résumé of the *Diagnóstica* was published by *CEREN (Cuadernos de la Realidad Nacional)* in early 1973. The complete *Diagnóstica* was published after the coup by Siglo XXI in Mexico City.

4. Two good articles on the illegal occupations were published in 1973 although they are difficult to obtain now. One was by Juan Carlos Marín in the first and last issue of *Marxismo y Revolución* published in Santiago in August 1973. Another was by José Bengoa in the magazine *Sociedad y Desarrollo* in late 1972 or early 1973. The article is entitled "Movilización Campesina: Análisis y Perspectivas," and the issue of *Sociedad y Desarrollo* is devoted entirely to the agrarian reform in Chile. *Sociedad y Desarrollo* was published in Santiago in 1972 and 1973.

5. These statistics are based on the author's own research for Lautaro County and on the *Diagnóstica* for Chile as a whole.

6. These statistics are based on the author's own research and on the 1965 Agricultural Census done in Chile.

7. See the bibliography on Mapuches in the Selected Bibliography.

Selected Bibliography

General

Bloch, Marc. *Feudal Society* (London: Routledge and Kegan Paul, 1961).
___. *French Rural History* (Berkeley and Los Angeles: University of California Press, 1966).
Dobb, Maurice. *Studies in the Development of Capitalism* (New York: International Publishers Co., 1947).
Duby, Georges. *Rural Economy and Country Life in the Medieval West* (Columbia, S.C.: University of South Carolina Press, 1968).
Emmanuel, Arghiri. *Unequal Exchange* (New York: Monthly Review Press, 1972).
Engels, Frederick. *The Origin of the Family, Private Property, and the State* (New York: International Publishers Co., 1968).
___. *The Peasant War in Germany* (Moscow: Progress, 1956).
Frank, Andre Gunder. *Capitalism and Underdevelopment in Latin America* (New York: Monthly Review Press, 1967).
___. *Lumpenbourgeoisie, Lumpendevelopment* (New York: Monthly Review Press, 1972).
___. "Dependence is dead . . ." *Latin American Perspectives* 1(1974):87–106.
Galeano, Eduardo. *Las venas abiertas de América Latina* (Buenos Aires: Siglo XXI, 1971).
Hill, Christopher. *A Century of Revolution* (New York: Norton, 1966).
Hilton, Rodney. *Bond Men Made Free* (London: Temple Smith, 1973).
Hobsbawn, Eric. *The Age of Revolution* (New York: Mentor, 1964).
Kautsky, Carlos. *La cuestión agraria* (Madrid: vda. de Rodríguez Serra, 1903).
Laclau, Ernesto. "Feudalism and Capitalism in Latin America." *New Left Review* 67 (1971):19–38.
Lefebre, Georges. *The Coming of the French Revolution* (Princeton: Princeton University Press, 1947).
___. *The French Revolution from its Origins to 1793* (New York: Columbia University Press, 1962).
Lenin, V. I. *Capitalism and Agriculture* (New York: International Publishers Co., 1946).
___. *The Development of Capitalism in Russia* (Moscow: Progress, 1967).
___. *Imperialism* (New York: International Publishers Co., 1939).
Mandel, Ernest. *The Formation of the Economic Thought of Karl Marx* (New York: Monthly Review Press, 1971).
Mariátegui, José Carlos. *Seven Interpretative Essays on Peruvian Development* (Austin: University of Texas Press, 1971).
Marini, Ruy Mauro. "Dialéctica de la Dependencia." *Sociedad y Desarrollo* 1(1972):35–51.
Marx, Karl. *Capital* (New York: International Publishers, 1967).
___. *Pre-Capitalist Economic Formations* (New York: International Publishers Co., 1964).
Marx, Karl and Frederick Engels. *Selected Works of Marx and Engels* (New York: International Publishers Co., 1968).
Pirenne, Henri. *Economic and Social History of Medieval Europe* (New York: Harcourt, Brace, 1937).
Sweezy, Paul. *The Theory of Capitalist Development* (New York: Monthly Review Press, 1942).

Sweezy, Paul, et al. *The Transition from Feudalism to Capitalism* (New York: Science of
    Society, 1963).
Tawney, R. H. *The Agrarian Problem in the 16th Century* (New York: Burt Franklin, 1912).
Williams, Eric. *Capitalism and Slavery* (New York: Capricorn Press, 1966).

Spain

Elliott, J. H. *Imperial Spain* (New York: St. Martin's Press, 1964).
Larraz, José. *La Epoca del Mercantilismo en Castilla* (Madrid: Aguilar, 1963).
Stein, J. and B. H. Stein. *The Colonial Heritage of Latin America* (New York: Oxford
    University Press, 1970).
Vicens V., Jaime. *An Economic History of Spain* (Princeton: Princeton University Press,
    1969).

Chile

Amunátegui S., Domingo. *Las Encomiendas de Indígenas en Chile* (Santiago: Cervantes,
    1907).
___. *El Nacimiento de la República de Chile* (Santiago: Balcells, 1930).
Bagú, Sergio. *La Economía de la Sociedad Colonial* (Buenos Aires: El Ateneo, 1949).
Baraona, Rafael, et al. *Valle de Putaendo* (Santiago: Ed. Universitaria, 1961).
Borde, J. and M. Góngora. *La Evolución de la Propriedad en el Valle de Puangue* (Santiago:
    Ed. Universitaria, 1956).
Feliu C., Guillermo. *La Abolición de la Esclavitud en Chile* (Santiago: Ed. Universitaria,
    1973).
Góngora, Mario. *El Origen de los Inquilinos de Chile Central* (Santiago: Ed. Universitaria,
    1960).
Jara, Alvaro. *Guerra y Sociedad en Chile* (Santiago: Ed. Universitaria, 1971).
Jobet, J. C. *Ensayo Crítico del Desarrollo Económico-Social de Chile* (Santiago: Ed. Univer-
    sitaria, 1955).
McBride, G. M. *Chile, Land and Society* (New York: American Geographical Society, 1936).
Meza Villalobos, Nestor. *Política Indígena en los Orígenes de la Sociedad Chilena* (Santiago:
    Universidad de Chile, 1951).
Pinto, Anibal. *Chile: un Caso de Desarrollo Frustrado* (Santiago: Ed. Universitaria, 1973).
Popcock, H. R. S. *The Conquest of Chile* (New York: Stein and Day, 1967).
Ramírez N., Hernán. *Antecedentes Económicos de la Independencia de Chile* (Santiago: Ed.
    Universitaria, 1959).
Schejtman, M., Alexander. *El Inquilino de Chile Central* (Santiago: ICIRA, 1971).
Sepúlveda, Sergio. *El Trgio Chileno en el Mercado Mundial* (Santiago: Ed. Universitaria,
    1959).
Vitale, Luis. *Interpretación Marxista de la Historia de Chile*, 3 vols. (Santiago: Prensa
    Latinoamericana, 1969-1971).

Mapuches

Alegría, Fernando. *Lautaro* (Santiago: Ed. Zig Zag, 1943).
Barella, Carlos. *Lautaro Guerillero* (Santiago: Universidad Católica, 1971).
Berdichewsky, Bernardo. "Antropología aplicada e Indigenismo en los Mapuches de
    Cautín." Santiago: mimeograph, July 1971).

___. *The Araucanian Indian in Chile* (Copenhagen: The International Work Group for Indigenous Affairs, 1976).

Campos, M., M. J. *Nahuelbuta* (Santiago: Ed. Francisco de Aguirre, 1972).

Cona, Pascual. *Memorias de un Cacique Mapuche* (Santiago: ICIRA, 1972).

Cooper, J. "The Araucanians." *Handbook of South American Indians* 2:687–760.

Domeyko, Ignacio. *Araucania y sus Habitantes* (Santiago: Ed. Francisco de Aguirre, 1971).

Farón, Luis C. *Mapuche Indians of Chile* (New York: Holt, Rinehart, and Winston, 1968).

Gonzalez de Nájera, Alonso. *Desengaño y Reparo de la Guerra del Reino de Chile* (Santiago: Andrés Bello, 1971).

Góngora Marolejo, A. *Historia de Chile* (Santiago: Ed. Universitaria, 1969).

Guevara, Tomás. *Historia de la Civilización de la Araucania* (Santiago: Anal. Universitaria, 1898).

Hilger, Sister Inez. *Araucanian Chile Life and its Cultural Background* (Washington, D.C.: Smithsonian Miscellaneous Collection, 1957).

Latcham, R. E. "Ethnology of the Araucanians," *Journal of the Royal Anthropological Institute* 39(1909):334–70.

Marion de Lobera, P. *Crónica del Reino* (Santiago: Ed. Universitaria, 1969).

Medina, J. *Los Aborígines de Chile* (Santiago: n.p., 1952).

Moesbach, P. E. *Idioma Mapuche* (Padre Las Casas, Ed. San Francisco, 1962).

Ovalle, Alonso de. *Histórica Relación del Reino de Chile* (Santiago: Ed. Universitaria, 1969).

Saavedra, Alejandro. *La Cuestión Mapuche* (Santiago: ICIRA, 1971).

Titiev, M. *Araucanian Culture in Transition* (Ann Arbor: University of Michigan Press, 1951).

Index